EMERGING
GENDER
IDENTITIES

"We are faced with a dizzying ongoing evolution in cultural understanding of and recommended responses to a kaleidoscope of emerging gender identities. This book offers richly informed and thoughtful Christian analysis of these phenomena, along with compassionate and challenging recommendations for ministry. Yarhouse and Sadusky have the breadth of knowledge and experience to challenge readers to move toward more theologically grounded and pragmatically effective engagement."

—**Stanton L. Jones**, Wheaton College (emeritus);
coauthor of the God's Design for Sex
family sex-education book series

"Yarhouse and Sadusky are unafraid of exploring the overlap of Christianity, psychology, and cultures, and equally unafraid of reaching out in peace. I admire such a version of Christianity. I have read every page of this book. I disagree with the authors' concept of suffering, but that is a minor point. I found myself nodding my head in agreement over and over. I greatly appreciated their breakdown of the theological positions (ultraconservative, orthodox, and liberal) and how these *positions* affect *gestures* toward those that carry gender-related questions. I endorse this book for ministers, parents, and gender-exploring youth."

—**Caryn LeMur**, a male-to-female transsexual
and a follower of the words and life of Jesus

"Julia and Mark have written a much-needed book about a beautiful and complex topic. Every page oozes with grace and wisdom. Mark and Julia not only have the academic credentials to speak into transgender-related issues, but they have also spent countless hours listening to and loving the very people they're writing about."

—**Preston Sprinkle**, author of *Embodied: Transgender Identities,
the Church, and What the Bible Has to Say*

"I am not overstating things when I say that this book is a page-turner. Yarhouse and Sadusky anticipate readers' questions. They carefully explore the historical and theological implications of the questions. But they never forget that they are writing about people with real pain who are seeking to understand a reality in light of their desire to love Jesus and retain their faith. Not everyone is going to like this book. But Yarhouse and Sadusky's challenge is for men and women of faith who work with children, young adults, and others who are experiencing gender identity issues to seriously grapple with the complexities so that they—as parents, pastors, health-care practitioners, and educators—will be known as people who will tackle difficult problems in such a way that the people of God will feel beloved."

—**Shirley V. Hoogstra**, president, Council for Christian
Colleges & Universities

"Yarhouse and Sadusky unpack one of today's pressing issues: transgender and emerging gender identities. As Christian psychologists, they integrate Christian insight with accurate scientific knowledge, offering well-informed and up-to-date understandings of a rapidly changing dimension of society. Current political and cultural discourse offers little room for critical engagement, and Yarhouse and Sadusky courageously offer wisdom and advice. They challenge Christians to move beyond getting theology right, even asserting that correct theological knowledge doesn't always translate into knowing how to minister to persons with nonnormative gender identities. With many examples, they encourage Christians to accompany others, not simply instruct or admonish them from a distance. They invite the reader to renew their encounter with a merciful God, as part of developing ministry that incarnates God's love. I came away with my faith strengthened, more certain that I can entrust my loved ones to Christ and that I can continue to question, learn, and wonder about transgender and gender expansiveness."

—**Jenell Paris**, Messiah College

"The many tensions and agendas that surround gender theories make it very hard to discern the truth through the forest of ideologies. And yet there are human beings in that forest, with an infinite dignity and a need for love and understanding. Drs. Yarhouse and Sadusky have worked hard to seek out the truth and to develop a compassionate approach to understanding and ministering in this very sensitive space. They provide a wealth of trustworthy information for us through their excellence in psychology based on their professional integrity, years of study, and substantial clinical experience. At the same time, they deliver this truth to us through hearts that have been shaped by the compassion of Jesus Christ, which they have internalized through their deep Christian faith."

—**Fr. Boniface Hicks**, OSB, Institute for Ministry Formation,
Saint Vincent Seminary

EMERGING GENDER IDENTITIES

UNDERSTANDING

THE DIVERSE EXPERIENCES

OF TODAY'S YOUTH

MARK YARHOUSE
AND JULIA SADUSKY

Brazos Press

a division of Baker Publishing Group
Grand Rapids, Michigan

© 2020 by Mark A. Yarhouse and Julia Sadusky

Published by Brazos Press
a division of Baker Publishing Group
PO Box 6287, Grand Rapids, MI 49516-6287
www.brazospress.com

Printed in the United States of America

Library of Congress Cataloging-in-Publication Control Number: 2019052620

ISBN 978-1-58743-434-1 (paperback)
ISBN 978-1-58743-495-2 (casebound)

Unless otherwise noted, Scripture quotations are from THE HOLY BIBLE, NEW INTERNA-TIONAL VERSION®, NIV® Copyright © 1973, 1978, 1984, 2011 by Biblica, Inc.® Used by permission. All rights reserved worldwide.

Some names and details have been changed to protect the privacy of the individuals involved.

20 21 22 23 24 25 26   7 6 5 4 3 2 1

CONTENTS

LIST OF SIDEBARS

PREFACE

As we sit down to write this preface, a noteworthy news story has come across our feed. Merriam-Webster has selected the pronoun *they* as the word of the year for 2019, after an unprecedented amount of online searches on their website to understand its meaning. In the context of emerging gender identities, *they* is a pronoun sometimes preferred by those who identify as gender nonbinary. Perhaps this speaks to the relevance of this book.

One of the greatest challenges in writing a book on emerging gender identities is that society and the field we work in (i.e., psychology) and the specialty we have in lesbian, gay, bisexual, transgender, and queer (LGBTQ+) studies is rapidly changing and expanding to reflect ever-increasingly diverse experiences of gender and sexuality. As you read this book, you may find that several more words and pronouns and approaches to care are being discussed than were being discussed at the time we finished our contribution. Work in the area of gender identity seems to be fast-forwarding at a rapid pace. It feels somewhat like trying to follow the plot of a favorite series by watching it at four times or ten times the normal speed. You just want to slow it all down so you can understand what is happening to your beloved characters.

Well, that is similar to what it is like as we engage in an effort to better understand and engage with gender identity, transgender experiences, and diverse gender identities. Theology and scriptural exegesis matter a great deal to us, but the focus of this book will be the ways our theological and scriptural understanding inform a range of approaches to living with, caring for, and ministering to those who struggle with these questions. For those of you who have been hoping for a book that presents a foundational psychological understanding as well as practical reflections, we hope this can help you feel more equipped to wrestle with the complexities you are facing. We are not trying to provide detailed and specific instructions for every step you take in supporting young people today; we feel such an approach would be reduced to pat answers and oversimplifications. Rather, we hope that you can come away with a more robust appreciation for how to position yourself alongside our young people as they navigate gender identity.

Some readers may feel, as we have at times, that it might be too little and too late for Christians to enter into this conversation. As clinicians, we sometimes say that providing clinical services is like trying to repair the engine of an airplane while it's at thirty thousand feet: there just does not seem to be time to land the plane and take the much-needed time to look over the engine in the maintenance hangar. But we enter in anyway, and we hope that you can take away meaningful information to help you "catch up" as best you can, so that your efforts to understand can bear fruit with the real people you love who will explore or have been exploring gender identity questions.

Others may feel that the church has nothing of value to contribute. You may approach this with the assumption that any reservations around the current landscape of gender identity are unfounded. We hope that you can take away a greater appreciation for the wrestling of many people today, both secular and Christian, as we seek to understand diverse gender identities.

Still others may believe that the church ought not engage at all, as it has already done so much harm to transgender people. We can relate to the fear of what could happen and sadness about what has already happened when ill-equipped persons engage around such intricacies. Our hope is that this book can provide long-overdue information regarding the experiences of those navigating a range of gender identities, raise awareness of the real challenges therein, and resonate with Christians who see themselves in these pages. We hope that such information, in the hands of parents, loved ones, pastors, youth ministers, and lay

Christians, can help equip church communities, so that young people do not feel as if navigating gender identity questions precludes them from a relationship with Christ or a home in the church.

This book is the result of the observation that work in diverse gender identities has rapidly expanded. The speed of this expansion has been difficult for families and challenging for churches seeking to engage in meaningful ministry. Back in 2015, Mark's book *Understanding Gender Dysphoria* offered an explanation of gender dysphoria. We have written this book to distinguish emerging gender identities from gender dysphoria and to provide an update on what has changed in the clinical landscape in the past five years, as well as to offer options for Christians who wish to lean in to this conversation. We hope that anyone who is seeking to genuinely appreciate the current terrain will find some clarity in this book, while knowing that no single resource could possibly provide answers for all of your questions about gender identity and faith. Nevertheless, we will offer distinctively Christian principles that are in keeping with a historic Christian anthropology.

We want to express our sincerest gratitude for the many people who have made this book a reality. We want to thank the countless students affiliated with the Sexual and Gender Identity Institute (formerly the Institute for the Study of Sexual Identity) who contributed hours to research, clinical work, supervision, consultations, and trainings. We want to thank the various professionals and specialty clinics who have been available to us over the years for consultation and for the hallway conversations that inspired our own wrestling with the changing landscape.

Most importantly, we hope this book honors the countless brave people and their families that we have met with over the past five years. We want to thank you for your vulnerability and trust, which has opened our eyes to the difficulties you face in integrating gender identity and faith. We have listened to and been grieved by the ways you have suffered due to the limitations of the people of God, and we see this book as an effort to help your faith communities better accompany you. For those who have been made to feel that you do not belong in Christian churches, we pray you will hold fast to the truth of how beloved you are to Christ.

PART 1

MAKING IMPORTANT DISTINCTIONS

CHAPTER 1

Transgender Experiences and Emerging Gender Identities

Ellie came to a consultation with her parents, not sure what to expect. Like many teens we meet with, she was on the defensive. Expecting to hear from us the same message she had heard from her parents, she came ready to prove that she wasn't identifying as transgender merely to get attention or rebel against the status quo. She wasn't a transgender activist marching at the front of a pride parade. She was simply "trans," she said.

Once she realized we weren't there to tell her she was a "bad Christian" for not exhibiting stereotypically female dress, interests, and mannerisms, she relaxed. Then she began to tell her story. Sixteen years old, she faced many of the same stressors as other teens we meet with: peer pressure, college applications, conflicts with siblings, and uncertainty over how to answer the question, Who am I? She had hobbies, passions, and goals for her life. She wanted to adopt a child one day, to give another child the kind of promising future her own adoptive parents had given her. And in addition to all this, she didn't feel at home in her body.

Ellie wasn't sure how she wanted to respond to her bodily discomfort. At present, she used her birth name and female pronouns. She wasn't ready to make any decisions regarding bodily changes, but she also couldn't see herself reflected in any of the female role models in her life, her church, or even her own family. She felt completely alone until she began to open up about her experience to peers and found some with similar stories. These peers offered community, fellowship, and belonging. This sense of belonging contrasted with the isolation she felt in her youth group, which (to her parents' dismay) she had not attended in months. She had enjoyed youth group when she was younger, but now she felt "so different" from the other girls. She didn't understand why she couldn't just "fit in the girl box," but she was tired of "trying to act like a girl."

Ellie's parents, like many other parents we meet with, were anguished. We were a last resort, a desperate final stop on their long journey of trying to understand their oldest daughter. How could a girl who once seemed to love all things "girly" now appear to be rejecting not only the label "girl" but also the "biblical foundation" so central to their lives? Their daughter didn't care to go to church and would do so only begrudgingly. They worried about her faith and whether she would go to hell for "believing a delusion." Every interaction in their home felt volatile, rife with miscommunication.

At one point in our consultation, Ellie began to answer a question about how she had reached the conclusion she was "trans." Seconds later, she was interrupted by her mother, who capitalized on the moment to quote from Genesis. Mom proceeded to declare, "God made you female. Why are you rejecting God's will for your life? Where did the good girl we all loved go?" The conversation went nowhere: Ellie shut down, and Mom became more and more frustrated. Dad sat silently, as if he had stopped listening ten minutes ago. This approach wasn't working. The question was, What could work?

When Christians talk about the transgender phenomenon and adolescents who identify as trans*, genderfluid, genderqueer, or agender, they often have no idea how to respond, let alone how to develop an approach to engagement and provide a Christian witness to the broader culture. This book intends to help readers understand and distinguish between current mental health concerns among youth that are tied to gender identity (e.g., gender dysphoria, a diagnosable mental health condition) and emerging gender identities that many young people like Ellie experience or are turning to for a sense of identity and community.

We also hope this book will help Christians critically engage one of the most challenging topics in our culture today. When we hear the stories of individuals like Ellie, as well as very different stories about gender, we need guidance in parsing out gender dysphoria from other diverse gender presentations without negating the real experience of those in either group. We also need wisdom in distinguishing theoretical conversations about gender theory from personal questions about gender identity, so that we are better equipped to critically engage aspects of gender theory through a Christian worldview. This book offers both (1) practical guidance for caring for and journeying with young people navigating gender identity concerns and (2) insight into how these concerns have been shaped by our dramatically changing cultural context.

A Departure from Conventional Gender Incongruence

In 2015, Mark introduced many Christians to the concepts of gender dysphoria and transgender experience with his book *Understanding Gender Dysphoria*. *Gender dysphoria* refers to the distress associated with incongruence between one's biological sex and gender identity; *transgender* is a broader umbrella term for many experiences of gender identity that do not align normatively with a person's biological sex. Mark argued that the experience of gender dysphoria is real and that something like gender dysphoria has probably existed throughout history and across cultures, though it has gone by many different names. Societies have variously classified dysphoria as sin, pathology, crime, divine gift, and so on.

The West in recent years has witnessed a remarkable shift from viewing such experiences in terms of mental health and morality to viewing them as signs of an independent people group and culture to be celebrated. This dramatic cultural shift alone poses a challenge for the church to navigate. But this shift isn't the end of the story.

Generational Gaps and Cultural Shifts

Toward the end of a fascinating documentary titled *The Gender Revolution*, Katie Couric brings together Renee Richards and Hari Nef for a conversation about gender.[1] Richards, a transgender woman who still openly reminisces about her early life as a man named Richard Raskin, had transitioned in 1975. She was a professional tennis player and the first transgender woman to compete in the US Open. She was eighty-two at the time of the Couric interview. Nef, twenty-three at the time of the interview, is an international model and star of the television show *Transparent*. Nef identifies as trans. Their conversation offers a paradigmatic illustration of some of the shifts in thinking and experience of gender identity that have occurred in recent years.

During their conversation, Richards and Nef discuss Richards's transition in 1975 and her efforts to publicly downplay her gender identity, comparing Richards's approach to the very different approach that Nef and others express today. These differences in approach, they recognize, are the result of shifts not only in societal acceptance but also in prevailing attitudes toward gender's fixity. Couric notes that Nef sees gender as something that is "fluid" and can "evolve." Richards responds incredulously, "I don't think [Nef] sees gender as fluid." Nef looks away, smiles, looks back, and states, "Well, I do."

As Couric reflects on her time with Richards and summarizes some of what she heard, she indicates that Richards sees gender as binary. Richards agrees: "I had a very happy life for forty years as a man and I'm having a very happy life for forty years as a woman. But that doesn't mean I'm genderfluid."

Nef offers a strikingly different perspective on gender and society: "It is absolutely a binary society that we live in, but I believe that no single person is absolutely gendered. . . . 'Male' and 'female'—it's just wisps of smoke. If something works for you in a moment, then you can embrace it. If other parts of it don't, you can get rid of it."

Richards offers her own take on gender and what it has meant to rely on the binary in her life: "I'm really not beyond the pink and blue stuff. To me, the idea of a binary is what I think the world is, it's the spice of life. It's what makes us keep going. And I think that it's appealing and I like it. I know there are in betweens, and I know that there are all kinds of percentages that people are and that's fine. But, basically, the fact is that we are born with either two [X] chromosomes or an X and a Y, and you can't undo that."

While acknowledging the chromosomal realities, Nef challenges Richards's positive view of the binary and its impact on Richards's life:

> Well, you can't undo chromosomes, but in terms of the binary, you know, you are saying you are comfortable with the binary, and you like the binary, but you know . . . isn't the binary something that has caused you a lot of pain in your life? If the binary didn't exist, would there have been so much drama about you being 'outed'? . . . So much secrecy? . . . If the world didn't have such a (pardon my French) 'hard on' for like men, women, boys, girls, pink, blue. If that fetish, and I believe it is a fetish, if that didn't exist, wouldn't your life have been easier?

Richards replies, "It wouldn't have been life. It wouldn't have been real." When asked by Couric what Nef really wants with respect to gender and society, Nef offers, "I want a gender-chill future. . . . I want community, a society, the whole world that just chills out about the freakin' gender thing."

The exchange is a fascinating reflection on the differences in perspective of sex, gender, and society, even among transgender people. Both Richards and Nef concur that their disagreement likely reflects a "generational divide" in how they view these topics.

This generational divide illustrates the substantial shifts in perception and experience of gender identity in recent decades. That is, people of different generations think differently about gender not only because they are different ages but also because the eras that shaped them have spoken of gender so differently. Thus, this exchange between Richards and Nef doesn't simply raise questions about the different generational experiences of sex and gender in society. It also necessarily intersects with how medical and mental health communities have understood sex and gender over time. These communities have certainly played a role in transgender history, which we turn to next.

KEY TERMS AND EMERGING GENDER IDENTITIES

Agender: Used when a person's internal experience of gender identity is not gendered or when a person does not have a felt sense of a particular gender identity. Sometimes referred to as *gender neutrois*.

Androgynous: Used when a person's presentation or appearance is not easily identifiable as man or woman, and their gender presentation either is a combination of masculine and feminine or is neutral.

Bigender: Used when a person's gender identity is a combination of man and woman.

Cisgender or cis: Describes those for whom gender identity and birth sex are in alignment.

Female-to-male (FTM/F2M): Describes a transsexual person whose birth sex was female, who identifies as male, and who has pursued gender confirmation (or sex reassignment) surgeries to facilitate expression of their preferred gender identity.

Feminine-of-center: Reflects a person's experience of themselves as more feminine than masculine, regardless of whether they adopt a gender identity as a woman.

Feminine-presenting: Not so much an identity label as a description of how a person expresses themselves (as more feminine).

Femme: An identity label or descriptor used by some persons to convey that they experience themselves as more feminine.

Gender creative: Typically applied to children who express or identify their gender in a range of ways that differ from societal and cultural expectations for them, when these expectations are based on their biological sex.

Gender diverse: A general term for those who may not adhere to societal expectations regarding gender identity.

Gender expansive: Describes youth who express or identify in a range of ways outside the male/female binary.

Genderfluid: Describes those who experience their gender identity as fluid—shifting to some extent—and who may identify and/or present in various ways, regardless of whether these shifts adhere to or are outside of societal expectations for gender expression.

Gender nonconforming: Describes persons who may not adhere to societal expectations for gender expression or models of masculinity and femininity.

Genderqueer: Used of a person whose gender identity is not man or woman, who exists on the continuum between genders, or who is a combination of various genders.

Gender variant: Describes someone who does not conform to cultural expectations for gender identity or expression.

Male-to-female (MTF/M2F): Describes a transsexual person whose birth sex was male, who identifies as female, and who has pursued gender confirmation (or sex reassignment) surgeries to facilitate expression of their preferred gender identity.

Masculine-of-center: Reflects a person's experience of themselves as more masculine than feminine, regardless of whether they adopt a gender identity as a man.

Masculine-presenting: Not so much an identity label as a description of how a person expresses themselves (as more masculine).

Pangender: Describes those who draw from many of the possible gender expressions to establish their own gender identity.

Stealth: Describes when someone who is transgender is considered cisgender (or not transgender) by others.

They/them: Pronouns that can be and have sometimes historically been singular that can be used by people who are seeking a nonbinary singular pronoun more familiar than "ze/zir."

Third-gender: Describes a gender identity other than male or female.

Trans: An abbreviated version of *transgender* that functions as an umbrella term for various ways people express their gender identity when it does not correspond to their birth sex.

Trans*: A purposefully broad and encompassing term extending beyond *transgender* to describe people for whom gender identity and/or expression vary from their birth sex and/or from cultural expectations of them based on their birth sex. The term is understood to have originated in 1996.[a]

Transgender: An umbrella term for many ways in which people experience, express, or live out a gender identity different from the gender identity corresponding to their birth sex. The term is understood to have originated in 1971 and is sometimes shortened to *trans*.

Transman or trans man: A biological female who identifies as male may use this identity label. Some individuals prefer *trans man* as it emphasizes that *trans* is an adjective modifying *man*.

Transsexual: Describes those who seek to change or who have changed their primary and/or secondary sex characteristics through feminizing or masculinizing medical interventions (hormones and/or surgery). Transsexual persons typically adopt a full-time cross-gender identity. The term is understood to have originated in 1949. It is more common in medical discourses and in Europe. Many American transgender people consider the word distasteful or offensive as it has been associated with psychopathology.

Transvestite: A word used to describe those for whom cross-dressing is motivated by sexual pleasure, among other possible motivations. The term is understood to have originated in 1910 by Magnus Hirshfeld. Many transgender persons eschew this word as it has been associated with psychopathology.

Transwoman or trans woman: A biological male who identifies as female may use this identity label. Some individuals prefer *trans woman* as it emphasizes that *trans* is an adjective modifying *woman*.

Two-spirit: Designation used by some Native Americans to describe people believed to have experiences of both genders.

Ze/zir: Pronouns used by some individuals who prefer gender-neutral designations that function as alternatives to "he/his" and "she/her."

a. Susan Stryker, *Transgender History: The Roots of Today's Revolution*, 2nd ed. (New York: Seal Press, 2017), 10–11. Stryker notes, "Its use originated in database and Internet searches, where the symbol functioned as a wildcard operator. That is, a query with an asterisk in it would find the specific string of characters being searched for, plus any others. . . . Using trans* rather than *transgender* became a shorthand way of signaling that you were trying to be inclusive of many different experiences and identities rooted in acts of crossing." Also see Stephen Whittle, "A Brief History of Transgender Issues," *Guardian*, June 2, 2010, https://www.theguardian.com/lifeandstyle/2010/jun/02/brief-history-transgender-issues.

Transgender History

Transgender is a broad umbrella term for many ways a person might experience, express, or live out a gender identity different from the gender identity congruent with their biological sex. As an umbrella term, *transgender* includes a wide range of experiences, and there is not always agreement as to which experiences belong under that umbrella. The broader accounts of transgender may include those who adopt a cross-gender identity with or without medical intervention, those who engage in cross-dressing behavior with or without a corresponding identification as another gender, those who engage in cross-dressing behavior motivated by sexual arousal, those who identify between the male/female binary, those who identify outside the male/female binary, and more.

Historically, public response to behaviors and self-presentations we now call transgender were sometimes closely linked to legal penalties for same-sex sexual behavior and related offenses. Homosexual behavior was criminalized in the United Kingdom in 1533 when Parliament passed the Buggery Act, and in 1885 the Criminal Law Amendment Act further criminalized private acts regardless of whether there was a witness.[2] According to Stephen Whittle, "People who cross-dressed became easy targets of the law because they were associated, in the public mind, with homosexual subculture."[3] LGBTQ+ theorist and historian Susan Stryker notes that in America there were laws passed against cross-dressing in the Massachusetts Bay Colony as early as the 1690s.

As society began fashioning laws in response to gender behaviors outside the norm, people navigating questions about their gender identity sought medical or psychiatric services: "As a result of these laws, people who were trans sought out doctors who could cure them and a whole new field in medicine developed: sexology."[4]

According to Stephen Whittle, "The first sexologist who took a special interest in the sexual impulses of trans individuals was probably [Richard von] Krafft-Ebbing (1840–1902), professor of psychiatry at Vienna. His *Psychopathia Sexualis* was published from 1877 to after his death. Krafft-Ebbing constantly endeavoured to give clearer classifications to the behaviours and individual histories of his patients."[5] Margaret Mead's work on "sex roles" across cultures was also significant and "introduced into the anthropological imagination the concept of a socially learned, psychological component to sex [that] set the stage for later notions of gender that emerged in the 1950s."[6]

Some of the earliest modern medical and psychiatric thought used terminology such as "transsexual" and "transvestic" to account for such experiences. Here is an account of part of that history:

> Through the work of the early sexologists such as Krafft-Ebbing and [Magnus] Hirschfeld, transsexuality became a recognized phenomenon available for study, discussion and treatment. Throughout the 1920s and '30s medical provision was very sparse, but still transsexual people managed to find doctors who would help them. At Hirschfeld's infamous clinic, the first sex change operations were performed by Dr Felix Abraham: a mastectomy on a trans man in 1926, a penectomy on his domestic servant Dora in 1930, and a vaginoplasty on Lili Elbe, a Danish painter, in 1931. The surgery was not easy, and Lili died less than two years later from complications.[7]

Endocrinologist Harry Benjamin observed a phenomenon he described as "a woman kept in the body of a man" and referred to this phenomenon as *transsexualism*.[8] In 1966, Benjamin published *The Transsexual Phenomenon*,[9] a groundbreaking book in its presentation of transgender experiences as unlikely to abate: Benjamin "essentially argued that a person's gender identity could not be changed and that the doctor's responsibility was thus to help transgender people live fuller and happier lives in the gender they identified as their own."[10]

Benjamin's assessment introduced into the Western sociocultural context a "medical paradigm" for gender identity conflicts.[11] According to today's transgender advocates, this "new university-based scientific research" program was steeped in a binary view of gender: "Access to transsexual medical services thus became entangled with a socially conservative attempt to maintain traditional gender configurations in which changing sex was grudgingly permitted for the few seeking to do so, to the extent that the practice did not trouble the gender binary of the man."[12]

In 1980, gender identity disorder was introduced into the third edition of the *Diagnostic and Statistical Manual of Mental Disorders (DSM-III)*.[13] This new classification was first applied only to gender identity disorder of childhood, while *transsexualism* was the term used for adolescents and adults. Gender identity disorder was subsequently refined in *DSM-III-Revised (DSM-III-R)* in 1987 and in the fourth edition of the *Diagnostic and Statistical Manual of Mental Disorders (DSM-IV)* in 1994: the category of "gender identity disorder of adolescence and adulthood, nontranssexual type" was introduced in *DSM-III-R* and subsequently removed in *DSM-IV*.[14] In *DSM-IV*, gender identity disorder of childhood and transsexualism were collapsed into a single diagnosis of gender identity disorder.[15]

Some members of the transgender community disparaged the pathologizing of their experience represented by these diagnoses, while others viewed diagnostic labels as a necessary compromise to facilitate access to health care.[16] The fifth edition of the *Diagnostic and Statistical Manual of Mental Disorders (DSM-5)*, published in 2013, introduced gender dysphoria as a diagnosis that focused not on cross-gender identity as itself disordered but on the distress experienced by some who reported incongruence between their gender identity and biological sex.[17] This diagnosis, too, was viewed by some transgender advocates as yet another compromise to receive medical services.[18] In this iteration, a person could actually have the diagnosis of gender dysphoria removed postsurgery, if indeed surgery resolved their experience of distress.

In any case, for the purposes of our discussion, it should be noted that the introduction of the gender dysphoria diagnosis also served to depathologize a range of experiences of gender incongruence, gender variance, and gender nonconformity. In *DSM-5*, a person may identify either with "the other gender" (thus still subscribing to the notion of a binary) or with "some alternative gender different from one's assigned gender" (thus leaving room for gender identities beyond or outside the male/female binary) without being diagnosed as mentally ill simply because of that identification.[19] The new diagnostic classification also adopted language that had been previously used in the medical community to describe intersex conditions where ambiguous genitalia at birth were sometimes surgically altered to "assign" a sex to the child. This same language of "assignment" was taken up in *DSM-5* to describe the "assigned gender" at birth of those who experienced gender dysphoria as well.[20]

Although it is impossible to do justice to all the relevant figures in the history of the evolving conversation on gender identity, we will highlight a few more key researchers and clinicians. Robert Stoller has been credited with developing in the professional literature the concept of gender identity, defined as "one's persistent inner sense of belonging to either the male or female gender category."[21] John Money viewed gender identity "as the private experience of gender role," while gender role was "the public manifestation of gender identity."[22] Money held that gender identity developed at a young age and was unlikely to change. While some key figures like Harry Benjamin viewed cross-gender identity experiences as largely biological in their origin (in terms of etiology or cause), others such as Stoller postulated a developmental theory for the etiology of gender identity concerns. Richard Green studied under both Money and Stoller and was influential in the earliest psychiatric conceptualizations of transgender identity—what was at that time referred to as *transsexualism*.[23]

Some of the clinical research conducted by Ray Blanchard and colleagues in the 1980s and 1990s focused on clinical differences related to the sexual orientation of those diagnosed with gender identity disorder.[24] For example, insofar as biological males who presented as female had a history of sexual attraction to men, they were considered to have a classic experience of transsexuality—that is, to be "women trapped in the body of men"—and were described as *androphilic* (or homosexual). In contrast, Blanchard described biological males as *autogynephilic* transsexuals if they had no history of sexual attraction to men but reported a sexual attraction to the thought of themselves as women. Autogynephilia was considered a kind of fetish, and it was associated with greater dissatisfaction with gender confirmation (previously known as "sex reassignment") surgery. Blanchard also recorded other less common forms of transsexuality, all of which were related to sexual orientation.

Despite arguments in favor of sexual-orientation-based typologies, some transgender advocates were outspoken critics of these typologies.[25] In particular, they rejected the idea that some presentations of transgender identity were more akin to a fetish than to an experience of felt gender identity per se. Academic peers such as Charles Moser also critiqued the typology.[26] Today clinicians are instructed by *DSM-5* to identify age of onset (early onset, late onset) rather than sexual orientation to describe subtypes of transgender identity.

These key developments in research and assessment of transgender identities have occurred alongside significant cultural shifts as well. One early shift, as we have seen, was from a legal paradigm in which nontraditional expressions of gender identity were treated punitively to a psychiatric paradigm in which they were an ailment requiring treatment. This psychiatric identity was replaced over time by a political identity, which ultimately became a public identity. According to Zein Murib, the shift from psychiatric to political identity was an intentional effort to distance what we now describe as the transgender community from medical and psychiatric diagnostic language and classification that had previously been used to account for transgender experiences.[27]

How did these shifts occur? In the early twentieth century, the psychiatric community catalyzed the shift from the punitive legal paradigm to the medical paradigm by distinguishing biological sex, gender identity, and sexuality. The first term, *biological sex*, was a reference to "embodied and inherited traits, such as chromosomes, genes, hormones, and physical markers." These sex traits were now distinguished from a person's experience of *gender identity*, a term that described the "internal sense of masculinity and femininity, and the social roles associated with each."[28] As Murib notes, the term *sexuality* was also distinct from either of these concepts and referred to "desire, attraction, and related behaviors."[29] This parsing of biological sex, gender identity, and sexuality helped provide language to describe a lack of congruence between biological sex and gender identity. However, since the concepts developed through this language reflected a psychiatric understanding of the experience of incongruence, they were criticized by some members of what would become the transgender community.

Critics of psychiatric and medical conceptualizations of gender identity incongruence sought a new political identity to challenge these prevailing narratives about their experiences. Murib argues that attempts were made by some activists to foster a political identity (in contrast to a psychiatric classification) by identifying a source of oppression that would draw people with diverse experiences under a broad umbrella of identity. But what could constitute such a source of oppression? According to Murib, the source of oppression named by these activists was existing norms regarding sex and gender. *Transgender* became an umbrella term for gender diverse persons that "marked an important shift away from the identity categories derived by doctors and psychiatrists and imagined a future for transgender as an explicitly public and political identity."[30]

We can begin to see how the medical and psychiatric distinction between sex, gender, and sexuality contributed to the later idea that there is no necessary relationship between biological sex and gender identity: "The sex of the body . . . does not bear any *necessary* or *predetermined* relationship to the social category in which the body lives or to the identity and subjective sense of self of the person who lives in the world through that body."[31] This linguistic shift opened up space for the creation of gender identities that reflected psychological experience, recasting emotional and experiential reality as a category of personhood ("I am a transgender person"; "I am trans"). Tey Meadow put the development this way: "Gender is no longer simply sutured to biology; many people now understand it to be a constitutive feature of the psyche that is fundamental, immutable, and not tied to the material of the body."[32]

According to Stryker, the position that sex and gender identity are not in a necessary relationship is political "precisely because it contradicts the common belief that whether a person is a man or a woman in the social sense is fundamentally determined by bodily sex, which is self-apparent and can be clearly and unambiguously perceived."[33] For a group who felt stigmatized and pathologized by medical and psychiatric communities, a political identity was thus an understandable response. Stryker adds further, "How a society organizes its members into categories based on their unchosen physical differences has never been a politically neutral act."[34]

In addition to changing language, activists took several other steps to move the transgender experience from a psychiatric or medical identity to a public identity vis-à-vis a political identity. As Jack Drescher notes, the political tack taken by transgender advocates advanced "normalizing arguments" that included

- adopting normalizing etiological theories, such as the belief that one is born . . . transgender;
- adopting a transhistorical approach that connects modern [transgender] identities to historical figures and cultures;
- using modern cross-cultural studies to show that [antitransgender] attitudes are culture bound;
- looking to statistics regarding prevalence to refute the notion that [transgender experience] is rare;
- underscoring the difficult, if not impossible, task of changing [gender identity], even through psychotherapeutic means;
- adopting and insisting on the use of normative language to replace medical terminology . . . ;
- labeling theories that contradict affirmative perspectives as unscientific;
- ad hominem and ad feminam attacks on professionals who either believe [transgender experience] is an illness or use pathologizing language to make sense of [transgender experience].[35]

The fact that transgender advocates have made and continue to make normalizing arguments about transgender experience neither proves nor disproves the veracity of their claims. Thoughtful Christians need to critically engage these claims and their underlying logic rather than accepting them at face value or rejecting them out of hand. Unfortunately, our current political climate does not lend itself to critical engagement with claims and logic. While we will cover some ground in this regard, a comprehensive critique of each argument is a task we leave for a future project.

Proponents of the deconstruction of existing sex and gender norms view parents who subscribe to their perspective as heroes in the "dismantling" of the "sex/gender system."[36] However, we view these parents as products of the very communities that praise them, because these communities have provided them with the language and categories necessary to dismantle existing cultural expectations. These parents may be hailed as heroes, but they are not the source of the gender ideologies they enact. They are not the ones who have an interest in "undoing" gender. Rather, they love their children and seek out advice about how best to express this love in relation to sex and gender norms. Regardless of where we find ourselves in the current debate around sex and gender identity, we do well to not villainize parents or identify them as the root of shifting gender perspectives.

Yet parents are drawn into the discussion as proximal agents and become keys to social change.

> The notion that "gender identity," or the felt sense of gender subjectivity, is fundamental, immutable, and not tied to the materiality of the body makes it possible for parents to begin to understand some children to be transgender and to alter their social environment to accommodate that subjectivity. Atypical gender was once considered a form of psychopathology; it was a failure of gender. Now for the first time, atypical gender is understood not as a failure of gender, but as a *form* of gender. Gender transgression marks the insufficiency of reified gender categories (male/female), and not of the individual who inhabits them. Gender nonconformity now constitutes social identity, rather than eroding it.[37]

The purpose of introducing these arguments is to ask the following question: How do arguments developed for political purposes become components of a public identity? A public identity is the natural consequence of a successful political identity, regardless of whether those who benefit from the public identity recognize its political history. Public identity refers to how people are known to others in their communities.

You might have a transgender neighbor or coworker, a gender nonbinary classmate or suitemate, or a genderfluid loved one—an uncle, aunt, son, or daughter. The way this person is known by you and by others in their community with respect to gender forms their public identity. The more common transgender identity becomes, the more it comes to be seen as a normal variant of gender identity expression. A normalizing argument is just that: it presents diverse gender identities as within the scope of what can be expected in one's cultural setting.

Those who adopted a political identity in relation to transgender experience worked to ensure that this identity was not treated as an inferior or disabled identity defined exclusively in medical and psychiatric terms. According to Murib, diagnostic shifts in psychiatry were essential to the emergence of transgender as both a political identity and a subsequently public identity.[38] To identify as transgender in a public way (rather than simply adopting a psychiatric diagnosis of disorder) reinforces the notion that there is no inexorable relationship between biological sex and gender identity. This brand of public identification is now often seen as the most reliable path for a transgender person to thrive in the world.

Ellie, the adolescent with late-onset gender identity concerns whom we discussed at the beginning of this chapter, reflects a public identity made possible by the political identity of transgender activism. Renee Richards and Hari Nef also reflect public identities born out of shifts in gender identity discourse from psychiatric and medical communities into the public domain via the political development of "transgender." Although Richards and Nef experience their gender identities differently and disagree on the merits of the male/female binary, both individuals participate in a dramatically changed (and continually changing) sociocultural context where such disagreements may take place and where cross-gender and otherwise variant gender identities are valued and celebrated.

This book moves beyond conventional presentations of gender dysphoria, beyond the plainest distinctions between cisgender and transgender identities. We are here discussing emerging gender identities, some of which coincide with older forms of transgender identity rooted in the male/female binary but many of which are part of gender-nonbinary and gender-diverse presentations that have only recently risen in prominence. Some of these identities are connected to gender dysphoria, while others may not meet diagnostic criteria for a gender dysphoria diagnosis, or professionals might disagree about proper diagnosis. Some emerging gender identities appear to be trending among adolescents and among those presenting at specialty clinics for assistance with gender identity. These atypical presentations are challenging existing models of care and challenging clinicians to rethink categories of gender and gender identity as well as to rethink the diagnostic labels and treatment plans they recommend in such cases.

How should Christians respond to the changes occurring within our culture? Do we view these changes simply as part of a larger LGBTQ+ agenda to deconstruct norms regarding sex and gender? Do we view them as necessary shifts in thought that reflect the latest scientific research? Or are there other options for critical engagement from a Christian worldview? Are there other ways of understanding these events and engaging the individuals and organizations reflected in our cultural moment? These are the practical questions that lay before us and will be taken up in part 2 of this book.

As we come to a better understanding of the history of transgender experiences and the shifts from political to public identity, we must explore how emerging gender identities have come about and whether these new linguistic categories for gender create new categories of people. We turn to this discussion in chapter 2.

CHAPTER 2

How Language and Categories Shape Gender Identities

A recent Minnesota Public Radio report introduces readers to Max, a thirteen-year-old who identifies as "agender."[1] Max explains the term this way: "What it means is I'm neither a guy or girl . . . and that's how I feel, which is different than terms like 'gender fluid'—which means you feel like a guy or girl at different times—because I don't feel like I'm both guy and girl. I'm neither." Two years ago, after initially identifying as a girl, Max discovered several gender identity labels, including *agender*, through social media. "I was like, you know what? This describes me a little better than 'girl.' . . . I've been rolling with that for over a year."

Agender is one of many emerging gender identities, on a list that also includes new terms like *genderqueer*, *genderfluid*, *bigender*, *gender expansive*, and *gender creative*. A few years ago, prevalence estimates for transgender self-identification ranged from 1 in 215 to 1 in 300.[2] More recent estimates put the rates for adults at closer to 0.6 percent—roughly 1 in 166.[3] It is unclear whether these studies capture all the variations of gender identity that exist today, since many emerging gender identities fall under the "nonbinary" category.

Rates of transgender self-identification among youth appear to be much higher than rates among adults, however. Recent prevalence estimates from the Centers for Disease Control (CDC) report that 1.8 percent of teens agreed with the statement, "Yes, I am transgender."[4] A survey from GLAAD conducted by the Harris Poll suggests significantly higher rates of transgender and gender variant experiences among younger people. Titled "Accelerating Acceptance," the 2017 survey suggests 12 percent of people between the ages of eighteen and thirty-four identify as transgender or gender nonconforming, more than twice the percentage of those between the ages of thirty-five and fifty-one.[5] These remarkably high percentages are questionable, in our view, but they illustrate what has undeniably been a dramatic shift in the prevalence of transgender identities in a relatively short span of time. If these estimates are accurate, emerging gender identities may reflect a cultural trend that is likely to add more confusion to the already challenging topic of gender identity.

How are we to understand these increases? How might we understand Max's experience? These are difficult questions to answer, but we want to offer some ideas to help make sense of these cultural trends and respond to Max in a more meaningful way.

There are at least two common and starkly opposed explanations for recent increases in the number of young people presenting at gender specialty clinics in several countries,[6] including the United States. One explanation attributes these increases to more exposure or awareness, while the opposing view credits the rising numbers to social contagion. Let's take a look at both accounts.

In trans-affirmative care circles, the most common explanation for the rise of trans self-identification is that young people use these labels more than older generations because young people are more easily able to publicly identify as transgender or gender nonbinary. According to this explanation, the rise in trans-identifying youth is not an increase in the *number* of young people whose experience defies cisgender norms; rather, this rising number represents an increase in *self-reporting*, because young people today live in a culture where they can safely be honest about gender experiences that have always existed but were previously taboo.

This explanation is rooted in an essentialist understanding—or, at least, an essentialist presentation—of what it means to be transgender or gender nonbinary. When we say "essentialist," we are speaking of the claim that these experiences are real and categorical, present across cultures and throughout history. Proponents of this view point to anthropological studies suggesting that something like transgender experience has existed in many forms and cultural contexts. In some cultures, such experience was accepted or even revered; in other cultures, identifying in opposition to sex and gender norms was catastrophic. Many individuals who have attempted to live within the gender binary have done so in great distress and with few people knowing about their struggles.

We mentioned in chapter 1 that we do believe gender dysphoria and transgender experiences have existed in some form throughout history and across cultures. However, the theory of increased awareness is not the only explanation for current trends in the rise of emerging gender identities and atypical gender identity presentations. A second, opposing explanation of the current trends comes from those who are most wary of these trends—especially the trend of late-onset dysphoria among natal females. Groups like 4thWaveNow describe the trends as a form of "social contagion."[7] Broadly understood, social contagion is the phenomenon by which "affect, attitudes, beliefs and behaviour can indeed spread through populations as if they were somehow infectious," and "this tendency towards homogeneity has been identified in a number of types of behavior" including smoking, risk-taking behaviors, criminality, and self-harm.[8]

A recent study by Lisa Littman, although heavily critiqued for its methodology and conclusions, nonetheless offers a perspective of "social contagion" in the context of gender identity:[9] "In the past decade, there has been an increase in visibility, social media, and user-generated online content about transgender issues and transition, which may act as a double-edged sword. On the one hand, an increase in visibility has given a voice to individuals who would have been under-diagnosed and undertreated in the past. On the other hand, it is plausible that online content may encourage vulnerable individuals to believe that nonspecific symptoms and vague feelings should be interpreted as gender dysphoria stemming from a transgender condition."[10]

While we do not think either of these accounts on its own captures all of what we see in the existing trends, they are certainly the two most prominent perspectives. They are opposed to one another in ways that will continue to fan the flame of the cultural wars regarding sex and gender, as people line up on opposing sides and reject suggestions outside of their own explanatory framework.

In our view, to say that what we are currently seeing is due merely to the freedom to label does not exhaustively make sense of the increasing and evolving heterogeneity in experiences of transgender identity. Neither does it explain the uptick of biological females who present as transgender or otherwise gender diverse but who report no history of gender-related questioning in childhood. To describe what we see as mere social contagion does not capture the story of the sixty-year-old person who has experienced gender-related questions long before they were popularized, does not want to transition, but is grateful to have language for an experience she thought of for many years as a sign of "psychosis."

A third way to think about the apparent increase in transgender and gender nonbinary identification and referrals to specialty clinics, especially among youth, is to recognize multiple layers of explanation that likely contribute to this increase. Certainly, we can acknowledge that some people are more likely to identify as transgender or gender nonbinary due to greater social awareness of the experience and greater social tolerance or acceptance of it. Some people who now identify as transgender or gender nonbinary have had such experiences all along but did not previously have the ability or opportunity to be known by others in the way they are known today.

To claim that this cultural shift accounts for the entire increase in diverse gender presentations would not be accurate. We see many young people who do not have a history of gender identity concerns, who freely admit that in another culture or social landscape they would not subscribe to such labels, and who did not think of themselves in such terms until the option was made available. Likewise, it would not be accurate to say that the sharp increase in diverse gender presentations is exclusively the result of social contagion, as though all new cases of gender dysphoria and all atypical gender presentations are really just a search for identity and community by teens who are troubled in other ways. Truthfully, not every teen sees this label as an avenue into community. Not every teen sees a transgender identity as a badge of honor. And frankly, we don't know any teens who woke up one day and thought, "I want to enhance my social status, make my parents proud of me, and get more likes on Instagram. I'm going to adopt a trans* label." This oversimplification of the trends we see is appealing because it reduces complexity and lets us dismiss these experiences as a mere fad. Yet if there is greater complexity at play, reducing this complexity is not only unhelpful but also unkind: it keeps us from responding in a nuanced and adequate way both to the underlying factors at play and to the people for whom these factors may have lasting impacts.

We believe several factors contribute to the gender identities we see emerging today. We do see an increase in some gender permutations that reflect a desire for the identity and community that teens may find within LGBTQ+ spaces. It is unclear whether LGBTQ+ identification can lead to gender dysphoria over time—that is, whether self-understanding as transgender could lead to greater emphasis on and distress around gender identity. We do see some cases of cross-dressing behavior that begins as a sexual fetish but can evolve over time into a persistent self-perception leading to actual gender dysphoria. This phenomenon is noted in the fifth edition of the *Diagnostic and Statistical Manual of Mental Disorders (DSM-5)*.[11]

Another factor likely contributing to emerging gender identities is the shifting terrain of masculinity, femininity, and sex and gender norms resulting from the sexual revolution and feminist movements. While shifts in attitudes about sex and sexual behaviors may seem somewhat removed from the present discussion, these shifts offered a sense of liberation, separating the body's capacity for sexual pleasure from its capacity for procreation. With the introduction of accessible contraceptive options, the body's procreative potential was rendered obsolete, and even viewed in some cases as a threat to women's equality with men.[12]

Such thinking is exemplified by feminists such as 1970s writer Shulamith Firestone, who calls for a kind of "feminist revolution." She begins by quoting German philosopher Friedrich Engels: "Everything is fluid, is constantly changing."[13] Her mission, she explains, is to change not only society but also human nature and human biology in order to eliminate the oppression of women. Women, being at the mercy of their biology, must be liberated from it; they must "outgrow nature" so that their reproductive capacity, which disadvantages them in relation to men, is annihilated.[14] As a solution to the oppression against women, Firestone calls for not only "the elimination of male privilege but of the sex distinction itself: genital differences between human beings would no longer matter culturally."[15] Perhaps her hope is being realized in recent shifts in norms of sex and gender. This vision is not far from the prominent narrative today that calls for a gender revolution.

Reacting in part to this deconstruction of sex and gender norms, some people have doubled down on rigid stereotypes of maleness and femaleness. Many Christian contexts have become especially reliant on gender stereotypes in their attempt to offer a distinctly biblical narrative of human gender and sexuality. Men's retreats are fraught with burly images of masculinity, presenting as the norm the hypermasculine lumberjack who refuses to cry. Rock climbing, beer drinking, football watching, and locker-room humor have been normalized in some circles as synonymous with being a "real man."[16] For women, some Christians have preached that a godly woman's life should look like a snapshot out of *Leave It to Beaver*: staying home with the children, dabbing on makeup and throwing on heels before her husband arrives home from work, keeping her opinions to herself, and certainly pleasing him sexually. Conversely, some women have heard that the godly woman is one who does not attend too much to her appearance for fear of vanity and who seeks modesty so as not to distract men by her beauty. It seems likely that the reactive strength of these cultural narratives also may contribute to the discussion about emerging gender identities.

We wonder if, for some teens, adopting an emerging gender identity is a way of making meaning out of the sense that they do not fit into rigid stereotypes of masculinity and femininity. A teenage boy who isn't drawn to sports will likely feel out of place among his male peers when the conversation turns to football. A teenage girl who isn't drawn to makeup might feel inadequate among her female peers when they start discussing *Cosmo* magazine. The more stringent their community's gender expectations—especially for young women who are told that they must be either stylish and fashionable or, conversely, meek and homely in order to be godly women—the more heightened their sense of displacement may be.

In adolescence, peer connections are central to the social and emotional lives of young people. They look around to see from their peers the options for their own self-expression. In what ways could the sense that they do not fit in the increasingly narrow (and even contradictory) "boxes" of stereotypical maleness and femaleness contribute to the uptick of emerging gender identities we now see, especially among women? If the only models a woman sees available to her demand radical self-sufficiency, total dependence and subservience, or sole emphasis on physical beauty, what becomes of the woman who finds all these paths unappealing? When Bible passages like 1 Peter 3:5–6 have at times become grounds for the abuse of women, might some women find themselves understandably repulsed by such a narrative? There is no question that the categories we have described leave little space for the development of a male or female identity in which all people can envision themselves thriving.

We tend to steer away from the language of "social contagion," as it seems unnecessarily antagonistic and doesn't account for other factors that could also be at play. It has been used to invalidate the lived experience of those who, for whatever reason, do not see themselves as male or female. Rather than thinking in terms of social contagion, we incline toward a framework developed by Ian Hacking, who identifies a broader problem in mental health that he refers to as a "looping effect." Let's consider this idea and whether it can be applied to emerging gender identities associated with transgender experiences.

The Looping Effect

The looping effect, according to Hacking, is a recursive dynamic between people and categories from the human sciences.[17] In essence,

COMPETING EXPLANATORY FRAMEWORKS FOR ATYPICAL GENDER PRESENTATIONS

Explanation 1: Newfound freedom and courage to self-identify
Explanation 2: Social contagion
Explanation 3: Multiple contributions, including a looping effect

looping is about how "changing ideas change people, and how changed people necessitate further changes in ideas."[18] The looping effect is conceptualized as a phenomenon that affects everyone. We all interact with language and categories that shape our experience of ourselves and the world around us. Hacking illustrates the phenomenon by giving an account of his own work studying early nineteenth-century demography and statistics; discussing the effects of counting and categorizing on different people, he notes how "people come to fit their categories."[19] In other words, people's behaviors changed in response to how they were categorized.[20]

Hacking also reflects on a looping effect in mental health categorization, where people react to how they are categorized. Reactions may be behavioral or conceptual or may affect identity insofar as assumptions about one's self and the condition are shaped by mental health nomenclatures. This shaping can come from many sources, including mental health experts, broader societal views, and taken-for-granted realities.

According to Hacking, a looping effect can be accounted for in five parts:

a. Classification
b. People
c. Institutions
d. Knowledge
e. Experts[21]

These five parts are illustrated in figure 1. Here is an account from Hacking that elaborates on the five parts using the example of multiple personality as a mental illness:

> We have (a) a classification, multiple personality, associated with what at the time was called a "disorder." This kind of person is now a moving target. We have (b) the people, those I call "unhappy," "unable to cope," or whatever relatively non-judgmental term you might prefer. There are (c) institutions, which include clinics, annual meetings of the International Society for the Study of Multiple Personality and Dissociation, afternoon talkshows on television (Oprah Winfrey and Geraldo Rivera made a big thing of multiples, once upon a time), and weekend training programmes for therapists, some of which I attended. There is (d) the knowledge: not justified true belief, once the mantra of analytic

Figure 1
A Looping Effect

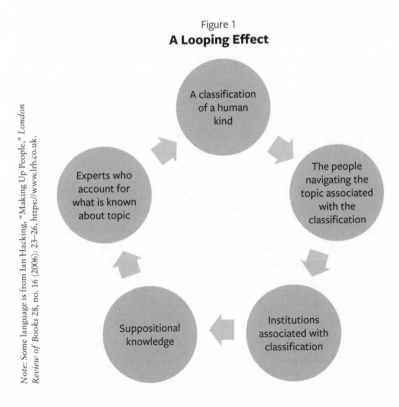

Note: Some language is from Ian Hacking, "Making Up People," *London Review of Books* 28, no. 16 (2006): 23–26, https://www.lrb.co.uk.

philosophers, but knowledge in Popper's sense of conjectural knowledge, and, more specifically, the presumptions that are taught, disseminated and refined within the context of the institutions. Especially the basic facts (not "so-called facts," or "facts" in scare-quotes): for example, that multiple personality is caused by early sexual abuse, that 5 per cent of the population suffer from it, and the like. There is expert knowledge, the knowledge of the professionals, and there is popular knowledge, shared by a significant part of the interested population. There was a time, partly thanks to those talkshows and other media, when "everyone" believed that multiple personality was caused by early sexual abuse. Finally, there are (e) the experts or professionals who generate (d) the knowledge, judge its validity, and use it in their practice. They work within (c) institutions that guarantee their legitimacy, authenticity and status as experts. They study, try to help, or advise on the control of (b) the people who are (a) classified as of a given kind.[22]

Let's step back and look at what a looping effect actually is. To begin, we want to follow Hacking in distinguishing between natural and human phenomena. Hacking's example of a natural phenomenon is the scientific categorization of a substance, such as a chemical compound. The compound does not respond to categorization. It does not react to the label being used, nor does it think about its own designation or the language used to describe it as a phenomenon.

In contrast, when scientists categorize people, these people are obviously able to respond to their categorization in ways that inert substances cannot. For example, when mental health professionals identify diagnostic categories for mental health concerns, we see changes in how people think about themselves, behave, and interact with their own designation. Mental health categories, like other forms of human categories, offer new ways for people to think about themselves, their identity, and their history. Put differently, "Language influences how psychopathology is framed, theorised, experienced and treated."[23] As a result, by expanding the language and categories we use to describe a phenomenon, we inadvertently expand the ways in which people can experience themselves and their history. This is a part of the looping effect.

Hacking offers a narration of the events surrounding multiple personality as he understands them:

> Around 1970, there arose a few paradigm cases of strange behaviour similar to phenomena discussed a century earlier and largely forgotten. A few psychiatrists began to diagnose multiple personality. It was rather sensational. More and more unhappy people started manifesting these symptoms. At first they had the symptoms they were expected to have, but then they became more and more bizarre. First, a person had two or three personalities. Within a decade the mean number was 17. This fed back into the diagnoses, and became part of the standard set of symptoms. It became part of the therapy to elicit more and more alters. Psychiatrists cast around for causes, and created a primitive, easily understood pseudo-Freudian aetiology of early sexual abuse, coupled with repressed memories. Knowing this was the cause, the patients obligingly retrieved the memories. More than that, this became a way to be a person. In 1986, I wrote that there could never be "split" bars, analogous to gay bars. In 1991 I went to my first split bar.[24]

We may begin with the creation of categories to account for the experiences of paradigm cases, but people interact with those categories. Categorizing people opens up new ways for people to think of themselves, new ways to behave, and new ways to think about their past: "Ways of classifying human beings interact with the human beings who are classified. . . . People think of themselves as of a kind, perhaps, or reject the classification. All our acts are under descriptions, and the acts that are open to us depend, in a purely formal way, on the descriptions available to us."[25]

Once people have been classified, institutions associated with classification inevitably arise. These can include specialty clinics, professional conferences, professional organizations, and related institutional endeavors such as task forces, working groups, and committees that reflect institutional thought and shape popular thought about a topic.

From these institutions emerge suppositional knowledge and theories defining what we know about a topic. This suppositional knowledge includes what is taught about a topic and how it is revised over time, and it gradually migrates into the broader cultural discourse about the phenomenon. This knowledge may be reflected in the entertainment industry, media, social networks, and so on.

As the body of knowledge increases, experts arise who weigh in on how we are to understand the phenomenon. In the case of mental health considerations, experts take the lead in determining what is factual about the topic, and they introduce interventions and methods of working with the phenomenon.

The principle of the looping effect suggests that certain kinds of people may increasingly "come into existence" through the creation of classifications and the ways in which people interact with those classifications. Extending this to discussions about mental health categorization, we might ask, Do looping effects help in any way to explain trends in mental health presentation over time? A looping effect does appear to account for the steep increase in multiple personality, as Hacking suggests: "In 1955 this was not a way to be a person, people did not experience themselves in this way, they did not interact with their friends, their families, their employers, their counsellors, in this way; but in 1985 this was a way to be a person, to experience oneself, to live in society."[26]

We want to suggest that a similar looping effect is occurring vis-à-vis what we have called emerging gender identities. Let's reconsider gender dysphoria and the relatively recent phenomenon of emerging gender identities in light of a possible looping effect.

Emerging Gender Identities

Let us clarify at the outset that we are not suggesting that society has created incongruence between people's gender identity and biological sex. Something close to this phenomenon has been reported throughout history and across cultures. We say "something close" only because gender identity is itself a relatively new concept. We want to be clear, though, that a subset of people is often recognized as diverging from sex and gender norms, and this reality appears to be reflected in a variety of cultural contexts throughout history.

Let us further elaborate our position that transgender experiences today are not completely invented by society. Hacking, in his discussion of the looping effect, frames a philosophical debate between nominalists and realists. Nominalists argue that new distinctions create new realities that "effectively came into being" alongside their nomenclatures.[27] To one extent or another, nominalists hold that "categories, classes and taxonomies are given by human beings rather than by nature and that these categories are essentially fixed throughout the several eras of humankind."[28] Realists, in contrast, hold that such distinctions have always been real and were simply waiting to be named and classified correctly.

We do not see either of these explanations as wholly satisfying. Neither did Hacking. He himself was drawn to a "dynamic nominalism" in which kinds of people were not so much *discovered by* science (or some other accounting, such as demography or surveying) as they were *evolving alongside* science; that is, "a kind of person came into being at the same time as the kind itself was being invented."[29]

Although Hacking is concerned with categorization and entities generally rather than with specific questions about gender identities, the principles at play in his philosophical framing are relevant here. As we turn to the transgender discussion and especially to emerging gender identities, we find that neither nominalism nor realism alone can explain all the current trends. We believe that something like gender incongruence has been reported throughout history and across cultures, challenging a strict nominalist position. Yet as the experience of gender incongruence is understood in evolving ways by society, as well as by individuals navigating gender identity questions, our vocabulary of gender identity also seems to shape people's perceptions and experiences of gender, challenging a strict realist position.

Is gender expression a preexisting reality that was only recently recognized by those developing surveys? Or are we discussing experiences of gender (e.g., gender expansive, bigender, gender nonbinary) that "came into being at the same time as the kind itself was being invented"?[30] Society's current fascination with gender identity, as distinct from identity as a sexed being (male or female), clearly follows the development of transgender as a political and public way of being in the world. So while some forms of gender incongruence certainly preceded our current moment, we are also suggesting that new and emerging gender identities are being constructed in part by the present cultural context.

Consider the recent history of categorizing gender incongruence as a mental health concern. Recall that the framing of *transgender* shifted from medical and psychiatric to public and political as the umbrella began growing to account for a wide range of gender identity experiences. If we fast-forward to more recent history, we see a shift from the previous edition (*DSM-IV-TR*)[31] to the most recent edition (*DSM-5*) of the American Psychiatric Association's diagnostic manual, which now classifies the *distress* potentially associated with gender incongruence as a disorder but does not conceive of incongruence or transgender identity as disorders in themselves. This shift in diagnosis occurred in part in response to interactions with members of the broader transgender community, who battled the stigma associated with medical and psychiatric labels and rejected the view of transgender identity as a signal of psychopathology.

As of this writing, the current psychiatric classification for the phenomenon under discussion is *gender dysphoria*.[32] As we noted in chapter 1, a similar phenomenon in the previous diagnostic classification was *gender identity disorder*. We say "similar phenomenon" because the diagnosis changed as the profession weighed in on how to understand gender incongruence.

The current psychiatric categorization of gender incongruence—that is, gender dysphoria—is not concerned with gender identity as such; to experience any kind of diverse gender identity is not the issue. The question is whether this experience is distressing or impairs functioning. In some respects, this focus on distress both narrows and broadens the psychiatric categorization. It narrows the categorization insofar as many people will not report distress; they will simply report their identification with one of many emerging gender identities, such as gender expansive or gender nonbinary. By connecting the diagnosis only to distress, *DSM-5* makes it possible for people to have or express gender identities that are not treated as mental health concerns but can be understood as alternative gender identities associated with the broader LGBTQ+ community.[33]

But the current account also broadens the psychiatric categorization, because it includes not only cross-gender identity—the classic transsexual experience of perceiving oneself as a woman trapped in the body of a man (or vice versa)—but also other gender identities outside of or in between the male/female binary.

Mental health professionals and the general population must navigate competing ideas about how to understand people who experience gender incongruence. All the more, those who experience gender incongruence themselves must navigate the language and categories available to them (in their social context) for gender and identity, determining how to make sense of their past experience and direct their future experience. They can and do interact with both the current psychiatric classification and the language associated with various categories of identity.

Recall that a looping effect can be accounted for in five parts:

a. Classification
b. People
c. Institutions
d. Knowledge
e. Experts

We illustrate the five parts as they pertain to the gender dysphoria diagnosis in figure 2. We begin with (a) a classification, gender dysphoria, the current psychiatric construct for what was previously called gender identity disorder. This classification is applied to (b) the people who experience gender identity incongruence, and they continue to interact (as they have undoubtedly been interacting) with their classification. As Tey Meadow observes, "As transpeople and their parents assert their identities in increasing numbers to medical professionals, they become installed as legitimate categories of being, analysis, and study. As they assert their identities to schools, churches, and communities,

Figure 2

A Looping Effect Associated with Emerging Gender Identities

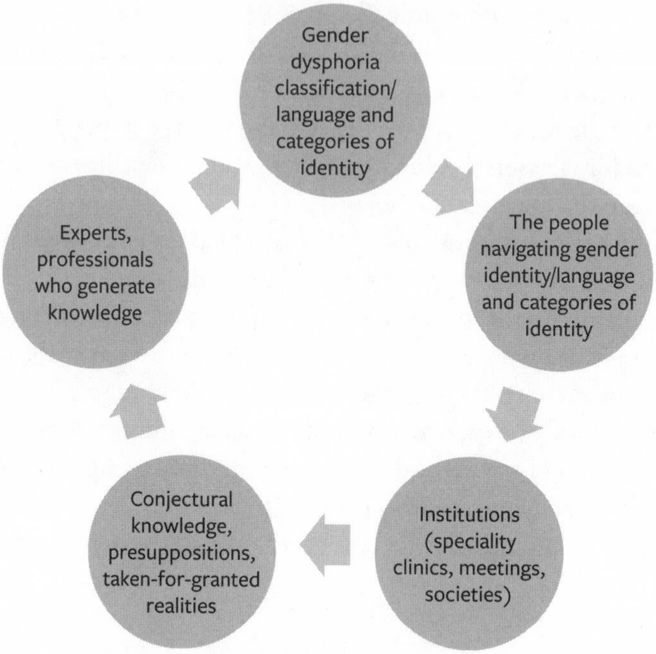

Note: Some language is from Ian Hacking, "Making Up People," *London Review of Books* 28, no. 16 (2006): 23–26, https://www.lrb.co.uk.

they change the architectures of those institutions, becoming embedded in the very ways they function."[34]

We also know of many (c) institutions, professional societies, and specialty clinics associated with the gender dysphoria diagnosis.[35] As Hacking notes, "Classifications do not exist only in the empty space of language but in institutions, practices, material interactions with things and other people."[36] Indeed, we have seen a rise of such specialty clinics in the US in the past ten years. The opening of new clinics is often a response to the growing demand for transgender care; many clinics are developing waiting lists, as they are overwhelmed by calls for consultations. Some common claims about experiences of gender incongruence are emerging as suppositional (d) knowledge, which Hacking defines as "the presuppositions that are taught, disseminated and refined within the context of the institutions."[37] In the realm of gender, suppositional knowledge includes illustrations like the genderbread person, the gender unicorn, and other tools that depict taken-for-granted realities about how young people may experience their biological (now-assigned) sex, gender, and gender identity.[38] We are not so much criticizing these resources as we are noting how their teaching shapes the possibilities for gender identity and, ultimately, people's sense of self. The curation of this knowledge about gender requires (e) the experts, who determine for society what counts as valid knowledge and who offer guidance about how to respond, including how best to use specific (d) knowledge in a clinical or applied setting and as a society.

What results from the looping effect of gender identity in our culture? Though the looping effect has many outcomes, one of the most significant is the development of transgender as an *industry*. This development of classification-based industry may not be embedded in Hacking's original looping effect, but it certainly exists by extension. Speaking favorably about such developments, Meadow offers the following synopsis: "Transgender children are popular subjects of reality television shows, the news media, documentary films, and children's books. . . . There are children's books about children who identify as members of the other gender or who enjoy dressing or playing in gender-diverse ways. There are guides for parents on raising a gender nonconforming child and a rapidly expanding literature for the clinicians who serve them. There are dozens of personal stories by parents and young people themselves. There are self-help books for teens and parents. In short, 'trans' is not just an identity; it's an industry."[39]

Although we could take this discussion in a number of different directions—including public policy, legislation, and religious-liberty debates—we will leave most of these matters in the hands of others. For our purposes in framing our discussion about how Christians can understand and relate to those facing gender identity questions, the development of transgender-as-industry is accompanied by a few other significant outcomes of the looping effect:

- an increase in the number of specialty clinics serving diverse gender identities

- an increase in the number of people reporting diverse gender identities
- greater diversity of emerging gender identities
- lack of consensus about how best to proceed with children and teens who experience gender incongruence
- backlash from some parents who are concerned about the speed and direction of care for gender-atypical youth

At this point, we caution readers to be aware of the impact that our rapidly changing culture may have on how people think about themselves, their gender identity, and the options that lie before them. None of us—including psychiatric professionals, even those who specialize in this area—fully appreciate how cultural forces can shape our categories of self-understanding.

Is gendering a biological or a social process? Whether you are an advocate of the changing norms that support transgender and emerging gender identities or a critic of these cultural shifts, you would be hard-pressed to deny that there are elements of both biology and social processes at play in gender.

Advocates of transgender and emerging gender identities are often drawn to biological arguments for gender (think of the "brain-sex" theory and recent MRI scans suggesting something like an intersex condition of the brain).[40] Advocates also acknowledge the existence of social processes of gender, which they see as doing great damage to transgender people, and they want culture to develop new social processes that support emerging gender identities.

Critics likewise often argue that gendering is a biological process—because, they say, gender ought to reflect the biological sex of the person under discussion. They acknowledge that social processes are in play, too, a dynamic often described in terms of "social contagion" in the development of transgender and emerging gender identities.

Our view is that elements of both biological and social processes are at play in gender identity development. We maintain that emerging social processes have contributed to emerging gender identities, which reflect a growing sense of personhood. These social processes bring significant implications for youth that both church culture and broader Western culture must grapple with. Young people are discovering and identifying their sense of self in a new way within their current sense of gender, and to approach conversations around gender identity with instant mockery or uncritical enthusiasm misses the complexities and nuances that would help us understand how to best support these young people. Gender has become an increasingly "iterative, interactive process" in ways that reflect the looping effect described by Hacking.[41]

We are also witnessing in some emerging gender identities not gender dysphoria but simply new language and categories for developing identity. It is as though, because there are "new storylines" available (with the deconstruction of norms regarding sex and gender), there can now be "new stories."[42] We suspect that some teens in particular are susceptible to stories that have only recently gained cultural salience. As these teens face challenges in their own lives, they may be more prone to adopting culturally salient ways of describing their identity and community. If a path is unavailable to a person, they do not choose it; when a path becomes available, someone facing other troubles or challenges may indeed choose to "express their difficulties" through that path.[43]

A great challenge for mental health professionals—as well as for the rest of us—is learning how to distinguish different accounts of transgender and emerging gender identities. Proper discernment of actual mental health concerns can lead to the identification of appropriate interventions that would be warranted for some teens but not others. Some teens' exploration of gender identity questions is motivated by experiences of gender dysphoria; other teens face a variety of difficult life circumstances that have led them to seek identity and community through existing culturally salient roles. While responding to dysphoria is an important intervention for the first group, it may be of little help to the second group. Children and teens may self-ascribe using terminology, language, and categories that do not tell us what is actually going on in their lives or how best to respond and care for them.

Alan Jacobs, in a brief reflection on the topic of emerging gender identities, observes how adults can attribute dramatic cultural shifts to children rather than considering how they as adults have contributed to the phenomena:

> One clever little specialty of adult humans works like this: You very carefully (and, if you're smart, very *subtly*) instruct children in the moral stances you'd like them to hold. Then, when they start to repeat what you've taught them, you cry "Out of the mouths of babes! And a little child shall lead them!" And you very delicately maneuver the children to the front of your procession, so that they appear to be leading it—but of course you make sure all along that you're steering them in the way that they should go. It's a social strategy with a very long history.
>
> So, for instance, when you hear this: "It's the children who are now leading us," said Diane Ehrensaft, the director of mental health for the clinic. "They're coming in and telling us, 'I'm no gender.' Or they're saying, 'I identify as gender nonbinary.' Or 'I'm a little bit of this and a little bit of that. I'm a unique gender, I'm transgender. I'm a rainbow kid, I'm boy-girl, I'm everything.'"—certain alarms should ring.[44]

What does Jacobs say in response? He offers this: "No child came up with the phrase 'I identify as gender nonbinary.' It is a faithful echo of an adult's words."

Jacobs is right, of course. The language used by children in the present context reflects language used by adults. This does not mean that we disregard the experience of the child who uses such words. Rather, we must take seriously the experience of the child that led to their being drawn to such words while also considering how the availability of these words within culture may impact a child's sense of self and notions of what will lead to their own flourishing.

Gender specialists often provide parents, too, with language to use in interactions with their children. This altered language may be intended to eliminate the hegemony of the sex/gender system and the male/female binary, which is seen as a source of oppression. We are, of course, concerned about children whose experience does not fit well into existing gender categories. We would never support belittling these children or denying the significant distress caused when they are made to feel that their experience is negligible. But we do not see the categories of male and female themselves as a source of oppression. We invite readers to respond to such children with care and compassion while retaining an appreciation for male and female gender categories. The alternative appears increasingly to be the deconstruction of all gender categories and norms, and in their place the social construction of ever-expanding iterations of gender, with a corresponding hegemony over those who retain any reference to a relationship between sex and gender.

Language and categories do not develop in a vacuum. The way we define, describe, and account for gender and related experiences develops in a specific sociocultural context and in interaction with those who are classified. Rather than relying entirely on either the "increased awareness" theory or the "social contagion" theory to explain the rise of emerging gender identities, we have suggested vis-à-vis Hacking that something closer to a looping effect provides the better, more nuanced explanation for how our current gender moment has come about. We now turn to how such insights can inform how we relate to and care for those facing questions about gender identity.

Our conclusion about the looping effect in diverse gender identities should not detract from the reality of gender dysphoria for some people. Whether gender dysphoria originates in childhood (early onset) or later in life (late onset), even if it appears to develop subsequent to other motivations for gender-atypical behavior, it is still a reality for that person and should be responded to with compassion. But insofar as society contributes to the creation of emerging categories for gender identity, it is worth noting that such efforts have real-world effects for which we must take responsibility.

As we bring this chapter to a close, we illustrate in figure 3 several possible presentations of diverse gender identities we have been discussing in this chapter. There are, of course, those for whom *transgender* is the best word to describe their experience of a gender identity that does not correspond with their biological sex. A subset of these individuals will be diagnosed with gender dysphoria, reflecting the distress of their experience of incongruence.

Figure 3

Multiple Presentations of Diverse Gender Identities

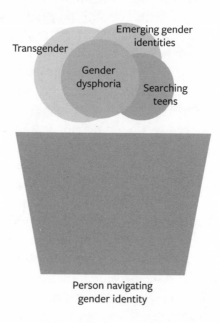

Person navigating
gender identity

We have also suggested that there are *emerging gender identities* (e.g., gender expansive) that reflect to some extent a looping effect in how people respond to the language, categories, and diagnostic labels used to account for their experiences. They may invest in identity motivations that can be fueled by a social construct they find resonance in. A subset of these individuals will also meet criteria for gender dysphoria.

Finally, we acknowledge that there may be teens dealing with other challenging life events not directly related to gender: for lack of a better phrase, we refer to this group as *searching teens*. In the past these teens might have turned to another cultural phenomenon in search of identity and belonging, but today transgender identity has cultural salience and offers a sense of community. They, too, may invest in identity motivations that find support in social constructs they connect with. Those in search of identity and community may thus find a home of sorts under the transgender umbrella.

Throughout this book, we will describe ways to relate to youth with gender diverse presentations. It will likely be beyond the scope of most Christian roles, whether professional ministers, parents, or laypeople, to distinguish whether the teen you care for reflects one or another of these possible presentations. Instead, we want to position you as a Christian to provide helpful accompaniment while the teen sorts out their concerns. True accompaniment will be at its best when it includes those of us who are family, friends, ministers, and even mental health providers to young people. Regardless of your role in a young person's life, and even though you may not always know how a teen's experience maps onto the possibilities we've discussed above, we hope the relationship strategies to come can equip you to accompany youth well in each situation you encounter.

CHAPTER 3

Controversies in Care

Artie, age five, was brought in by his parents for a gender identity evaluation. He had been displaying gender atypical interests for the past two years. These interests were initially dismissed as either "within limits" of what any boy might do or "just a phase" that would end once preschool began. Several months into preschool, the behavior had not changed. If anything, it seemed more pronounced. The parents, both Christians, struggled with what was best for Artie.

Bertrand, age eleven, was brought in by his parents for a consultation. He had been demonstrating gender atypical behavior and interests for several years. He was nearing the onset of puberty, and his parents were struggling with whether to "block" puberty and give Bertie (and themselves) a little more time to decide the best way forward in terms of gender identity.

Carissa, age fifteen, was brought in by their mother because they had disclosed a gender nonbinary identity to their parents four months ago, after being confronted about a picture posted on Instagram. Carissa is insisting on gender-neutral pronouns and chest reconstruction surgery to remove their breasts. Carissa's mother is absolutely overwhelmed by the weight and pace of the questions she is fielding.

These cases reflect three distinctly different and controversial areas of care today. This chapter provides an overview of the currently disputed areas of care for transgender youth, including whether to encourage children to adopt a cross-gender identity, whether to block puberty, and how to approach debates about "rapid onset" gender dysphoria. We will explain each of these controversies and offer some guidance for engaging with those who are questioning, even in cases where many unanswered questions about care remain.

While these particular controversies are specific to mental health care and not engagement broadly, it can be helpful to be familiar with the professional discussions that are taking place, including the controversies in the field, as you or those you care for face difficult decisions like Artie's family. Perhaps as we increase our understanding of the issues, we will be better positioned to come alongside families and youth.

For parents who have a loved one who is navigating gender identity questions, it is also important for you to understand some of the discussions and controversies in the mental health field, particularly as you hope to be informed consumers of mental health services and to support your loved one in decisions you and they face or may be facing in the years to come.

Care for Prepubescent Children

For a child who has yet to enter puberty, we have previously discussed three broad trajectories:

1. Reinforcing gender identity that corresponds to birth sex
2. Watchful waiting
3. Facilitating gender identity as expressed[1]

In this section we provide an update on the options available to families and some of the controversies surrounding them.

Reinforcing Gender Identity That Corresponds to Birth Sex

One trajectory of care allows for the possibility that a child can be assisted in resolving their gender incongruence with their birth sex. This has been referred to as the "live in your own skin" approach; it assumes that a child has a "malleable gender brain," and the common accompanying assumption is that living as transgender or with gender incongruence is more challenging on many fronts than identifying with birth sex.[2] Such an approach is dependent on current cultural understandings of gender expression and roles for boys and girls. Those culturally valued expressions and roles are reinforced in ways that are meant to be helpful to a child, with the end goal being a kind of congruence between the child's self-perception and their birth sex.

Legislation in many states has opposed sexual orientation change efforts, and in some cases it has included gender identity change efforts, which could affect practitioners drawn to this kind of approach. Insofar as such models are framed as a form of "conversion therapy" akin to making a gay person straight, we anticipate increasingly fewer practitioners will provide such services. The assumption that gender identity is like sexual orientation is predicated on an essentialist assumption that transgender is a discrete category or kind that is distinct from cisgender, understood to be such at an early age, and must not be intervened against in a way that could do harm to a child. Said another way, those who are critical of efforts to reinforce a gender identity that corresponds to one's birth sex would presume that the child really is "transgender." Guiding the child to live in accordance with their birth sex is to attempt to "change" their true gender identity.

A recent policy statement (titled "Ensuring Comprehensive Care and Support for Transgender and Gender-Diverse Children and Adolescents") from the American Academy of Pediatrics (AAP) stated that gender identity change efforts "are used to prevent children and adolescents from identifying as transgender or to dissuade them from exhibiting gender-diverse expressions."[3] This policy statement has been critiqued, too, as we will discuss below.

Watchful Waiting

A second trajectory of care is to take a "wait and see" posture toward the child or teen. This model "allows that a child may have knowledge of their gender identity at a young age, but should wait until the advent of adolescence before engaging in any full transition from one gender to another."[4]

Watchful waiting essentially provides a range of options to the child, who then makes choices about play and activities, even if these activities are gender atypical. The child is supported in their interests without attempts to direct or reinforce in one direction or the other. The goal here is to avoid shaming the child toward or against one set of interests; for instance, if a boy is interested in gymnastics and playing with Barbie dolls, a parent taking the watchful waiting approach would not force him to play baseball and only expose him to G.I. Joe dolls.

Consider how this approach might be applied in the case of Artie, the five-year-old introduced at the outset of this chapter. If Artie was making decisions about clothing for the day, he might have three outfits laid out for him, varying in colors and themes. One outfit would reflect a style preferred by many boys, with a second outfit reflecting what many girls might select, and a third outfit more neutral in color tones and themes. Artie could select any of the outfits for that day. Or if Artie were playing with toys, he would have a range of toys available to him, including items we stereotypically associate with boys (e.g., trucks), items we stereotypically associate with girls (e.g., dolls), and items our culture regards as gender-neutral (e.g., coloring books).

Surprisingly, the AAP, in its controversial 2018 guidelines, took issue with watchful waiting as well, calling it an "outdated approach" to gender incongruence in youth: "This outdated approach does not serve the child because critical support is withheld. Watchful waiting is based on binary notions of gender in which gender diversity and fluidity is pathologized; in watchful waiting, it is also assumed that notions of gender identity become fixed at a certain age."[5]

Again, we will offer a few thoughts below in response to the AAP policy statement.

Facilitating Gender Identity as Expressed

A third trajectory of care is to reinforce a person's emerging gender identity. This evolving approach, which is becoming a trend in many professional circles, stems from basic principles of what is sometimes called "trans-affirmative" or "gender-affirmative" care: "In this model the role of parents and socialization agents is not to shape or reinforce a child's gender identity or expression, but rather to facilitate it, mirroring back to the child the messages that the child communicates about their preferred gender expressions and articulated gender identity."[6] Such an approach "includes allowing children to speak for themselves about their self-experienced gender identity and expressions and providing support for them to evolve into their authentic gender selves, no matter at what age."[7]

Facilitating a child's expressed gender is the approach recommended in the AAP policy statement noted above. Clinicians are advised to "facilitate exploration of complicated emotions and gender-diverse expressions while allowing questions and concerns to be raised in a supportive environment."[8] The policy statement goes on to underscore the importance of communicating that

1. transgender identities and diverse gender expressions do not constitute a mental disorder;

2. variations in gender identity and expression are normal aspects of human diversity, and binary definitions of gender do not always reflect emerging gender identities;

3. gender identity evolves as an interplay of biology, development, socialization, and culture; and

4. if a mental health issue exists, it most often stems from stigma and negative experiences rather than being intrinsic to the child.[9]

The policy statement is worth reading in its entirety. We cannot summarize it fully here, but given that it originates from the largest pediatric organization in the US, it deserves careful reading. We turn now to a few reflections on the models of care and, specifically, the AAP report.

Reflections on the Models of Care

A critique by clinical psychologist and sexologist James Cantor published shortly after the release of the AAP policy statement noted several limitations.[10] Although it is difficult to fully appreciate the critique's arguments without reading it in its entirety, we will summarize two key points related to the three trajectories discussed above.

First, in response to the AAP's denunciation of what it calls "conversion" therapy—that is, attempts to reinforce the gender identity corresponding with birth sex—Cantor observes that no studies have been conducted of such practices related to gender identity: "Studies of conversion therapy have been limited to *sexual orientation*—specifically, the sexual orientation *of adults*—not *gender identity*, and not *children* in any case."[11] Cantor is saying two things. First, he is saying that the studies of conversion therapy conducted to date have examined attempts to change only sexual orientation, not gender identity. Second, he is saying that studies conducted to date have studied only adults, not children. In other words, there is no research that can speak to or inform the academy's denunciation of gender identity "conversion" therapy with minors.

To help us evaluate the merits of efforts to support a gender identity corresponding with a person's biological sex, researchers have gathered accounts from people for whom gender dysphoria *persisted*. These people tell us that birth-sex-affirming interventions were not helpful to them and at times were shaming or even harmful. It is important to listen to these accounts and not take lightly the impact of forcing a child to adopt stereotypically masculine or feminine interests or play. However, researchers haven't yet gathered accounts from people for whom gender dysphoria *desisted*. We are not stating that birth-sex-affirming interventions are necessarily the reason these children's gender dysphoria desisted; still, it also isn't clear that such steps were necessarily harmful. We know very little about what causes a child's gender dysphoria to desist and what impacts their ability to adopt a gender identity corresponding with their birth sex. Thus, we agree with Cantor's critique that the policy statement from the AAP is ahead of the science in making claims that have not been studied empirically.

Second, Cantor observes that the policy statement omits relevant research on the watchful waiting approach, which the statement portrays as "outdated." Indeed, the statement references only one of the eleven follow-up studies of children with gender dysphoria and makes no mention of the findings from any of those studies. What were the findings? In every published study, the majority of gender dysphoric children "ceased to want to transition."[12]

Cantor's conclusion is that the policy report "is advocating for something far in excess of mainstream practice and medical consensus. . . . [It] is a systematic exclusion and misrepresentation of entire literatures. Not only did [the policy] fail to provide *extraordinary* evidence, it failed to provide the evidence at all. Indeed, [the policy] recommendations are *despite* the existing evidence."[13]

This account makes clear that we are in the midst of a cultural and professional debate about sex and gender and about how best to care for young children who experience incongruence between their biological sex and gender identity, including those who meet diagnostic criteria for gender dysphoria and those who express any number of emerging gender identities.

We see the gender-affirmative model as well intentioned, in that it wants to reduce shame for kids who do not experience their sense of self as congruent with their birth sex. In practice, however, we are concerned that it is overconfident in the ability of children to reliably share their gender identity and experience. It makes children the experts on their own experience, and the experts on appropriate steps forward, at an age when we understand children to be changing and growing a great deal. We are also concerned that, in practice, some clinicians may treat any expression of gender atypicality in essentialist categories, defining every child as either fully and permanently transgender or fully and permanently cisgender. When children are treated in terms of such essentialist categories, children with some gender atypical interests may find themselves urged into more such behavior and urged away from behavior stereotypical to their birth sex, even if they would not have felt the need to take such steps if left to their own devices. The implications of cross-gender identity and expression are significant and not to be taken lightly.

It is clear that the current trajectory of services is toward gender-affirmative models of care that work with young children toward accepting a cross-gender or other gender identity. Whether that trend will shift or be challenged in the future is unclear.

Older Children and Whether to "Block" Puberty

In 2007, hormone blockers as an intervention for gender dysphoria were first introduced in the US by pediatric endocrinologist Norman Spack.[14] They had been used for several years prior to that in the Netherlands and had originally been developed for the treatment of precocious puberty (early pubertal development). According to Courtney Finlayson, a pediatric endocrinologist interviewed in the 2015 *Frontline* episode "Growing Up Trans," "Pubertal blockers are the medicines that suspend puberty. So, the idea is that we can push the pause button on puberty and let children have a little more time to grow and develop and be more confident of their gender identity."[15]

The question of whether to "block" puberty is the second major controversy in care for children who experience gender dysphoria. Mark has provided an introduction to puberty blocking in *Understanding Gender Dysphoria*.[16] "Blocking" puberty entails altering a child's body chemistry using hormone blockers (i.e., gonadotropin-releasing hormone analogs) that delay puberty by preventing the release of sex hormones. These blockers are given just as a child begins to show early signs of entering puberty (at what is referred to as the Tanner 2 stage of development). Blockers keep the gonads from making either estrogen or testosterone, thus preventing any additional physical changes associated with puberty. A boy will not grow facial and body hair; his voice will not deepen. A girl will not develop breasts or start her menstrual cycle.

The use of puberty blockers was originally intended to create a "holding pattern" of sorts for children with gender identity concerns.

Blocking was a strategy for buying time, providing children with another year or so to decide whether to resume pubertal development in keeping with their birth sex or to take additional steps to facilitate a cross-sex or other gender identity.

Part of the controversy of blockers involves the question of whether they should be regarded as a form of medical intervention and handled with according caution. To some minds, the use of puberty blockers constitutes the first actual medical intervention, since the body is chemically altered. However, supporters do not see blocking puberty as an intervention—at least, not in the same way as they do the introduction of cross-sex hormones. They see blocking as a way of extending the decision-making time for everyone *prior to* medical intervention.

The case for supporting blocking is that, if a child ends up adopting a cross-sex gender identity, blocking puberty allows for a more seamless physical transition. For instance, if a biological male were to wait until adulthood to transition, height, bone structure, and development of an Adam's apple would make it more difficult to pass as female. Delaying puberty could prevent the need for some common gender confirmation surgeries meant to undo bodily changes that occurred in puberty.

Philosopher Maura Priest argued in a recent article that transgender adolescents ought to have the legal right to puberty-blocking medications without parental consent. Her take on the debate is that blocking has become the "standard physical care" offered to such teens and is warranted by research. While parents normally have the authority to give legal consent to medical interventions, they should not refuse standard physical care for their children, meaning that their authority "should not encompass denying gender-dysphoric children access" to blockers.[17]

Those who have expressed concern about blocking puberty point to the lack of research on this intervention's effects on older children. The long-term impact of puberty blockers on bone density, cognitive development, and fertility hasn't yet been studied, they argue.[18]

An additional concern with puberty blocking is that children who begin any kind of medical intervention, including delaying puberty with puberty suppressors, appear far less likely to adopt the gender identity corresponding with their birth sex. That is, instead of creating more time for children to decide either to adopt the gender identity corresponding with their birth sex or to adopt a cross-gender or other gender identity, blocking puberty seems to weight the decision, making children far more likely to ultimately choose a transgender or alternative gender identity. In one study conducted in the Netherlands, all the children who went through hormone-blocking treatment decided to adopt their preferred gender identity rather than to align their gender identity with their birth sex.[19]

Perhaps puberty blocking, rather than creating space for two equally likely outcomes, simply provides parents with more time to support the eventual outcome of a cross-gender or other gender identity. We believe parental support of their loved one is important. However, it is unclear that delaying puberty is helpful in all cases. It seems that this approach tends to confirm and consolidate an alternative gender identity to a child's biological sex rather than allowing for neutrality and exploration of multiple options without a fixed outcome. This is a striking reality considering that, historically, most children who experienced gender dysphoria did not continue to experience it in adulthood, because their dysphoria seemed to resolve at puberty.

It is also unclear whether the benefits of puberty blocking that have been touted are empirically supported.[20] Evidence appears to be both limited and mixed, with much of it not yet published.[21]

The documentary "Growing Up Trans" features the Lurie Clinic at the Children's Hospital in Chicago for its work with children navigating gender identity. In an interview related to puberty blocking and gender exploration, Finlayson, an attending physician at the clinic, observes, "So these kids really are a new generation who are being cared for completely differently than children were in the past. And that is . . . exciting for them to have opportunities that somebody wouldn't have had even . . . 10 years ago. But it's also very challenging for the medical community to find the right way to do this."[22]

Lisa Simmons, a physician in adolescent medicine at the Lurie Clinic, notes that "the majority of children with gender dysphoria will not grow up to be transgender adolescents or adults, but I think the challenge is that we're not able to definitively predict for whom gender dysphoria will continue and for [whom] it may not continue."[23] Her honesty is refreshing, given the current climate of overconfidence about what we know and don't know about gender identity.

To make puberty blocking the standard of care may significantly reduce the likelihood that gender dysphoria will resolve in concert with biological sex, as it historically has in most cases.[24] There just would not be the opportunity for the full exploration of one's natal sex through the experience of puberty. This means that many more children may pursue a cross-sex or alternative sex identity, increasing the likelihood that additional lifelong interventions will be selected.

An article published in *Endocrine News* speaks to the possible impact of increasingly recommended "next step" interventions (the use of cross-sex hormones) on fertility: "Although the treatments are considered safe, they are not risk-free. Most [transgender persons] become infertile as a result of the hormonal switching medications. Estrogens diminish sperm production in males, and testosterone's cessation of menses can cause polycystic ovaries in women; these changes usually lead to infertility. Some late-pubertal male patients have opted for sperm banking, but equivalent options for women are limited. Egg freezing is an arduous and expensive procedure requiring ovarian hyperstimulation with HCG, akin to women undergoing in vitro fertilization, and not as likely to be successful, especially if the ovaries are immature when GnRH-suppressed."[25]

In other words, the chemical delay of puberty processes, while widely considered benign and reversible, can have consequences if paired later with cross-sex hormones. The risk to fertility in particular is a concern.[26] However, some caregivers believe this risk is worth incurring in order to escape the greater risks associated with nonintervention. The article ends with a poignant comment from Walter Meyer III, a psychiatrist who works with young people with gender identity concerns. Meyer concludes, based on the high risk of suicide for transgender children, that more harm is done if puberty blockers and possible cross-sex identity are not considered.[27] For many, though, the risks and implications for fertility and other concerns are noteworthy and not to be passed over.

The Debate about "Rapid Onset" Gender Dysphoria

Those who work with transgender persons and persons warranting the diagnosis of gender dysphoria have noted a dramatic increase[28] in the number of cases presenting at specialty clinics: "The field of interdisciplinary treatment for gender nonconforming children and youth has not just expanded at an astronomically fast rate; to switch metaphors, it has rather been such as a tsunami, with a swell of children and families seeking support and services and stretching existing gender clinics and programs at their seams."[29] The increase has been most dramatic among biological females who do not report a history of gender atypicality. Such a teen would be considered late onset if diagnosed with gender dysphoria.

On August 16, 2018, the journal *PLOS ONE* published a paper by Lisa Littman about a phenomenon she and others have described as "rapid-onset gender dysphoria."[30] We discussed this study briefly in chapter 2. What we didn't discuss in that chapter is the extent of the controversy sparked by the paper. Within a month of the paper's publication, Brown University, where Littman is a professor, removed a press release about the study from its website. The dean of Brown's School of Public Health posted a notice citing concerns about the study's design and methodology, as well as its potential to harm transgender youth.[31] A revised version[32] of the publication that provides additional context was published in March 2019.[33]

What made the study so controversial? According to Littman, parents surveyed reported that about one-third of youth were in friendship groups in which roughly half began to identify as transgender. Littman interpreted this apparent trend as "social contagion" and proposed that this contagion was contributing to the increase in natal females coming to specialty clinics in recent years.

To those who opposed the study, Littman's argument was troubling in part because of its introduction of the term *rapid-onset gender dysphoria*, which sounds official but is not an actual diagnosis. Also noted as a concern was the potential to delegitimize the experiences of transgender youth.[34] In other words, many critics believed that the teens described in the study had always been transgender but had been forced until late in their development to hide their gender identity from those around them. The critics worried that the same stigma that had previously kept these teens quiet about their gender identity was now being used to delegitimize that gender identity and its expression.

In addition to these concerns about protecting transgender youth, critics of the study also raised concerns about the study's methodology. The data in the study were gathered by seeking out specific groups that already reported the "social contagion" phenomenon that researchers wanted to identify. The introduction to the survey also described the phenomenon that the survey was meant to demonstrate, thus priming respondents to answer in a specific fashion instead of seeing if "social contagion" emerged naturally as a theme from a wide array of respondents.

In Search of Wisdom: A Critique of Current Trends

How are we to make sense of the trends in care today? We have shared our thoughts on three current controversies, but we wish to pull back from the particulars of these debates into a broader critique. We suggest that the extreme voices on both sides of the discussion are likely overstating their cases and that the truth about transgender experiences and emerging gender identities lies somewhere in between.

An image that comes to our minds and has been discussed elsewhere is that of an art gallery.[35] A trend in some art circles today is to invite the public to function as art curators. Ellen Gamerman, in the provocatively titled *Wall Street Journal* article "Everybody's an Art Curator," writes, "Not an art expert? Not a problem. Museums are increasingly outsourcing the curation of their exhibits to the public—sometimes even asking the crowd to contribute art, too. The institutions produce quick and often inexpensive shows that boost ticket sales. As crowdsourcing initiatives go mainstream, the roles of the museum and the artist are getting rethought. It's no longer only the highly trained professionals who decide what belongs on the gallery wall, but the audience, too."[36]

How does this movement connect to our discussion of current trends in the care of transgender and gender nonbinary youth? We propose that something like crowd curation is happening in response to young people navigating gender identity questions today. The curation of gender identity in the field of transgender care has been "outsourced," in a manner of speaking.

Do we really outsource the curation of gender identity to the public? To some extent, yes. At least in the modern era in the West, many gender identity options available to youth are "on display" like pieces of art. This display has become increasingly intricate over time: first, cisgender is separated from transgender; next, transgender experiences expand to make room for genderfluid, genderqueer, agender, and bigender expressions; and finally, we have newly emerging gender identities like gender nonbinary, gender creative, and gender expansive. The gender display in society has never been more complex. Yet this display lacks knowledgeable curators of the art it exhibits. Experts who might ordinarily be relied on as curators have turned to children with transgender and gender diverse experiences for guidance, making these children the curators of their own gender possibilities. In the words of trans-affirmative psychologist Diane Ehrensaft, noted in the previous chapter, "It's the children who are now leading us."[37]

Of course, the brief accounts we have offered and the sources we have cited here cannot capture the complexities of care provided at any specialty clinic, and there is no sense providing a truncated account of such services. But in many clinics a very real tendency exists to rely on children and teens to curate their own gender identity. Inevitably, these children and teens use linguistic constructs fashioned by society to explain their experience and identity. We argued in chapter 2 that a "looping effect" may account for some emerging gender identities, as individuals navigating gender identity interact with the language and categories we use to account for them and then reinforce those categories by adopting them.

There has been backlash against some of the postures taken in trans-affirmative care, especially among parents who are concerned about pressure they face to approve invasive procedures for their children.

Some conversations are also taking place among concerned medical professionals who feel they don't yet have sufficient research to confidently provide input to families about the best way to respond to children with emerging gender identities. Like art critics at a crowdsourced museum, they feel that certain questions have been left to the opinions of those perhaps unqualified to answer them. Unlike concerned critics in the museum analogy, however, some medical professionals worry that life-altering decisions about gender identity and body transformation have been left to young people who lack the proper guidance to answer them.

We approach gender dysphoria as a real experience—a diagnosable disorder—that can be quite painful for a person.[38] If gender dysphoria does not resolve on its own by late adolescence or early adulthood, we consider interventions to gender dysphoria as residing on a continuum of options for managing distress. We do not begin with medical interventions; rather, we begin with a wide range of coping strategies, including faith-congruent coping strategies, in response to an undeniably painful experience. If a person is not sufficiently helped by noninvasive coping strategies—strategies that are often utilized in a stepwise manner, moving toward increasing alignment with a transgender identity—a person might consider more invasive coping responses, such as medical interventions (e.g., cross-sex hormones, gender confirmation surgery).

Although some people today see medical interventions as steps to be celebrated as confirmation of one's authentic self, most Christians we have met with who pursue them do so with trepidation and from a place of desperation. In acknowledging that such interventions exist and are available, we are not necessarily commending them, but we also recognize that people who pursue such interventions may see them as palliative (i.e., they could reduce suffering that cannot be alleviated any other way). In any event, we do not see these interventions as optimal. This is, in part, for practical reasons—medical interventions are often irreversible and would include a lifelong regimen that is expensive. There are also research-related questions in terms of the number and quality of outcome studies for younger people. This is also due to questions we wrestle with related to the moral and ethical implications

FOR PARENTS: THINKING ABOUT THE OPTIONS

Parents, one concern you may be facing is how to weigh whether specific coping strategies are morally permissible. This is a topic that more and more Christians are weighing in on. The book *Understanding Transgender Identities* offers four views from Christian authors on the topic of transgender experiences and gender dysphoria, and the various views reflect different approaches to the topic, including some discussion of gender presentation, behavior, and intervention.[a] We have sat with families who are wrrestling with these questions and who have struggled, perhaps like some of you have, to see Scripture speaking explicitly to the topic of gender dysphoria and what kinds of steps would be morally permissible or morally impermissible. We would contend that there is enormous complexity here, so if you are feeling tension and confusion, you are not alone. Still, we do see broad and important principles throughout Scripture that we bring to these discussions.

First, we appreciate the importance of male-female distinctions intended by God at creation. There is an integrity and sacredness to the human body and to the ways that God communicates to humanity in and through our particular bodies. His capacity to be glorified in our bodies is still present in the fallen world we live in. At the same time, we take seriously the range of variations in gender identity and especially the dysphoria that may be associated with incongruence and is often attributed to the fall. What you may be wrestling with is how to

of these steps in every case. Still, we can appreciate rare situations when discernment led a Christian to take these steps. We have met with such people and have been struck by how profoundly difficult their decision was.

We appreciate how the present discussion of gender identity draws our attention to the potential needs of people suffering from gender dysphoria. We can also benefit from expanding expressions of masculinity and femininity so that we do not limit gender expressions and roles in ways that do a disservice to the wide range of children's self-expression. We do not want to see churches or families double down on gender stereotypes when a child expresses gender in ways that are "outside proceed in navigating options in the fallen world in which we live, especially in specific cases where enduring gender dysphoria is present.

We encourage you to stay connected to those you can trust to pray for and support you in your faith community and to pray that God will give you timely wisdom and prudence in decision-making. We also recommend that you take a step-wise approach to any possible coping strategy, as you prayerfully and thoughtfully consider the ethics of the options before you and the biblical reasoning that goes into evaluating them. Whenever possible, we help people find the least-invasive means (e.g., general coping; adjustments in presentation, hairstyle, and dress) to manage the distress of gender dysphoria. We acknowledge, though, that there are limited resources for individuals with severe gender dysphoria who have tried less invasive coping skills and continue to experience immense distress. As parents, you can position yourself alongside your loved one as they may today or down the road be considering a specific step; you can help them identify what has been helpful or unhelpful in providing them with some comfort or relief, as well as weighing the sense of peace that guides their conscience concerning specific steps they are considering. Above all else, we encourage you to draw near to Christ, who cares deeply for you and your loved one and will not abandon you in this process.

a. James K. Beilby and Paul Rhodes Eddy, eds., *Understanding Transgender Identities: Four Views* (Grand Rapids: Baker Academic, 2019).

the box" of what might be expected. Therefore, sparking interest in these discussions about gender and sex is important. It is demanding, certainly, but necessary if the church is to respond to the needs of youth today.

But we are seeing more than increased awareness. We are seeing a cultural move toward adults letting young people take the wheel of the gender conversation and steer the car, often without offering much guidance beyond a promise to get out of their way. This brand of youth empowerment is not unlike what we have seen in movements toward minors making reproductive decisions without parental guidance. One gender identity expert at a specialty clinic shared with us that "no one wants to be the one to say no to a teen who wants what they want." We believe this attitude is ubiquitous among many professionals providing care, and it removes from the clinic the responsibility of helping in the curation of care. It puts care in the hands of teens themselves, who may not be getting the kind of guidance they need from those entrusted with their care.

Complaints from Parents

Some clinics are evaluating complaints from parents that they may be hurrying young people toward a cross-gender or other gender identity without first adequately assessing several potentially important variables. For example, in 2018 a group of parents voiced their concern that the Tavistock Clinic in the United Kingdom "should do more to consider young people's personal histories, notably by examining whether they are on the autistic spectrum, have experienced trauma or are being influenced by social pressures, before helping them on the path to transition."[39]

Tavistock had apparently already begun an internal review of their procedures, but the parents expressed concern that the sheer number of new referrals made it difficult to adequately assess the needs of young people: "Given the pressure under which [the Tavistock Clinic] now works, we believe there is a real danger that the cohort of young people who enter [the Tavistock Clinic] post-16 may be fast-tracked on to adult services in an attempt to reduce caseloads."[40] In particular, the parents asked about environmental considerations, social pressures, the "popularisation of trans issues on social media," past trauma, and other considerations that might (in their view) have been overlooked during assessment because of clinicians' eagerness to provide what teenagers were requesting, which was frequently medical intervention.

The Tavistock Clinic defended its practices with an argument we have seen at other clinics: with challenging cases, rather than simply provide what teens requested or what the parent group refers to as "fast-tracked," there is often an attempt to pace out services, to extend care so that the clinicians can determine if the gender identity concern is enduring.

Surprisingly, the clinic statement also included the following: "Nevertheless, we are always mindful that gender dysphoria is not in and of itself a mental health diagnosis."[41] This is surprising because gender dysphoria is precisely the diagnosis given (at least when referencing the fifth edition of the *Diagnostic and Statistical Manual of Mental Disorders* [*DSM-5*])[42] from a mental health standpoint when warranted. But the clinic was likely thinking that gender identity disorder had been the diagnosis under the *International Classification of Diseases*, tenth edition (*ICD-10*), and was in the process of being reconceptualized as "gender incongruence" and relocated from the category of "mental disorders" to "sexual health" in the eleventh edition (*ICD-11*).[43]

Most specialty clinics are walking a fine line between the priorities of their stakeholders. On the one hand, many stakeholders want clinics to provide a thorough assessment and to consider possible social trends and psychosocial realities that may contribute to gender identity questions. On the other hand, some stakeholders believe that questions about gender identity have little if anything to do with the mental health community, and there has been a concerted effort to remove mental health professionals from the gatekeeping role they have held for so many years.

We suspect that some of the complaints made by parents against clinics reflect the emerging diversity of gender presentations that we described in chapter 2. An older child or teen who identifies with a transgender or emerging gender identity may not meet criteria for gender dysphoria, yet they may still be requesting highly invasive procedures. Medical professionals have not adequately reflected on the nuances of different teens' experiences in the realm of emerging gender identities. Until more time and effort are invested into discernment and cultivation of clinical prudence in such cases, complaints will likely continue.

Informed-Consent Models of Care

Part of what works against increasing nuance is efforts to sideline mental health professionals in these discussions. There is a tremendous push today to embrace informed-consent models of care that remove mental health professionals from their gatekeeping role of deciding whether certain interventions are merited. The idea of an informed-consent model is captured in Andrea Long Chu's provocatively titled *New York Times* op-ed, "My New Vagina Won't Make Me Happy: And It Shouldn't Have To." Chu is critical of the "right-wing narrative of clinical delusion" that suggests that trans-affirmative care should be refused to transgender youth because transgender identity is a delusion.[44] But she also rejects the mental health care model steeped in a "liberal counter-narrative" of suffering, in which trans-affirmative care is offered to relieve suffering. Such a counter-narrative may be an improvement on the "clinical delusion" model of care, Chu argues, but it still places care and critical decision-making in the hands of the medical, psychiatric, and psychological communities rather than yielding to transgender people themselves: "A gender-affirmative model will almost certainly lead to more and higher-quality care for transgender patients. But by focusing on minimizing patients' pain, it leaves the door open for care to be refused when a doctor, or someone playing doctor, deems the risks too high."[45]

In other words, once the concession is made that care is about alleviating suffering, the gatekeepers have a role in determining who is a good candidate for which interventions, presumably based on research that predicts likely outcomes. Yet the considerations gatekeepers have in mind when they approve medical interventions are not the same considerations that Chu herself has in mind. Chu's own goal in pursuing transition is not about alleviating pain: "I still want this, all of it. I want the tears; I want the pain. Transition doesn't have to make me happy for me to want it. Left to their own devices, people will rarely pursue what makes them feel good in the long term. Desire and happiness are independent agents."[46] One of the problems with medical and psychological gatekeeping, according to Chu, is that the history of care has been one of condescension: "As long as transgender medicine retains the alleviation of pain as its benchmark of success, it will reserve for itself, with a dictator's benevolence, the right to withhold care from those who want it. Transgender people have been forced, for decades, to rely for care on a medical establishment that regards them with both suspicion and condescension. And yet as things stand today, there is still only one way to obtain hormones and surgery: to pretend that these treatments will make the pain go away."[47]

Having argued that medical and psychological gatekeeping can no longer continue, Chu makes her case for the informed-consent model. In short, she argues that once people know the potential benefits and risks of various interventions, they can take responsibility for the outcomes of those interventions: "I believe that surgeries of all kinds can and do make an enormous difference in the lives of trans people. But I also believe that surgery's only prerequisite should be a simple demonstration of want. Beyond this, no amount of pain, anticipated or continuing, justifies its withholding."[48]

We recognize that there are differences between adults and adolescents asking for invasive procedures, so this discussion can and should be shaped by the age of the person in question. But we also don't want to be naive in assuming that arguments about informed consent are limited to adults, because we see this line being crossed over and over again. There is a trend toward putting mental health and related health care decisions into the hands of adolescents rather than restricting access to such care for adolescents. The shift is to take the informed-consent model that is used with adults and apply that same model to adolescents. We are concerned about such a shift. When the assumption is that any level of restriction is arbitrary and not in the best interest of young people, we may miss the reality that mental health professionals are positioned and trained as such to support people of all ages in making decisions for their long-term well-being, even if these decisions differ from what a person might desire in a particular moment.

The role of mental health professionals seems particularly (potentially) valuable given the reality that teens who adopt transgender or emerging gender identities may do so for a variety of reasons, not all of which include a diagnosis of gender dysphoria. At their best, mental health professionals bring insight that can help anticipate potential advantages and pitfalls of each course of action, especially when they are faced with requests for irreversible invasive procedures. We call mental health professionals' role "potentially valuable" because we consider the role valuable only insofar as these professionals assess for and provide feedback regarding diverse motivations for gender identity questions, and as they acknowledge the current lack of consensus on atypical gender presentations. The reality, however, is that current trends in care appear to contradict this assumption about what mental health professionals should offer their clients. We are thinking here of trends in reproductive health, parental notification laws, issues with consent, and so on. Care for transgender minors has moved and will undoubtedly continue to move in this same direction. Anything short of trans-affirmative care will likely come to be considered unhelpful, unethical, or even illegal. Such a trajectory leaves little room for mental health professionals, and professionals in general, to speak into decisions minors are making and to facilitate thoughtful and appropriately paced decision-making.

Not too long ago we sat in on a two-day advanced training in trans-affirmative care. In the jurisdiction where the training took place, it is legal for a teen as young as fifteen to pursue gender confirmation surgery without parental consent. Since this jurisdiction was an outlier at the time, we discussed the implications of such legislation. There were different opinions in the room, of course, but we found that the most experienced mental health providers tended to agree on one thing: they did not encourage invasive procedures for teens without parental support (and certainly not without parental knowledge of the procedures), because experienced clinicians know that the best predictor of transgender teens' well-being over time is the quality of their relationships with their parents. Well-meaning trans-affirmative care has at times become unbalanced in not recognizing that teenagers are located in social networks, and one of the most important of these networks is their family. We understand that not all trans teens have families who will offer adequate support to promote their well-being, and some teens may already be displaced or be in a contentious relationship with their parents. Still, we believe that greater emphasis should be placed on restoring those relationships and working toward mutual understanding and respect. Legislation that limits parental participation in a teen's decisions could exacerbate tensions in already-fragile relationships—the most important relationships for that teenager's well-being.

One reason we favor a gatekeeping role for mental health professionals is that mental health professionals—at least those who are balanced and competent in this area—can see the big picture, can appreciate the way a teenager is situated in a network of relationships, and can offer dispassionate recommendations for care. The mental health professional's distance from situations helps to foster a long-term view in decision-making about gender identity, allowing for discernment without presuming a sense of urgency in every case. Of course, the value of a mental health professional is negligible (and, in our view, may contribute to harm) if the professional does not offer appropriate cautions or if they fail to address issues of pace, timing, and the reality of diverse trajectories among people navigating gender identity.

A related reason we see value in a mental health professional's involvement is that there may be multiple motivations for gender-atypical expressions. Think of an iceberg: gender atypical expression (often cross-dressing) is what we see above the surface. But what motivates gender atypical expression is what resides below the surface. Teens may engage in atypical expression to manage gender dysphoria, reduce anxiety about body image, express a sense of "true self," experience sexual arousal, seek entertainment, or respond to boredom. Moreover, some teens do appear to be in a search for identity and community.

From a developmental perspective, adolescence is the time of identity formation. Young people try on different identities and ways of being known in different circles. They might be one way at home and another way at youth group. They might relate one way with their peers and another way with extended family. The end point of identity exploration is a stable identity across the various groups they interact with. For some teens, a transgender or emerging gender identity will be one of the identities they test during this formative period. Although it is hard to estimate the prevalence of this rationale, some teens who are searching for identity and community may find that the trend toward diverse gender identities provides some sense of belonging. They may subsequently invest in identity motivations that can to some extent be fueled by social constructs that resonate for them.

This trend can be helpful to those who experience gender dysphoria because it validates their experience and helps them find support. We think of a sixty-year-old woman we evaluated for gender dysphoria who had since childhood felt as if she was "crazy or psychotic or something." It wasn't until she heard the stories of transgender people portrayed in the media that she thought to seek confirmation of this diagnosis and learned that she was not alone. It was noteworthy, though, that she had no interest in medical or surgical procedures or even in a social transition. She sought out other ways to cope with her experience, and over the course of many years had already found strategies that worked. Simply receiving validation that her experience was real helped her manage the distress without such intense shame.

But for others, this same trend might be potentially harmful. Encouraging those who might not experience gender dysphoria to find solidarity with those who do experience dysphoria may draw some teens into avoidable forms of trauma. For these teens, if there were not a trend toward transgender and other emerging gender identities, some of them might be searching for identity and community elsewhere, perhaps in a less tumultuous arena with the potential for significant commitments including medical and/or surgical interventions that sometimes accompany a cross-gender or other gender identity.

A final reason we see value in a mental health professional being involved in the exploration of gender identity is equifinality. *Equifinality* refers to the idea that multiple pathways can lead to the same end point. Is it possible that multiple pathways can lead to the same end point of gender dysphoria? We argue that the answer to this question is yes, perhaps in even more ways than are currently known. Dysphoria diagnoses are already divided by age of onset, indicating that early onset and late onset represent two pathways of dysphoria. In addition, typologies based on sexual orientation are controversial, but they suggest the possibility that some of the different phenomena that look like dysphoria may be better conceptualized as something else. This is the case when cross-sex behavior is tied to a pattern of sexual arousal rather than evidencing a cross-sex or other gender identity. Even in these cases, the *DSM-5* notes that gender dysphoria can develop from what has been called "transvestic fetishism." In other words, sometimes a person has a fetish associated with cross-dressing behavior; but it is possible that an identity concern can develop from a long-standing fetish. While we do not see this scenario as commonplace, it is important that a mental health professional assess the precise nature of each client's gender identity experience, as well as acknowledging the multiple pathways that may have brought them to their current experience.

What happens when the principle of equifinality is brought into conversation with current trends in transgender and emerging gender identities? Based on recent observations about the social and environmental elements present in some cases of late-onset gender dysphoria, particularly among natal females, is it possible that we are witnessing yet another pathway to the experience of gender incongruity or gender dysphoria? This question ought to give us pause, challenging the level of confidence with which many professionals apply a one-size-fits-all approach to managing gender dysphoria and making treatment recommendations. In observing that social and environmental factors may contribute to the recent rise of transgender and emerging gender identities, our desire is not to invalidate the experience of any given person but to take seriously the experiences of all people. We want to be realistic about what we know and don't know in each case, in order to seek out the best approaches to addressing their concerns.

We are pleased that there continues to be a low rate of regret for surgical procedures among those who have had them, and we appreciate what we can learn from research about who is likely to be satisfied with the results of surgery and who may be at greater risk of regret. We have written elsewhere on the range of available studies attending to the question of regret, which fail to provide the long-term follow-up we would hope to see.[49] Nevertheless, the available studies do indicate overall satisfaction with surgical interventions in the short term. For many Christians, much is left to be discerned about the ethics of such interventions. From the mental health perspective, we tend to think that these low rates of regret are related in part to the lengthy process

FOR PARENTS: CONSIDERING MORE INVASIVE PROCEDURES

Parents, we recognize that one of your greatest fears likely has to do with more invasive procedures, such as the use of cross-sex hormones and various surgical procedures. These steps have been popularized in entertainment and social media in ways that make the conversation about them nearly inescapable, and this is an area where the trend appears to be toward making more and more services available to minors, even without parental consent. We can appreciate your fears. Your mind may be jumping ahead several steps to specific decisions that cause you great distress. We have found it more helpful to take a step-wise approach in which each management strategy, each coping strategy, is weighed and given serious consideration before it is implemented, and in which each implemented strategy is monitored over time, evaluated, and moved away from if it is found unhelpful.

For different parents, different steps may cause more or less anxiety. We recognize that these are difficult questions to wrestle with, and as we shared earlier, we do not see much explicit guidance from Scripture on the topic of gender dysphoria or specific interventions, which can be understood in many ways. Some parents might conclude that the lack of guidance means that no step that reflects any cross-gender or other gender identity or expression is permissible, while others might conclude the opposite—that the lack of guidance makes everything permissible. In our experience it has been more complicated for parents who have voiced the fears you may have. You are not alone. Other parents have prayed about what is morally permissible, what is pleasing to God, what relieves their loved one's distress, or what improves their loved one's quality of life. We encourage you to slow down and take one step at a time rather than focus on the most invasive procedures or getting ahead of where you and your loved one are in decision-making. It's the getting ahead of ourselves that can cause more anxiety. Any decision in this area can be a difficult one to weigh, and we encourage you to not face these decisions alone, to be in prayerful reflection with others who love you and your loved one and who can demonstrate wisdom and maturity in decision-making. Input from these sources can be incorporated with the input from competent mental health professionals as you face these decisions together. Insofar as you conclude that specific interventions such as cross-sex hormones or gender confirmation surgeries are morally impermissible, we encourage you to entrust your loved one to Christ, remain available to them if they do take such steps, and seek to accompany them moving forward in ways that are congruent with your convictions.

that surgical candidates have gone through with a team supporting their decision-making. This lengthy process has been put in place not to create an arbitrary obstacle but to increase the likelihood of the best intervention and the best outcome. The trend to move away from this approach is troubling in part because we cannot yet predict the impact of such a move on outcomes for a range of medical and surgical interventions. These outcomes matter, especially as societal trends increasingly encourage these interventions for people of younger and younger ages.

PART 2

SEEING THE PERSON

CHAPTER 4

Foundations for Relationship

In part 1 of this book, we discussed transgender experiences and emerging gender identities. We introduced three explanatory frameworks for the rise in prevalence estimates and referrals to specialty clinics. We disagreed with the account that says all of these identities have always existed but only now do people have the courage to self-identify. We do believe that some teenagers are coming forth who might not have done so a generation ago, perhaps due to increased cultural support for such experiences. However, we see the "newfound courage" explanation of these trends as a naive view, because it adheres to an essentialist understanding of gender identity: an understanding not shared by many of those now adopting transgender and emerging gender identities. We also disagreed in part 1 with the account that says these new cases are caused by social contagion. We do believe some teenagers who are searching for identity and community find these things in transgender and emerging gender identities; that is, they can personally invest in identity and community motivations that are supported by existing social constructs that they find compelling. But we do not see increases in transgender and emerging gender self-identification as solely a reflection of peer group influences and socialization.

Our view is that multiple contributing factors must be accounted for as we encounter each individual who is navigating gender identity. Some teens do suffer from gender dysphoria, and research is meant to inform best practices for working with these teens, as controversial as clinical interventions sometimes are. We may be seeing some increase in the number of teens adopting transgender or emerging gender identities because of greater awareness and exposure to the language and categories associated with gender dysphoria; even so, gender dysphoria is still a relatively rare phenomenon. Some teens who adopt transgender or emerging gender identities without experiencing gender dysphoria may be reacting to rigid stereotypes of masculinity and femininity that leave little room for any degree of gender atypicality. Still others may be searching for identity and community to cope with life challenges and turning to identity groups defined by shifting norms of sex and gender, including emerging gender identities. It is unclear whether these latter groups of teens would be good candidates for the interventions common among teens diagnosed with gender dysphoria.

As we suggested in part 1 of this book, some of the emerging language and categories for gender identity have developed within a larger looping effect: people interact with the language and categories available to account for their experience. The interactive and dynamic nature of the looping effect provides important insight into how emerging gender identities may have come about. We ended part 1 by offering reflections on the various treatments available to those who present with gender dysphoria, the controversies associated with these treatments, and the research on individuals' short-term satisfaction with these treatments. Of course, we know that subjective satisfaction with a choice may not resolve the question of whether these interventions are morally permissible for the Christian, and we anticipate great variability in how Christians and churches respond to the range of options available today.

Seeking Practical Wisdom

We turn our attention now to how Christians can care for those navigating the complicated area of gender identity. In his recent book *Restless*

Faith, Richard Mouw reflects on the idea of practical wisdom (*phronesis*).[1] Practical wisdom "requires a strategy that integrates various kinds of sensitivities and insights: theological, pastoral, ethical, spiritual, social, scientific."[2] As we consider engagement in this space of gender identity, we want to keep in mind that we will continue to draw upon multiple sources, relying on practical wisdom, in the development of a nuanced approach.

Our approach is also informed by an insight from Ian Hacking, who identifies two important pressure points arising from two "vectors" of the relationship between labels and people. One vector moves down from "above": that is, it describes the work of experts who label people and create what "counts" as knowledge about a topic. The other vector moves up from "below," and it depicts the "behavior of the person so labeled."[3] A nuanced approach to relationships has to keep these two vectors in view and respond to both. This means attending to the factors that inform which "knowledge" about gender identity is deemed valid by individuals and culture. It also means attending to the various ways transgender individuals live in the world, which may inform how transgender identity is perceived by outsiders and how people who adopt this identity choose to express it.

In the spirit of Hacking's view of "dynamic nominalism," we have argued that people both have experiences prior to being labeled and also adjust to the labels given to them. Thus, we have resisted the impulse to say that being transgender simply means seeing reality and one's true self more clearly, as if science is merely discovering gender categories that have always existed. At the same time, we have also resisted the impulse to say that all experiences of gender incongruence are created through trends toward cultural acceptance of these experiences, as the "social contagion" model might hold. Neither explanation is nuanced enough to account for all experiences, nor would either sufficiently capture the experience of any particular person.

We propose that gender incongruity and transgender identity are best understood through a combination of two coexisting realities: (1) advances in science that provide language for real experiences worth understanding and (2) an increase in emerging gender identities due to social acceptance and sociocultural influences. The experiences of those with emerging gender identities should not be considered an objective and stable fact in every case, nor should it be invalidated as mere social contagion. There is a complex interaction of many factors that we must weigh as we shape our engagement with those who adopt emerging gender identities.

Holding in mind Hacking's two vectors, we want to take seriously the pressures from above and below that impact how a person behaves in accordance with a label. For example, if a person identifies as genderqueer or genderfluid, we want to consider the outside influences and internal experiences that have shaped this identity instead of immediately objecting to the person's exploration of gender identity. Distinguishing a person's claimed gender identity (or gender identity questions) from the vectors influencing them can help us reserve judgment on pathways they might take. We may also find, if we listen long enough, that the person before us is not actively pursuing pathways some of us would find concerning. In fact, many people with gender identity concerns are merely looking for someone to venture with them on the journey of understanding their current experience. And even if they are looking for more than that, such as approval of a particular pathway, offering your presence in itself gives more than you realize. This approach, in the spirit of discipleship, will offer a tangible reminder that God, too, is ready to accompany them on this journey and cares about the decisions they make around gender identity, just as in every other area of their lives.

Keep in mind that the person you care for is interacting with all the dynamics we have described previously. Their gender identity questions could very well have surfaced in another cultural setting and time. However, because their gender identity questions have arisen in this current cultural context and time, they are subject to the current dynamics of our expanding gender identity categories, and their process may reflect new language and ways of making meaning out of their gender identity. These influences add another layer to the already complex question—Who am I?—that we all wrestle with, especially in adolescence and early adulthood. Today's young people face unique cultural challenges;

they could certainly benefit from some compassion and wisdom as we accompany them on this difficult terrain.

Considering Theological Foundations

In this chapter our goal is to help you find your bearings for journeying with those who have questions in the area of gender identity. To set up that discussion, we begin by examining the relationship between correct thinking and correct practice.

Considering our foundational theology of sex and gender is important. Being able to think through theological anthropology, ethics, and so on is an essential starting point. You may be reading this book and believe you have the theological foundation around sex and gender down pat. You may be confident, then, that because you have the theology right, you have helpful answers for the person navigating gender identity or expressing an emerging gender identity. In our experience, confidence about having the right theology about sex and gender unfortunately does not translate into knowing how to minister to people with nonnormative experiences or avoiding enacting pastoral hurts in these realms.

We will build on the three lenses Mark initially outlined in *Understanding Gender Dysphoria,* which are understood as three ways of thinking about gender identity (see table 1).

Table 1. Three Lenses through Which People "See" Transgender

Integrity Lens	Tends to respond to gender identity with reference to the integrity or sacredness of sex differences established by God at creation. The emphasis here is on Genesis 1 and 2 and restoring creational intent. Cross-sex identification is often framed as a moral concern.
Disability Lens	Transgender experiences generally reflect variations that occur in nature. Gender incongruity is a nonnormative, nonmoral reality that can be responded to with compassion. Christians who gravitate toward this lens tend to emphasize the effects of the fall on all of creation, including sex and gender.
Diversity Lens	Transgender and emerging gender identities reflect variations of gender experiences that should neither be condemned nor viewed as "less than." Rather, gender diverse experiences should be celebrated by society.

Lenses and Various Theological Foundations

The three lenses often form the foreground for disagreements among thoughtful Christians. The lens an individual adopts can lead to radically different conclusions about how best to engage with those who are navigating gender identity questions. In families, churches, and societies, disagreements rooted in these lenses can lead to miscommunication, hostility, and significant hurt. What we have discovered since the introduction of the three lenses several years ago is that Christians whose theological position may be considered, for lack of better terms, ultraconservative/fundamentalist, orthodox, or liberal will each draw on the three lenses as a kind of prescription for "corrected vision"[4] on the topic of gender identity. In table 2 we offer a range of theological positions and how each position draws on elements of the integrity, disability, or diversity lens to help account for its view of gender identity and gender dysphoria.

Ultraconservative/Fundamentalist Foundation

Those who engage this topic from an ultraconservative/fundamentalist theological position do not simply express the integrity lens; rather, ultraconservatives/fundamentalists can be thought of reflecting elements of the integrity, disability, and diversity lenses—offering a prescription, if you will, for seeing the topic more clearly. The integrity lens is seen in the affirmation of the male/female binary as a good of creation that is tied to genital structure and chromosomal determination. Their take on the disability lens is that there is a moral brokenness to the disability that makes nonnormative gender identities irredeemable apart from reinstituting God's original creational intent for that person. In terms of the diversity lens, in which people often explore questions of identity and community, diversity is celebrated within a narrow bandwidth for gender-role expression. If anything, the diversity between men and women is highlighted, but the diversity among different men and among different women is perceived as a threat to the binary. Goals, then, are directed solely toward aligning gender identity to biological sex. In cases in which a person has already transitioned,

Table 2. How Each Lens Is a Different Prescription by Theological Position

LENS	THEOLOGICAL POSITION		
	Ultraconservative/ Fundamentalist	Orthodox	Liberal
Integrity	Prioritizes the creation account; affirms male/female binary as God's creational intent; construes authentic gender identity as derived from male or female genital structure and chromosomal sex determination; views all deviations from the binary as sin (see "Disability").	Prioritizes the creation account; affirms male/female binary as God's creational intent; accepts multidetermination of sex (genetic, anatomical, neurological, psychological, sociological, and potentially others) as male or female; sees gender identity as complex and potentially problematic on any of multiple dimensions because of the fall for each person to varying degrees.	The male/female binary is viewed as descriptive rather than prescriptive (God's original creation is not necessarily exclusive or restrictive or perhaps captured fully by the Genesis account); gender identity is minimally tethered to genital structures or chromosomes; greater weight is given to psychological, self-affirmed identity as blessed by God.
Disability	Departures from the male/female binary are construed as willful disobedience and sinful; nonnormative gender identities are judged irredeemable expressions of moral brokenness and disability (those who express nonnormative gender identities are manifesting active and ongoing rebellion against God's standards and directly challenging the truthfulness of Scripture).	Departures from the male/female binary are considered as multicausal; nonnormative gender identities are a tragic reality for some, but such experiences do not diminish the infinite value of the human person and the potential to give glory to God with their lives, even with ongoing challenges in this aspect of life. The Christian call for compassion is critical to an adequate response to those exploring gender identity.	Departures from the male/female binary are to be celebrated as manifestations of human diversity and God's creative capacity; construing such diversity as disability or, worse, as moral brokenness is seen as disparaging or oppressive. One's response must include ongoing community affirmation to foster self-acceptance and counter both the morality and the disability narratives.
Diversity	Only more rigid understandings of traditional roles are construed as appropriate and valid; departures from traditional gender-role definitions are questionable if not sinful; diversity is celebrated only within a relatively narrow range of gender role expression tied to one's genitally and genetically related gender identity. The emphasis is placed on the distinction between men and women rather than the varied ways of being a man or a woman.	The lives of those who acknowledge God's original creational intent yet whose gender identity is a departure from normative experiences are celebrated as potential contexts in which God's grace and love can be multiplied and manifested, which is often though not exclusively manifest in an encounter with God's love for them in the midst of suffering. Their unique witness is powerful and ought to be shared as a reflection of their personhood, even while they may not necessarily reflect gender expression that is seen as more typical.	The lives of those whose gender identity is a departure from normative experiences are celebrated as manifestations of human diversity and God's creative capacity. Those Christians who challenge this narrative are seen as failing to love like Christ does. The only appropriate Christian response is one of affirmation, in light of the reality of diversity, in much the same way as Christians ought to affirm the dignity of each person regardless of race, social status, and so on.

goals are directed toward repentance and a corresponding return to one's original gender identity or gender identity that reflects one's male or female genital structures and chromosomes.

Liberal Theological Foundation

Likewise, the person on the other end of the theological spectrum, the person whose view of diverse gender identities is informed by a liberal theological position, is not exclusively conveying the diversity lens; rather, this person will in some ways incorporate elements of the other lenses again as a prescription for seeing the topic more clearly. This theological position understands the male/female binary of the creation stories to be descriptive of what was rather than prescriptive of what ought to be. Gender identity is viewed as equally if not predominantly based on psychological and self-affirmed identity rather than solely on one's genital structures or chromosomes. The "disability" language is viewed as disparaging while the "brokenness" language is viewed as oppressive. Departures from the male/female binary are alternatively viewed as reflections of human diversity and God's creative capacity. Goals, then, are directed toward self-awareness and self-acceptance of one's gender identity, as well as the creation of a supportive ecclesiastical and public culture in which diversity can thrive.

Orthodox Theological Foundation

What we encourage as an anchor for a nuanced Christian response to questions about gender is what we are referring to as a broad orthodox foundation that, again, attempts to integrate elements from each of the three lenses. An integration of the three lenses should help us see this topic more clearly, but we have to think through a biblically faithful integration of these lenses.

An orthodox theological position reflects the integrity lens insofar as it begins with giving greater weight to the creation accounts and, as a result, affirms the male/female binary as God's creational intent. There is meaning imbued in male/female sexual difference that is a reliable guide in most cases and communicates theological truths worth reflecting on. The experience of gender identity, however, is complex and potentially problematic for a percentage of people due to the range of variables that impact gender identity and consequently the range of ways in which the effects of the fall can be experienced in one's gender.

Christians who uphold an orthodox theology draw upon the disability lens to recognize the departures from the male/female binary are real and may be due to many contributing factors, none of which detract from or diminish the person's infinite value or worth or potential to explore how they might give glory to God with their lives. Particular difficulties with gender identity ought not be attributed solely as a sign of moral depravity, although those exploring gender identity certainly are touched by the fall and capable of engaging in things that are cause for moral concern, just like anyone else.

For those who adhere to this theological position, the diversity lens illuminates the many ways in which a person's life is the context in which God's grace and love can be multiplied and manifested, offering identity, community, meaning, and purpose in each unique experience of gender identity. Part of discovering meaning and purpose can be through an encounter with God in the midst of suffering. Not only that, but this lens helps us recognize that the range of manifestations of our particular personhood, including personality, traits, interests, and passions, ought to be celebrated as a reflection of God and need not be restricted to stereotypes or cultural norms. This fosters a posture that is fairly open-ended and nuanced, recognizing that there are many experiences and decisions faced by young people navigating gender identity and faith. The point of emphasis here is that each person, no matter their experiences of gender, ought to be able to discover life-giving identity, community, meaning, and purpose in and through the life of faith.

Moving beyond Getting Theology Right

Our experience is that when we are talking about journeying together as fallen people with fallen people in a fallen world, things are never as simple as they were in Eden. We turn now to why we think that getting our theology right is only a part of effectively accompanying those exploring gender identity.

Getting theology "right," or aspiring to, is an important part of discipleship. The Christian life, however, has never been merely about getting theology right. To settle matters of theology, ethics, and anthropology on paper or in our heads is not sufficient for navigating life in our fallen world. It's not sufficient in the face of any human suffering, let alone the questions that arise around gender identity. Believing marriage is a covenantal union for life does not always translate into a step-by-step guide for interacting with those who find themselves in troubled marriages. Believing drug abuse is detrimental to spiritual wholeness does not tell us how to journey with the addicted young man in our small group who just showed up high. Believing Jesus died for all, including the disabled man in the pew behind us, does not offer instruction on how to communicate the love of Christ to that man in particular.

We recognize the tension that emerges between *knowing* theology, ethics, and morality and *being* effective ministers of the gospel: *How do I know what is immoral and what isn't? When should I say what a person is doing is wrong? How should I communicate my concern? When should I speak up about the concerns I have?* In some cases, individuals—or even whole churches—who have a heart for following Christ stake their claim in one camp at the expense of the other. For the ultraconservative/fundamentalist position, this means prioritizing a theoretical theology of gender grounded in Scripture without considering the impact and costliness of this theology for those on the fringes. The liberal position emphasizes so highly the importance of walking with people that it might treat as irrelevant the moral and ethical implications of a person's decisions for fear of casting judgment. An orthodox position says that we need not throw out theological considerations but that we also must not exert all our energy into categorizing the morality of gender identity decisions, thus leaving no energy to invest in relationships with the real people making those decisions.

We would challenge you that, even if you think you have the theological and ethical answers, now is the time to pause and reflect on what exactly your answers are and how you plan to share them. Perhaps for some of you, your theology indicates that any form of cross-gender expression—for example, hairstyles, clothing, cosmetics, names, pronouns, cross-sex hormones, or various surgical interventions—is morally problematic. Even still, much remains to be said about how to respond to a person who has pursued those things, will do so, is considering doing so, or is not considering doing so but is looking for other options to integrate their gender identity and their faith. Alternatively, if your theology does not find any of the possible cross-gender expressions we see today as morally problematic or concerning, we invite you to wrestle with how you might minister to a person who is navigating gender identity questions and finds the solutions you offer to be in conflict with their own beliefs and values.

Many people have been casualties of an approach to relationships that merely presents doctrinal positions, devoid of the merciful love that radiated from Christ's every encounter. In the words attributed to the Christian theologian and mystic Bernard of Clairvaux, "There are those who seek knowledge for the sake of knowledge; that is Curiosity. There are those who seek knowledge to be known by others; that is Vanity. There are those who seek knowledge in order to serve; that is Love."5 Reflecting on and seeking a deeper theological understanding of gender can be thought of as *seeking knowledge in order to serve, in order to love*. Even after seeking knowledge about gender identity, the loving part is where the rubber meets the road and where things can get more complicated.

American Christianity has certainly been impacted by postmodern thought, and especially by moral relativism. Moral relativism is the notion that absolute truth does not exist. As a result, absolute truth is often thrown out, and experiential knowledge is given the primary place in coming to know reality. "My truth" and "your truth" are given greater importance than absolute truth with a capital *T*. In light of this, some Christians reactively discount that anything true can be learned from phenomenology, or the subjective experience of the person. Youth today are watching to see how Christians respond in the messiness of lived experiences, just as Jesus's contemporaries watched how he related to the people the Pharisees had counted as lost. Is Christianity still relevant, today's youth ask? Does it apply to the one person currently in front of us and account for their experience? Many young people prioritize the one over the ninety-nine and will discount absolute truth if it does not create space and apply to the specific people in their lives. Christ struck a balance between asserting moral truths and inviting relationship with those who questioned or even rejected these moral truths. This must mean that we can strike the same balance.

Moving toward a Flexible Relational Approach

Andy Crouch, in his book *Culture Making*, shares a helpful distinction between "postures" and "gestures" that we first came across when reading *The Good News about Conflict* by Jenell Paris.[6] *Posture* refers to how a person holds themselves. It has to do with positioning the body in a particular way. *Gesture* refers to a movement of the body, perhaps a hand or arm movement that conveys a welcome or farewell.

Crouch's point is that having a good posture allows for a wider range of gestures. He applies this principle to how the church positions itself in relation to changing culture and how we shape and create culture as Christians. He urges the church to adopt a flexible posture that allows it to respond to a changing culture with ease, much like a runner evades potholes on difficult terrain. The posture we take matters because it gives us flexibility in our changing cultural context.

We want to now more explicitly extend the principle of postures and gestures in relationships with transgender youth and youth who experience emerging gender identities. Your current posture might reflect one of the three lenses we introduced earlier: integrity, disability, or diversity. We want to revisit those lenses now in order to illustrate how rigid adoption of one posture over another may limit our gestures. We propose that an integrated approach offers the flexibility in gesture that is so desperately needed when working with those navigating gender identity questions.

We turn now to postures that emerge from these different lenses. Each lens limits gestures to some extent, and we also want to explore what it could look like if we again integrate the best of each lens.

Integrity-Leaning Posture

The integrity lens emphasizes God's creational intent in creating humans male and female, viewing those outside of or in between the male/female binary as not reflecting God's will for their personhood. Because gender incongruity is regarded in this way, it is often thought of in moral categories and as a violation of the created order. Those who see through this lens often adopt a posture that identifies individuals navigating gender identity concerns as being willfully disobedient. Gestures that flow from this posture tend to be rather limited and are often characterized by disputation (of incorrect thinking) and correction (of incorrect behavior). Thus, care for the person navigating gender identity involves encouraging that person to embrace their biological sex in an attempt to restore the creational intent for their gender identity and expression.

This posture's strength lies in its attendance to scriptural references from Genesis 1 and 2 and the way they inform a normative ethic of gender. Strong in theology, it leaves much wanting with regard to pastoral-care gestures. Integrity-leaning postures can create challenges in appreciating and working to compassionately alleviate the potential difficulties a person could face in trying to live according to their biological sex. The integrity lens's emphasis on avoiding wrong behavior can cause people to rely on cultural stereotypes as moral guides, devoid of a positive vision for expression of gender identity. If integrity-leaning gestures call people to embrace their biological sex, it may be helpful to thoughtfully consider what additional gestures could make environments more conducive to this embrace. Those who favor the integrity lens might want to consider the value of debunking rigid stereotyping around masculinity and femininity rather than doubling down on these.

The integrity-leaning posture tends to be weak in providing gestures that cast a vision of thriving life for those who experience gender incongruity. This lens may also struggle to provide a thorough account of experiences such as gender dysphoria and intersex conditions. It emphasizes the rule, often demanding that those who present exceptions get in line with the norm, even if that norm is informed by stereotypes that many do not fit in to.

If an integrity-leaning posture is to be effective, it must develop gestures that answer questions of identity, community, and belonging for the person who does not experience their gender identity as cleanly fitting in the male/female binary. Remember, a posture, to be effective, must allow for gestures that respond to the reality of difficult terrain in front of a runner. As we consider questions of gender, an effective posture must attend to the reality of the person before us. In the words of Thomas Merton, "The religious answer is not religious if it is not fully real."[7] The answers we offer out of the integrity lens must respond to the real questions of transgender youth as much as any other youth. Youth will likely dismiss our gestures—and the posture they flow from—if our gestures don't adequately address the reality that young people find themselves in.

Consider the situation where a transgender teen enters a youth group four years after having transitioned. Would the only available gesture be to urge that this teen discontinue cross-sex hormones and undergo surgery reversal? Would the teen be allowed to attend and participate in the faith community, and if so, what expectations would guide their participation? If the gesture made toward this teen is rooted in disputation, the posture behind that gesture will likely become more contentious in the eyes of this teen and others in the youth group. There may be times when asking the teen good questions, guiding them toward additional resources, or encouraging further identity exploration would be helpful. However, a posture that relies solely on the integrity lens could be limiting those who want to care for this teen to disputatious gestures. These gestures often alienate young people and leave them no room to delve deeply into the very questions we want them to consider.

Disability-Leaning Posture

The disability lens holds that gender incongruence, transgender experiences, and emerging gender identities typically reflect variations that occur in nature. For Christians drawn to this lens, these variations are accounted for by the fall. Distress around one's gender is not imbued with the same moral significance as is often seen with the integrity lens. Taking seriously Genesis 3, this lens provides a posture that can account for less common tendencies, including hormonal imbalances and neurobiological abnormalities. Many people view intersex conditions through this lens, understanding them as birth defects—and therefore products of the fall—but not believing that they imply some moral failing or spiritual deficit on the part of the intersex person. Likewise, those who see gender incongruity through the disability lens might say that gender dysphoria is a rare natural exception, and the appropriate response is one of compassion. Within this posture, an individual is likely agnostic about the causes of gender dysphoria, so their gestures would not spend much time trying to solve the question of causality.

Overarching gestures from this lens tend to communicate empathy, compassion, and acknowledgment of the hard choices faced by individuals who experience gender incongruity. These hard choices may include the potential use of medical interventions to manage gender-related distress. We have sometimes likened these choices to the choices of a parent whose loved one is diagnosed with seizures, neurofibromatosis, multiple sclerosis, or any other qualifying medical condition in which they might consider utilizing medical marijuana when they never would have thought of doing so otherwise. Friends might offer gestures that communicate "I am with you wherever you go" and be present to listen to parents as they journey with their child through this terrain. The pursuit of any interventions could be seen through this lens not as a "moral good" but as a necessary concession for managing a chronic experience.

Specific gestures, then, might include individual prayer and ongoing discernment for the person suffering, prayer at small groups or Bible studies for the family, and community support as the family explores the challenges of all paths. For parents of those navigating gender identity questions, it has included revisiting requests made by their teen around clothing, hairstyle, preferred name, and pronouns. We have known many parents who initially would not have thought of referring to their loved one by a different name (perhaps even a nickname from childhood) but, when asked to do so by their teen (who has shown many signs of depression or anxiety), made that decision and found that their loved one responded well to it in ways that they had not anticipated. Gestures may also include thinking with a friend about what helps them bear their distress, listening to and accompanying a person who pursues various treatment options (including more invasive steps), and viewing these treatment options as ways of coping with a condition out of medical necessity. Those offering support from the disability lens will want to realistically appraise how a person could cope with dysphoria while living in accordance with their biological sex, and they would seek to understand why the person might avoid atmospheres where their gender-related distress peaks (as, for instance, when a woman who experiences gender dysphoria avoids attending events where she might be expected to wear a dress). Communities shaped by this posture would engage in communal efforts to reduce rigid gender stereotypes and to think critically about how certain comments about gender could exacerbate the pain a person feels. Those who view gender incongruity through a disability lens, if they are not favorable toward gender identity transitions, can consider how a stepwise approach might be useful in coping with distress on a case-by-case basis.

For example, imagine a pastor working with a family whose child has socially transitioned. This pastor might allow the child to have a single room on a youth retreat rather than be assigned to a gender-specific room where they might not be comfortable among their peers. This could also mean providing a mentor to the child (and their family) who consistently checks in on them and anticipates future needs and concerns. The key is that someone navigating gender identity concerns is not left to do this task alone. This type of intentionality and fore-thought provides a communal atmosphere for a person to make new meaning out of their challenges, seeing themselves as belonging to the faith community instead of feeling invisible in these settings.

The strength of a disability-leaning posture is that it offers empathy and takes seriously the way all our experiences, including gender, are touched by the fall in varying degrees. However, this posture may find limited gestures to offer a person who wonders how they could derive a sense of identity and community by thinking of themselves as "fallen" or "disabled." If churches today struggle to care for individuals with other enduring challenges, such as grief, chronic illness, or disability, we would expect that there is much work to be done in providing a path for identity, community, and meaning-making gestures through this lens. Such a posture could also lead to gestures that communicate pity for the person, only isolating them further from the body of Christ.

Also, the disability-leaning posture may at times focus so much on gestures of empathy and compassion for the individual that adherents may feel conflicted about the place of gestures that take the form of teaching theological anthropology and related norms regarding sex and gender. This tension can have implications for ecclesiastical settings, Christian education, and the effective development of relevant church policies.

Diversity-Leaning Posture

The diversity lens views variations in gender identity and expression as a reflection of natural diversity that the culture should celebrate. For those within the LGBTQ+ community who identify as Christian, emerging gender identities exist alongside transgender experiences more broadly and are frequently considered the handiwork of a creative God. This perspective is the Christian form of the dominant lens in our culture today. One strength of this posture is that its gestures provide a compelling vision for youth navigating gender identity questions. Within the LGBTQ+ community, individuals are often told that they are invited into the "family," which communicates that they finally belong somewhere. The diversity-leaning posture is compelling to many because it offers meaning-making structures that inform identity and connect to a kinship network committed to navigating this identity together. Within this lens, an emerging gender identity is linked to transcendent meaning.

Gestures emerging from this posture would likely involve encouraging individuals to transition as an avenue toward self-actualization. The gestures would assure the young person and their family that the gender identity the young person asserts is "who they really are" and would express love through openness to any resolution of gender identity without critique. Messaging might include, "You are special. You are unique. This is who you are, and you are home here at our church, regardless of the degree to which you conform to your biological sex." Many who engage out of this lens would communicate that choices about gender identity should be resolved in the direction of one's authentic self, one's experienced gender identity. Ministry groups would likely want to distance themselves from strict binary rules of male/female sexual difference, which would be viewed as sources of oppression. Instead, they might encourage both cross-sex identities and identities between or outside the male/female binary. Likewise, they might adopt policies for youth ministry, bathroom usage, and conversation about norms of gender that reflect the normative nature of emerging gender identities.

This posture can also limit gestures, though. If love for others means indiscriminately reinforcing every way a young person expresses themselves or their gender, it could become self-contradictory as the young person's experiences shift, or it could tend to stunt the evolution and growth that young people naturally experience over time. Enthusiastic approval may be an appreciated gesture with one teen but not with another. The gestures associated with this lens are sometimes overly optimistic about people's capacity to perfectly know what is best for them. As Christians who take seriously the fall, we know that people are not always reliable judges of their own well-being. The diversity lens's tendency toward unrestricted affirmation may limit those who adopt it from asking helpful questions or providing resources beyond transitioning. This poses a particular challenge when we may be supporting youth who don't experience gender dysphoria and who could perhaps find the identity and community they seek without committing to irreversible bodily changes.

A diversity-leaning approach is strong in its emphasis on the call of the Christian to seek out and serve marginalized groups and to fight for social justice for those who have felt oppressed. When it draws from Scripture, it emphasizes the moments where Christ cautioned believers from casting judgment on others and called them to love unconditionally. It also leads a person into a community of support and encouragement with what can be an enduring reality. By way of analogy, when a person is born blind or deaf, a portion of the blind or deaf communities may deny that their experience is a condition or calamity. That being said, the majority of individuals with these experiences do recognize that eyesight and hearing are meant to be consonant with the two corresponding sense organs. Nevertheless, identification with either the blind or deaf communities, and the corresponding experience of support and dignity, is helpful in at least some ways that may compare to that of a gender atypical experience.

But the diversity-leaning posture falls short if a Christian fails to consider how Genesis 1 and 2 and historic theological notions of essential maleness and essential femaleness have been so readily uprooted by emerging gender identity experiences. Experiential narratives are prioritized as the reflection of absolute truth, a shift that potentially emerges from moral relativism and postmodern thought more than from Christian anthropology. Another concern lies with how the diversity lens can tend toward a humanistic philosophy that asserts we know ourselves best, leaving unanswered questions about what aspects of identity, community, desires, and behaviors we are called to submit to God and discern, rather than gauging the goodness of an act based only on our own will and sense of self. It is noteworthy that scriptural and historic Christian references are not central to the claims of this lens. The lens seems to assert that Christian love is the same thing as affirming every thought, desire, action, or decision an individual wants to make. This posture could also be limited in its ability to communicate a theology of a healthy gender identity to a broad body of believers.

Our hope in offering these reflections is multifaceted. First, we hope you can locate yourself in one of the three lenses or locate aspects of your thinking within multiple lenses and their interaction with a range of theological perspectives, as the categorizations might be restrictive. Second, we hope this model offers a pathway for perspective-taking as you consider why you or a loved one might be drawn to one of the three lenses and how people operating within other lenses might view the world differently. This exercise fosters healthier engagement in dialogue if we and those we love can understand the strengths of each of the lenses. Finally, we have found that integrating the best of each of the three lenses allows for postures and gestures that can create a more nuanced relational approach.

An Integrated, Flexible Posture

The integrated, flexible posture we want to model is one of accompaniment. This posture signifies that we want to understand where a person is, enter into their present experience with them, and commit to journey with them regardless of where they go from here. We recommend accompaniment in part to avoid reducing care for a person to one goal (behavioral modification, theoretical or scriptural knowledge of particular principles about gender, acceptance of any resolution of gender identity, or refusing to speak into gender identity at all by assuming that Christianity has nothing to offer). We can appreciate the desire to focus on one goal, of course. But we believe that no single goal is sufficient to provide the kind of support today's youth need in the realm of gender identity. In these and all cases, there is space and a call for discussing actions that may be impeding personal holiness, scriptural exegesis, and identification of moral and ethical guidelines to structure a faith community.

An inherent limitation to accompaniment is that it most naturally suits a situation in which parents are supporting their teen or adult child, or an individual or family is helped by a friend or pastoral point person. There are complexities, however, when a pastor or Christian leader must preach from the pulpit, develop doctrinal statements or policies, or teach a traditional view on gender in Christian education settings. So too, when a loved one is younger, such as a small child, the guidance and perspective of parents and other trusted adults is important and would not manifest as much in accompaniment as it would when that child grows older. Rather, we would advocate for a "scaffolding" approach, which would mean setting up a frame of support for the

FOR PARENTS: ACCOMPANIMENT IN FAMILIES

Accompaniment can be more complex to navigate in families where there are multiple perspectives on specific steps a young person may take. We met with one mother, Sue, whose nineteen-year-old, Kent, a biological female who identified as gender-queer, was seeking cross-sex hormonal treatment and was using a male name and pronouns. Kent did not have a history of gender-related distress in childhood, was unwilling to seek therapeutic support in making his decision, and was moving quickly to more invasive means. Sue was wrestling with how to accompany Kent while still being honest about her fears and convictions. Kent had no concerns about the ethics of cross-sex hormones, while Sue saw this step as morally impermissible. Kent was asking for Sue to financially support the use of cross-sex hormones, and Sue was sincerely struggling with whether she could do so.

This is an example of a point of tension where Christian family members may land in different places with regard to what accompaniment looks like. We encouraged Sue to seek ways to accompany Kent, even if her convictions make it difficult to celebrate the steps Kent is taking. Sue decided that she could check in with Kent after he begins hormones to hear about the process, she could seek to understand what drew Kent to this intervention, and she could continue to commit to spending quality time with him to connect over activities they enjoy doing together. She also agreed to use a nickname, "K," to address him, even though she was not able to commit to using a male name and pronouns. Rather than focusing on what she was not ready to do—namely, financially support the hormonal treatment—Sue was able to shift her attention to what accompaniment she could offer, and Kent was grateful for her willingness to journey with him, despite their differing perspectives on the intervention he was choosing.

child that positions parents to later shift to accompanying a loved one as they enter into later adolescence and young adulthood.

With these important caveats in mind, we want to develop accompaniment as a model for an integrated, flexible approach. As we move forward with our discussion, we are going to assume a biblically faithful, orthodox foundation as we have described above. Keep in mind that we may not know the factors contributing to a person's gender identity questions. As we discussed in part 1 of this book, it may be unclear if someone suffers from gender dysphoria, or if they are navigating confusing gender stereotypes, or if they are facing other challenges unrelated to gender and turning to emerging gender identities as an emotional "home" and a place of safety. Given how little we may understand about what is going on for a teen with gender identity concerns, we should be cautious and tentative rather than overly confident, imprudent, and reckless in our early interactions. Accompaniment lends itself to the exercise of prudence in future encounters. It does not exclude opportunities to guide, teach, and explore theology, but it would not end there.

Considering Our Aims

We turn now to considering our aims. What does it mean to effectively witness? How are the principles of gauging effective witness transferable to those navigating gender identity? Is our care for another most effective when we engage in consistent refutation of a person's labels, stated identity, or decisions—a strategy tried by some Christians today? When we ban certain people from our churches? When we discard all notions of norms of sex and gender to avoid judgment? These are among the questions we invite you to reflect on in the next few chapters. And we believe that answering these questions will require ongoing discernment long after you finish this book.

For some, care is effective insofar as it brings healing or restoration of God's creational intent. Those who adhere to a more ultraconservative/ fundamentalist position often land here. For others, care is effective when it allows us to walk with people in their suffering. We see this as more of the orthodox position. Its goal is to abide with the person and identify God's provision in their life, including the relationship we form with them. For still others from the liberal position, care is at its best when it creates an atmosphere where all are welcome, no matter where they are theologically or spiritually. It aims to create an atmosphere of inclusion and celebration of each person as they are.

We often speak with pastors who, drawing from ultraconservative/ fundamentalist theology, tend to engage in practices that can function as gatekeeping and restriction. They believe that the purpose of discipleship is to outline behavioral expectations for living a virtuous, godly life and to determine whether each person under their authority is open to taking steps to meet these expectations. In this approach, a person's access to continued relationship hinges on their compliance with particular moral and ethical standards of Christian faith or their willingness to become compliant. If young people are told or made to feel that they must have correct theology in order to be in relationship with other Christians, be part of a faith community, family, or peer group, then their wrestling with theology could preclude them from being cared for. In the case of a young person navigating gender identity, we could imagine a youth pastor telling a bigender person that they would not be welcome in a church small group unless they presented themselves in alignment with their biological sex and "repented" of their identification with the bigender label. Enforcing a policy like this would certainly keep relationships cleaner, but it will leave that youth to continue exploring gender identity apart from a body of believers who could offer valuable perspective.

From an orthodox theological foundation, what those who emphasize an integrity framework may do a better job with is constructing a social environment that helps direct the seeking, questioning youth who do not have gender dysphoria, insofar as guidance offered may help them land in more adaptive, traditional gender roles. But this same environment may be difficult for those who have gender dysphoria and find it difficult to manage within traditional gender roles. This is where the ultraconservative/fundamentalist approach in particular may run aground. A nuanced, nimble relational approach is essential.

When it comes to youth ministry approaches, some ministry staff have taken the diversity-leaning approach by stressing that the goal of their ministry is an open-door policy. All are welcome in the church, with little attention given to what can be said about morality and virtue when a person enters. In these cases, assigning moral value to a person's choices might be perceived as judgmental, harsh, and unloving. Thus, decisions about ministry to people with gender identity questions are driven by fear of judgmentalism. Motivated by this fear, it is easy to imagine a church deciding that no norms can be taught in relation to emerging gender identities, and the church can give no guidance to the way Christians reflect their gender identities in and through their lives. This position is increasingly appealing for many churches, as it creates a comfortable environment where people are welcome to be "in process" and don't feel pressured to have landed on ethical decisions.

We have witnessed the harm done if ministry, or any relationship, becomes solely focused on a list of behavioral expectations or a welcome sign on the door. In general, people who attend a faith community or profess Christian faith are seeking guidance around what Christ has to say about their lives, the way they live, and the decisions they make. After all, many are aware that the Christian life is set apart precisely because Christians submit to Jesus for guidance on, well, everything. The how-to of being his disciple is not always clear and is certainly costly at times. People want to know what costly obedience looks like, and trite or oversimplified answers one way or another leave them disappointed and lost.

When it comes to Christians navigating gender dysphoria, the same is true. Some have shared with us that they do not feel satisfied when Christian ministries or fellow Christians tell them all gender identity management strategies are either diabolical or of no moral consequence whatsoever. They want guidance from respected Christians on how to cope with dysphoria in a way that glorifies God, and some of them consider certain methods outside the bounds of morality. However, these Christians have struggled in churches, families, and Christian communities that make behavioral demands before people can begin to be shepherded or belong. In such interactions, Christians navigating gender dysphoria might get the sense that love is conditional and that certain people, certain behaviors, and certain desires make someone beyond the reach of God's love. This sense only heightens their already-present angst about making a decision that may be damning, especially since there is little clarity about which decisions would qualify as damning. Conversely, for them, ministry that stops at a welcome sign has left them wanting.

The goals we set for ministry, care, and relationship matter, as they can be barriers to certain individuals receiving the fruit of Christian charity. For this reason, we caution against defining rigid goals of either demanding behavioral compliance or offering blind affirmation of every choice a person makes. We would not deny the possibility of relationship to people on the basis of disagreements we may have initially, and we would not limit our care to people who already agree with us or agree with our desired goals, as if these things must be agreed upon in advance of relationship. Neither would we decline to engage with someone because we don't at the outset know the best way to accompany them. Imagine how few people the early disciples would have reached if they had functioned this way.

Returning to the tension between correct thinking and correct practice, we seek to find the mean between extremes. Opening the door to relationship and inviting everyone in does not mean that standards are irrelevant, nor does it mean that we ought to throw out careful reflection on what is moral and virtuous merely because standards of morality are difficult to accurately discern. Christian leaders do need to articulate a theological anthropology and offer clarity regarding norms for sex and gender. This is no easy task. Even attempting to discern how to apply a historical Christian ethic will be rebuked by some. This only magnifies our need for wisdom, prudence, and discernment to apply orthodoxy in the here and now as we aim to encounter and accompany each and every person we meet.

The orthodox, integrated posture of accompaniment can get messy, to say the least. It means not always having all the answers about how to engage with someone ahead of time or being fully cognizant of what the outcome will look like. Yet engaging in relationships without having all the answers isn't a bad thing, and it doesn't signify a lack of preparation. Instead, it means that we are invited to believe God will provide help along the way. It also signals to those we serve that, for the Christian, there is no more worthy pursuit than journeying with others toward being more fully alive and integrating God's plan for humanity—for their particular humanity—into their lives.

A Christ-Centered Approach

Christians claim Christ as our model for life and for our witness as Christians. Thus, our ministry (whether that is professional or vocational ministry or more informal relationship building) too must reflect Christ. No matter our particular spheres of influence, Christians have historically attempted to reflect Christ's roles as priest, prophet, and king. The priest offered sacrifices on behalf of the people at the altar of God. The prophet communicated messages between God and humankind. The king demonstrated the intended unity between God's kingdom and earthly powers that ought to submit their authority to God. These roles, perfectly embodied by Christ, lay a foundation for our own Christian witness and present three distinct aims for how we reflect Christ in our everyday lives. Let's consider how we ought to embody these roles.

Priestly Witness

In Scripture, Christians are chosen to "declare the praises of him who called you out of darkness into his wonderful light" (1 Pet. 2:9). In living out our priestly role, we who have received mercy are called to declare this freedom and offer God's saving light and mercy to others (2:10). Here we pause, reminded that an essential and ongoing key to fruitful ministry is found in receiving mercy from God. Only when we encounter God's mercy as an ongoing reality in our lives can we authentically share it with others. This means "humbly coming to terms with our daily sins and imperfections and experiencing Christ's mercy [which] makes us more merciful towards others and their faults."[8] Not only that, but humility before God's mercy allows us to "acknowledge that God's saving love must be 'mysteriously at work' in them—because we have experienced his love at work in the midst of our own daily struggles."[9] Contemplating God's mercy, then, is a point of essential reflection as we approach any ministry, especially ministry with individuals exploring gender identity. To bear witness to the wonderful light that is life in Christ, we must encounter again and again our dependence on God.

A priestly witness is not one where we act from a place of superiority, approaching others in a patronizing way. We must remember that our great high priest, Christ, descended to humanity, and as a result he is not "unable to empathize with our weaknesses" but knows them intimately (Heb. 4:15). Thus, we too do well when we minister out of a place of solidarity with others, asking God for the desire to understand the depths of their pain, failings, and struggles, and journey alongside them from a place of deep humility. This fosters authenticity, rather than a person feeling as if they have to "say the right things" to receive care and support. In the case of gender dysphoria, we want to create a space where a person can share vulnerability about their questions, even if some of these questions include considering interventions that many Christians would have concern about.

Extending mercy in response to another's repentance—the humble coming to terms with daily sins and imperfections—is certainly part of the ministry out of a priestly role. Broadly, we can foster a spirit of repentance that identifies vices and spiritual challenges not exclusively related to one's gender identity. When it comes to repentance and gender identity concerns, what can be especially complicated is that the people we minister to may agonize over what constitutes sin in responding to gender incongruence. As people try to identify ways to manage gender dysphoria, they may wonder what specific steps they have the freedom to pursue and what steps would be against God's best for them. They are not always sure what they ought to be repenting of, insofar as it relates to gender identity questions and ways of coping with distress. Is the urge to cross-dress sinful? Does the decision to adjust one's hairstyle or wear light makeup necessitate repentance? You may also be unsure about this. Many honest pastors, parents, and loved ones have conveyed a level of confusion and uncertainty around this. We can pray for mutual wisdom in understanding the big picture, as well as prudence in particular decision-making. We can pray for guidance, discernment, and mercy if and when decisions are made that some would believe to be cause for moral concern.

One acquaintance who did pursue medical interventions for her gender dysphoria later confessed that she wasn't sure whether she sinned in making that decision many years ago. She wondered what she should do now, as the decision to pursue medical interventions was the result of intense gender dysphoria and heightened risk that she would take her life. She was asking a good question, and it was unclear to some who knew her well what the right answer was. If someone feels led to repentance, as we join with them we must be careful not to act as if we are in possession of the mercy we offer; instead, we freely give what was freely given to us. To have mercy, *misericordia*, means to be moved within the depths of one's heart at the sight of the misery of another.[10] This movement is a movement toward the other, not merely a dispassionate assessment of their misery from a distance. Aiming to fulfill our priestly role protects us from adopting the attitudes of the Pharisees, who placed heavy burdens on others without helping them carry them (Matt. 23:4).

If a person repents of a behavior, it is also unclear what that means for subsequent behavior. Let's say our acquaintance felt convicted over time that she made a mistake in pursuing medical interventions years ago. Should our acquaintance reverse those steps, even if they were taken fifteen or twenty years ago? What if those steps were thought to be life-saving at the time? It may be difficult to discern answers to such complex questions, but ministry out of a priestly role places emphasis on God's mercy throughout the discernment process, recognizing different people may feel led to different decisions as God speaks to them about pathways to encounter and receive his mercy.

Prophetic Witness

Fulfilling the prophetic role means becoming a teacher who delivers the message of God to the people of God. This knowledge of God's message requires prayer and sacrifice and, most importantly, listening to him. This exercise in trust takes great courage, as we never know what we will be told to do until we ask, and we will often be asked to do and say things without having all the answers. Many Christians we encounter earnestly want to know what God would have them say to a person navigating gender identity, and they feel ill-equipped to do so.

This lack of confidence in ourselves does not relieve us of our prophetic witness in ministry; it just means that we are invited to place our confidence in God alone. We should remember what he commanded and promised Moses: "Now go; I will help you speak and will teach you what you are to say" (Exod. 4:12).

It is difficult to know all of what might be said specifically in terms of prophetic communication. Some truths may have to do with a Christian theological anthropology, norms regarding sex and gender, or what it means to live "in between the times" (or in between the fall, in which we wrestle with the reality of our fallen sexuality and gender experiences, and the return of Jesus and his making all things new). It might mean sharing what we understand God to have been doing in establishing essential maleness and femaleness, even if the embodiment of these do not fall cleanly into rigid stereotypes for most of us and are a source of great pain for some of us. We may be sharing about the reality of suffering and offering examples of other Christians who have lived with enduring realities and found meaning and significance precisely there. We may also emphasize those faithful Christians who have felt forsaken or abandoned by God, only to later speak of how they grew in faith or their capacity to believe in God's guidance and provision even when it was not readily apparent in particular moments of pain.

Prophetic communication is not a Christian leader shouting "Integrity!" at people who are facing such complexities. Through our own walk with God we ask that the Holy Spirit expand our capacity for wisdom and prudence about *what* is said, *how* it is said, and *when* it is said. For example, if you feel led to speak into the meaning and significance found in enduring suffering, ask God for wisdom and prudence in what to say, how to say it, and when to say it; study how enduring suffering has been experienced by others, and take note of the advice they would give from their own sorrow and how that journey unfolded for them, as well as when certain truths were accessible to them through the work of the Holy Spirit over time. C. S. Lewis, in the aftermath of his wife's death, shared this: "Talk to me about the truth of religion and I'll listen gladly. Talk to me about the duty of religion and I'll listen submissively. But don't come talking to me about the consolations of religion or I shall suspect that you don't understand."[11]

An honest friend once shared that talking about gender dysphoria and considering how to engage with a loved one navigating it made him feel as if he wanted to give up. "It is too complicated," he said. He did not feel equipped. This made him want to skirt the issue, avoid his family member, and not think about the complicated questions again. Yet he couldn't dodge the topic forever, and on some level, he knew God was inviting him to engage, even if he did not yet know how to. He was not unlike Moses, wanting God to send someone else. He, like Moses, was chosen, and surely would not be left without the assistance he so desperately needed. God is not surprised by our current culture. He is not confused or puzzled by the complexities we face. He has promised the grace of assistance in moments of perplexity so that we can fulfill the prophetic role that our situation demands.

Kingly Witness

The kingly role of the Christian looks quite different from the roles of many of the rulers we see in our world today. Still, it applies to us even if we are far from royalty. Christ himself was quite a different king than was expected. And while other earthly kings are not our model, Christ certainly is. He was gentle and humble of heart, yet with boldness and conviction in moments that silenced even Pontius Pilate.

The aspiration for the Christian, then, is not a tyrannical kingship but a suffering servant's heart: "You know that the rulers of the Gentiles lord it over them, and their high officials exercise authority over them. Not so with you. Instead, whoever wants to become great among you must be your servant, and whoever wants to be first must be your slave—just as the Son of Man did not come to be served, but to serve, and to give his life as a ransom for many" (Matt. 20:25–28). How can we serve those among us navigating gender identity questions? How can we offer our very selves as companions on the journey, with the humility of the God we serve? How can we seek to bring glory to God in how we respond to them?

Ministry that is kingly can commit to the person in humility. We serve them in walking alongside them, assuring them that they need not journey alone. We do not make our accompaniment contingent on the outcome. Rather, we enter into a sustained relationship in which we reflect the value and worth and dignity of the person before God. Inviting them to continually rediscover what it means to be adopted as a child of the King, and thus an heir, is a healing force for the person who has wondered if their questions preclude them from a relationship with God. In the face of their doubts, we can convey a level of confidence and unwavering faith in the Father's love for them and their belonging in God's family.

This brings us to a point of synthesizing the foundational goal for Christian ministers. We believe ministry at its best embodies and makes incarnational the love of God for humanity. Out of the priestly role we can reflect mercy in times of desperate need to fellow Christians and non-Christians alike, especially those impacted by the current gender identity landscape. To do so, we must renew our encounter with a merciful God, offering to others the mercy that God has so freely given to us. Out of the prophetic role we are invited to enter into dialogue around these difficult topics, to pray earnestly, and to trust in God's assistance and guidance for what to say. When we are invited to speak, we can humbly and confidently share about the love of our God, including what we know and do not yet know about how God's vision for the world informs our gender identity conversations. Out of the kingly role we can enter boldly into relationships, not for our own gain or to prove our knowledge or doctrinal compliance, but rather to live as a humble servant to others, even those we too often have seen as the least among us.

All three of these roles, to which each Christian is called, require nuance in responding to the particular person in front of you. This is where we desperately need supernatural help. Listening to the voice of God in particular moments and calling on him to guide us is the aspiration here, rather than discovering a cookie-cutter model for approaching gender identity. But if we are to seek a cookie-cutter model, let it be a model that leads with the fundamental dignity of persons. After all,

Christ embodied the radical theology that each person is made in the image and likeness of God. If we lose sight of this essential truth in how we relate to those who are navigating gender identity questions, our entire foundation will be for naught.

Love as the Goal

Regardless of our particular roles, postures, or gestures, each Christian is called to participate in the twofold command of Christ to love God and love others as ourselves (Mark 12:30–31). After all, the whole of our life is meant to be a fulfillment of this command. And when it comes to loving others, Christ gave no exception for the ones among us adopting emerging gender identities. When we avoid those who seem at face value to be different from us in some way, or even those who seem to be living in a way contrary to God's law, we must not claim Christ as the rationale behind our avoidance. The real mark of the Christian is how well we model our response after Christ, who entered into relationships with people everyone else had discounted as unworthy of love.

You may not know what you think about emerging gender identities or how to respond to them. You may not be sure what you agree or disagree with. Or you may feel strongly about what, and whom, you disagree with. Regardless, we invite you to call to mind the person whose presence or opinion makes you most uneasy in the gender identity conversation. When was the last time you showed the love of Christ or shared the good news of his saving love with them, not merely in what you say about theology, but in the way you look at, talk to, or talk about them? You might be tempted to argue that your lack of love is the other person's fault: if *they* were kinder or more open, then you would convey love through the way you relate to them or speak about them. We would challenge this, encouraging you to remember that unconditional love, charity in our posture and gestures, applies even to the most unkind, closed hearts among us.

If you are wondering whether this integrated and Christ-centered approach makes relationships messy—yes it does. If we are honest, perhaps our discomfort with messiness is why many of us are drawn toward one lens to the exclusion of the others. To this point, Christian pastor Caleb Kaltenbach articulates a challenge to integrity-leaning Christian churches in his book *Messy Grace*: "Jesus did not die on the cross to create a little country club where we have weekly gatherings, pat ourselves on the back for our good behavior (while hiding our bad behavior), and meet in clusters during the week but do nothing to reach out to the community. That's not the kind of church Jesus wants to build here on Earth."[12]

When we interact with people who don't live in obedience to the call of Christ, we need not panic. As Kaltenbach observes, if you resonate with the integrity lens, you already "have people in your life who are doing things or living certain ways that you don't approve of. Chances are, some of these people are friends and family. If you want to follow the example of Jesus, you will not give up on them or love them less."[13] With a relationship as a foundation, and with grace, anything is possible.

In another section of his book, Kaltenbach highlights our tendency to "get trapped in the wrong thinking. We think that we are not supposed to love people who live in a way that is contrary to what God says. . . . These are people we are fearful to get involved with because it seems so messy."[14] Gently, Kaltenbach reminds us, "It's a good thing Jesus didn't decide that we were too messy to get involved with." He even asserts that "a real mark of spiritual maturity is how we treat someone who is different from us."[15] This applies to those drawn to the integrity lens as much as to those drawn to the diversity lens.

We close this chapter by reflecting on Christ's approach with the adulterous woman in John 8:1–11. He loved her first. He defended her even before she showed any sign of repentance. He challenged those who reduced her dignity to her behaviors that violated the religious law. Where the religious leaders saw a monster who embodied the rejection of the God-given law by which they lived each day, we can imagine that Jesus saw a child of God. He saw a sinner among many sinners. To her, he spoke as the great high priest, emphasizing mercy, not condemnation. His strategy was prophetic in that he boldly commended to her the pursuit of virtue, but only after an encounter with him where he initiated an unmerited love. We imagine that there is a reason she did not balk at his message to "go now and leave your life of sin" (v. 11). It came after an encounter with real love, the love she had been searching for all along. The King of her heart was standing humbly before her. In serving her, his love compelled her to serve him from that point forward.

An integrated, flexible posture of accompaniment aims to reflect Christ above all else. It conveys through its gestures that each person is dignified and worth accompanying by the very nature of their humanity. It moves away from a fixed outcome as a prerequisite for love and relationship. It highlights compassion and a desire to suffer with the person, determining how to alleviate suffering whenever possible. It seeks to help uncover a path of thriving, even if paving that path will involve trial and error, make things messy, and take a lot of work from the entire body of Christ. With this model of accompaniment in place, we now turn to the nuances in particular areas.

CHAPTER 5

Locating Your Area of Engagement

In chapter 1 we discussed some of the history of language and categories that reflect a shift from treating gender incongruity as a medical or psychiatric phenomenon to regarding it as a public and political identity. We want to come back to some of these distinctions to help you locate your scope of engagement.

Three Potential Areas of Engagement

We have found it helpful to identify three potential areas of engagement in relation to gender identity: (1) political identity, (2) public identity, and (3) private identity.[1] While all three of these areas are relevant to the broad cultural conversation about transgender and emerging gender identities, all three are not equally relevant to each person who experiences gender incongruity, and not every Christian is called to engage equally in all three. Most of us will have opportunities to know people who adopt a public identity as transgender or gender nonconforming. Some of us will walk with people who are navigating the tensions of a private gender identity. Fewer of us will likely be called to engage with gender identity at the level of political identity and public policy. In each of these areas of identity, it is helpful to think about specific people who adopt such an identity so as not to lose sight of the particular image-bearers of God whom we encounter in each area of engagement.

Manny is a transgender adult who has been an outspoken critic of local policies in the school system. (Political)

Rachel is your neighbor. She lives two houses down from you. Her teenage child, Asa, recently transitioned and now presents as transgender. Asa has reached out and offered to babysit for you. (Public)

Chris is a teenager in your church's youth group. He has apparently been struggling with questions about his gender identity and faith and was encouraged by his mom to reach out to you, a youth minister, to mentor him. (Private)

Manny, Asa, and Chris represent three different identities and potential opportunities (and challenges) for engagement. All three areas of engagement seem to demand some sort of response, although you may not be called to accompany within each. This chapter distinguishes between the three to help you identify your specific call. People like Manny, for whom being transgender has become a political identity, can be some of the most outspoken advocates for the deconstruction of norms regarding gender identity. Insofar as this is Manny's goal, encounters with him may too quickly devolve into arguments about policies and advocacy. In contrast, those who have a public transgender identity, like Rachel's teenage son, Asa, might be neighbors, coworkers, or family members. Because they are part of our lives independent of any political debate and may not be seeking Christian counsel, gender identity may or may not be discussed in these relationships. Lastly, those who have a personal identity like Chris are those for whom gender identity questions are a current source of struggle, and they are likely reaching out for support in how to navigate their struggle. We will help the reader identify their scope of influence and the challenges and opportunities of engagement in each of these three areas.

Political Identity

When we think of a political transgender or emerging gender identity, we are thinking of individuals who support shifts toward transgender identity and experience being a protected class within society and identifying transgender people as a community needing advocacy in the political sphere. A person who represents a political identity would likely operate within the political arena, seeking reform in the ways government and society think of sex and gender norms. Active political voices might be those who believe that sex and gender norms are oppressive and that the connection between biological sex and gender is merely a result of social construction. As a result, they are the voices promoting policy shifts that protect groups they believe to be marginalized because of their gender identity. In the psychological community, these same voices may call for the removal of gender dysphoria as a diagnostic category. They fear that the use of this diagnosis pathologizes a normal variation in nature and mistakenly perceives illness where we ought to see an aspect of diversity to be celebrated. They might believe that the only appropriate response to a person with an alternative gender identity is to support transition in whatever way the individual desires.

These voices are prominent in media, urging that society indicate its respect for gender diverse presentations by permitting public bathroom use based on gender identity and giving people absolute autonomy to make changes to their anatomy as they see fit. These voices may also see traditional sex and gender norms as a threat to progress in this area, calling for these norms to be challenged and eradicated from schools, churches, and society as a whole. We have sat in dialogues with leading psychologists who represent these voices. They have heralded that "your biology is not at all instructive of your gender identity" and called for a "gender revolution" where individuals have absolute autonomy over their gender identity.

Maybe you have met someone who represents this kind of political identity, or maybe you are only interacting with them through a recently shared article on social media. Maybe you are hearing them in a television interview while you and your children are watching the evening news. Because your children are involved, you may feel pressure to make this a teachable moment, even though you have struggled in the past to do so from a place of Christian charity because of your strong feelings of disagreement.

As we stated above, to avoid the likelihood of depersonalizing this dynamic, we want to take a particular person into account. Earlier, we introduced you to Manny, a transgender person who has become a vocal critic of school policies. Let's imagine he has decided to protest outside of your church in response to the recent school policies he disagrees with about bathroom access. His belief is that your church's position on gender, while not directly cited in the policy debates, still reflects a binary view that is oppressive. How do you look at Manny when you leave church? How do you talk about him, whether he is in earshot or not? If he speaks to you as you leave your service, even criticizing the faith you subscribe to, how will you respond?

You have probably heard about people like Manny who adopt a political identity. What you have probably heard, though, is not exactly helpful. People like him may have been spoken about from the pulpit as a threat to "family values." We appreciate the caution of Caleb Kaltenbach, who challenges us to avoid speaking about those who directly challenge our beliefs in language such as "they," "them," "those people," or "the other side." For Kaltenbach, it is important "to stop thinking of 'them' as the enemy. 'They're' not the enemy."[2] He goes on to say, "'They're' not even all that different from us. We shouldn't be putting up barriers or maintaining a safe distance from 'them.' We need to lose our us-versus-them mentality."[3] If we move away from seeing Manny as an enemy, what can we move toward?

Affirming Personhood

Christians adhere to a radical belief that God became man and elevated our fallen humanity. We believe with scandalous certainty that each person has irrevocable dignity and value because they are created by God. Thus, an essential starting point is holding in mind the sacredness of each human person we encounter. They are the neighbor we are called to love. The Christian philosopher Edith Stein explains, "Whoever is near us and needing us must be our 'neighbor'; it does not matter whether he is related to us or not, whether he is morally worthy of our help or not. The love of Christ knows no limits. It never ends."[4] Manny, too, is our neighbor.

How will you respond to Manny? In a way that honors his dignity as a child of God, that affirms and holds in mind his personhood? The simplest and most important of responses to Manny might begin with a silent prayer: *How can I show this person the love of Christ? When I look at Manny, help me show him eyes of compassion, empathy, and desire for relationship, rather than eyes that look with scorn, reproof, or hatred.* This pause and self-assessment can anchor us, regardless of the identity of the person we encounter, and make room for the Holy Spirit to work in and through our interactions.

Some of those who adopt a political identity may, like Manny, have strong objections to the theological and anthropological assumptions within Christian faith. Yet the clarity with which Jesus calls his followers to love does not qualify. He did not say, "Love your enemies and pray for those who persecute you, except for Manny and others who disagree with you on ideological, political, social, or anthropological grounds." He did not say, "Scorn, mock, tease, or slander those who persecute you because they have their theology wrong." On what grounds would some Christians engage with people like Manny in this way?

Perhaps Manny would seem more worthy of charity if he talked more kindly, dressed more modestly, or didn't shout so loudly. Yet we Christians are the ones who claim that each person has sacred dignity and integrity. It is on this ground that we defend human life at every stage. The burden is on those of us who believe in a Christian anthropology to see the image of God in Manny rather than to discount his dignity until he "acts more dignified." We must remember that we all suffer when we fail to see the dignity of the person we regard as "other." To be consistent is to look with love on Manny, knowing full well that both he and some other activists may not talk as kindly, dress as modestly, or speak as respectfully as they could. But then again, if we are honest, neither do we.

Asking Forgiveness

Bishop Robert Barron has thoughtfully described our current socio-cultural stalemate as being rooted in our loss of the art of disagreement. In this sociocultural climate, he argues, we respond to disagreement with one of two polar extremes: either we violently oppose those we disagree with or we blandly tolerate them. He emphasizes that both approaches are dangerous to the aim of healthy argumentation. In a podcast on this subject, he proposes a middle ground of "rational, peaceful engagement through the mind."[5] The goal in any argument of this kind is seeking a better and more informed position in hopes of finding common ground. Healthy argument must include engagement around matters of great importance to everyone, capacity to hold in mind one's own perspective while honoring and taking seriously the perspectives of others, and commitment to loving others, which Barron describes as "willing the good of the other" over our desire to "win."

Perhaps many of us wonder if it is possible to truly love someone and also disagree with them. In an increasingly relativistic society, people might deny this possibility more than ever. But we believe you can absolutely love someone and disagree with them, even about deeply important matters. Every married couple embodies this reality. How we disagree, the respect with which we do it, and the desire we have to take on the perspective of the other person—all these things inform whether we will disagree in a way that upholds the dignity of the other as worthy of love. In fact, how we argue matters even more than the degree to which we disagree. Much damage is done if we do not figure out the difference between love and agreement.

However, we also acknowledge that Christians often struggle to disagree respectfully. Many of us need to apologize for the ways we have hurt others when we have disagreed disrespectfully or when we have responded with hate, disgust, or mockery of transgender people. Perhaps it is time to admit that, when it comes to the transgender people we pass on the street or the advocates we see on the news, we have often failed in love.

Insofar as we have failed, we can repent of our own sin. Not only that, but we can commit ourselves to growing in our ability to see the dignity of others. In this growth process, we benefit from interacting with Manny and others, building relationships that allow us to learn to offer charity.

Perhaps an apology is long overdue for the pain Manny and others have suffered at the hands of people like you and me. Even if Manny bashes the faith we love and mocks the tradition we subscribe to, could we respond with the same patience and grieved love that Christ does to all of us when we mock a child of his? As we are reminded by Archbishop Fulton J. Sheen, "God loves everybody, not because everybody is lovable—but because He puts some of his own love into each person. That, in essence, is what we have to do: put some of our love into others. Then, even an enemy becomes lovable."[6]

It is not the responsibility of the Christian to feel loved by each person we encounter or to feel affirmed in our theology by each story we hear. Rather, it is the call of the Christian to practice charity in our interactions, to see the image of God in each person, to respond accordingly, and to repent when we fall short of the call to love.

Perspective-Taking

At a recent conference, a transgender speaker and political advocate whom we will call Jane came forward to share her story about being a victim of sex trafficking for many years. She said many things in the talk that Christians would disagree with. Jane deconstructed sex and gender norms, calling them irrelevant and a source of violence in our world. She mocked Christianity as a whole and those who believe it. We disagreed about aspects of theology, anthropology, and philosophy—that was for certain. Yet her story was captivating just the same.

Jane shared about being repeatedly abused by a family member from the age of three and being kicked out of her home when she told her Christian parents that she was transgender. She used drugs for many years to cope with her painful experiences, was roped into sex trafficking by a pimp who showed her affection, and contracted HIV as a result. After twelve years, she escaped from sex trafficking and slowly began to rebuild her life. She spoke with a trembling voice about her abusive experiences and the comments she heard as a prostitute from passersby leaving a local church. The pain was visceral as she shared. We couldn't begin to fathom her pain, but we certainly empathized with her loss.

As Jane began advocating for protection of transgender people like her, her voice grew stronger and louder and more convicted. Her advocacy was clearly an act of resilience, as she stated, "I am no longer a victim as I stand before you today." She advocated differently than we would have, with different presuppositions, and our differences matter. Yet if she were protesting at your church with Manny, how could your knowledge of Jane's story help inform your response?

Perspective-taking involves trying to see through the eyes of the other, to consider how Jane and Manny might have come to the place they are, understanding that they are driven by the desire to protect transgender persons, many of whom have been marginalized, abused, and mistreated. Some persons have been so mistreated, so abused, and so marginalized that they see suicide as the only outlet for their pain. Jane and Manny have experienced this mistreatment, and Jane was marginalized for many years. Thus, they are motivated by the protection of something good, even if their strategies are different from yours. Can we invite Manny and Jane to lunch after church, modeling our response after Jesus, who ate meals with tax collectors even when he was scrutinized for doing so? Can we ask to hear their story and spend the meal mostly listening to their perspective, even if we feel attacked by the presuppositions underlying it? Can we calmly and passionately articulate points of disagreement with public policies we find troubling without villainizing Jane, Manny, or others who might disagree with us?

Perspective-taking does not preclude us from points of contention, including at times strongly disagreeing with the way others construe their lives. We would not lead with these areas of disagreement, but we will also want to be able to articulate divergent views with conviction and respect. Obviously, Jane is unlikely to be mistaken about the horribly painful and traumatic experiences of being abused or trafficked; however, that does not mean that in other areas of construing her perspective she is always going to be right. We want to be able to demonstrate empathy and compassion for Jane, to show that God loves her, and we do that best through our relationship with her. At the same time, we may genuinely disagree with her about ways she construes her perspective on gender identity, her view of Christianity in particular, and on norms regarding sex and gender. We need to be nimble and flexible in our encounters with Jane, as we ask God to guide us in whether we are to communicate aspects of disagreement and, if so, how best to communicate with her in these spaces—again *what* to say, *how* to say it, and *when* to say it—particularly about norms regarding sex and gender, as well as a broader Christian view of life and ways in which God's guidance leads to human flourishing.

Discovering Superordinate Goals

Other writers have spoken on the value of building bridges with the LGBTQ+ community. Moving beyond our disagreements, can we find superordinate goals with Manny and Jane when they ask, "How can Christians talk about love if they hate trans* people? Isn't Christianity evil?" Although we may think about solutions differently, we can acknowledge our shared desire to make the world safer for every human, not least by ending the hatred many Christians express toward transgender people. While we might disagree about which steps will make the world safer, we can agree that a society where people are mocked, ridiculed, and beaten because of the way they look, dress, or act is not acceptable.

Kaltenbach again offers a helpful reflection by articulating all the commonalities Christians have with the LGBTQ+ community that we too often have alienated. These commonalities include creativity, love for others, fervor to fight for justice, strong commitment to a cause we believe in and to holding events for this cause, intentionality about sharing our perspectives with those we love, commitment to communal living, willingness to be known for our beliefs no matter the cost, passion for being understood by others, involvement in groups that bolster our understanding of our beliefs, and communication of these beliefs through resources in media.[7] Coming together on superordinate goals

TRANSLATING A FOREIGN LANGUAGE

Entering into relationship with young people exploring emerging gender identities can feel like learning a foreign language. Tey Meadow, in a book on trans youth, describes a mother who acted as though the author and her transgender son shared a foreign language that she could not speak. The mutual understanding between author and son amounts to "a fluency in a foreign language, a kind of bodily and psychic knowing that inhered in the particularity of our genders." The author writes of the mother, "She needed a translator."[a] This may be how you feel.

What does it mean to learn the foreign language of emerging gender identities?

What does it mean to function as a translator of this language in the church?

What does it look like to become a student of culture without internalizing every current cultural narrative as absolute truth?

We are not suggesting that the newly developed language is "correct" or that you should adopt a new doctrinal position in response to changing language. Rather, we are suggesting that you become familiar with the relevant language so you can be conversant with the people with whom you engage.

a. Tey Meadow, *Trans Kids: Being Gendered in the Twenty-First Century* (Oakland: University of California Press, 2018), 15.

may help us discover even more how we can partner with the broader LGBTQ+ community, appreciating both our similarities and our differences with greater reverence.

How can we join with Manny in advocating for the protection of people who adopt an emerging gender identity, even if we believe that certain areas of their life and decision-making are outside of God's best for humanity? This is an important question to answer. If theologically conservative Christians were as committed as politically active LGBTQ+ people are to developing and upholding policies that protect all people, including vulnerable transgender people, in matters like bathroom access and workplace violence, perhaps our current polarization could be attenuated, even if we still experience disagreements about human anthropology and the like.

As we transition from political identity to public identity, we realize that in all three identities—political, public, and private—we are focusing primarily on one-on-one approaches or the person who feels called to a loving, personal, and sustained engagement with another person. We would be remiss if we failed to acknowledge that there are other callings and priorities that are quite independent, having to do with ministry broadly construed and separate from the three typologies we discuss here. For instance, we know that the pastor who speaks on this issue from the pulpit must have the well-being of every person in mind as he or she speaks, and there may be ways in which shaping church culture may take precedence, as often happens in the development of doctrinal positions or specific policies in the areas of sexuality and gender. We hope our emphasis on the individual (or micro level of interpersonal engagement) will inform such preaching and drafting of policies (or macro level of institutional policy), but we recognize that these are different individual callings and endeavors.

Public Identity

People with public transgender or emerging gender identities exist all over our world. They might be coworkers, friends, relatives, or neighbors who identify publicly in a category outside, beyond, or between the gender binary. The person walking in front of you at the grocery store or your child's friend who asks for a ride home from school might be among this group. They might be new to youth group or attending the Bible study at your home. They are not inviting you into the process of exploring their identity, name, or pronouns; they have already done this exploration without you and have reached at least enough conclusions to choose an identity they are comfortable publicly sharing with others. They introduce themselves or present themselves to you a certain way, and from what you can tell, their public identity is not up for debate.

We introduced you to Rachel and her child, Asa, earlier in this chapter. Rachel is your neighbor. She introduces you to Asa, who has recently socially transitioned from Adam to Asa, and is now Rachel's daughter. Asa may or may not ascribe to the notion that sex and gender norms ought to be deconstructed, and Asa may or may not advocate for the public policy shifts that have caused great tension and concern on all sides in recent years. You may never have these political conversations with Asa or Rachel. Rather, you are their neighbor. Your relationship with them is focused on things unrelated to gender identity. To artificially make your exchanges with Rachel or with Asa about their (or your) perspective on public policy will likely represent a missed opportunity to reflect the love of Christ to them. Frankly, you may not ever get the chance to embody the love of Christ for them.

But assuming you have the opportunity to be in relationship with them, you might wonder how to respond as a Christian. Imagine that you have put out a flyer asking for a babysitter for date nights and Asa offers to babysit.

Prior to thinking of how you might respond, let's consider how a range of Christians have responded to similar situations. Within certain Christian communities, people like Asa have been villainized, blacklisted, or prayed for with pity. Other communities have celebrated those who transition as brave and epitomizing self-realization. In communities with a traditional view of gender identity ethics, using the preferred name and pronouns of a person like Asa could be seen as threatening their theology of God's creational intent for male/female sexual difference. To allow Asa to babysit, or even to call her Asa rather than Adam, could be seen as ignoring the way she has violated God's creational intent.

Engagement has taken a variety of forms in these interactions. We have heard of a Christian saying, "No, but what is your real name? The one you were born with?" This is done, we imagine, in order to challenge the person to course correct. While we have never heard of this strategy being effective, it is often used to make a statement about essential maleness and femaleness. It tends to be received as hurtful, and the theology lesson is likely missed. We have heard of some Christians refusing to interact with such a person or, if they do, speaking about the person in hushed tones with others afterward, making the person a spectacle to be watched rather than a human to be known. None of these approaches would likely be received by any of us as fostering a meaningful relationship if we were on the receiving end. What might be?

Hospitality

Perhaps the guiding principle here can be hospitality. Hospitality acknowledges the person before you, Asa, as she is and relates with her as such. It fosters a relationship where you ask questions to get to know someone, are kind, and genuinely welcome them. This curiosity about Asa sends the message, "I see you and desire to know you," rather than, "I approve of every decision you may have made." Many Christians could struggle with some of the decisions Asa and her mom have made around gender identity. In fact, you may flatly disagree with the ways Asa has decided to adopt a gender identity that departs from her biological sex. You may question her philosophical assumptions that led her to adopt a different name and pronouns than the ones by which she was known previously. A spirit of hospitality allows you to use the name and pronouns that Asa uses for herself, even if you do not affirm her choices in this area or think of her in those terms.

When Asa offers to babysit or introduces herself, she is probably not seeking approval or validation that she made the right choice. Perhaps, over the course of a relationship where you grow in mutual trust, she might share with you how she came to choose the path she did. She may share her sense of confirmation of her choice or, conversely, her fears that she made the wrong decisions. You may disagree with her, no matter what she shares, and yet you may also gain an understanding of how she came to her current place. This could allow for a relationship that thrives, where you can support her in fostering her relationship with God, self, and others.

Warmth

Of course, you may never get to discuss Asa's personal faith with her. The moment she offers to babysit is powerful either way. Never underestimate the power of one positive interaction with a Christian believer or one conversation that leaves a significant wound. If many of us never return to a restaurant after one poor interaction with a waiter, imagine the power of one antagonistic interaction with a person of faith on Asa's own sense of God's love for her. Perhaps a posture of warmth from you would contrast many previous interactions where Asa was admonished, looked at with disgust, and perceived as a threat. What a gift it could be to welcome her warmly, without seeing that warmth as endorsing every aspect of her view of the world.

The warmth we might show to Asa is similar to how we might approach any newcomer at church, or cashier ringing us up, or individual we strike up a conversation with at the doctor's office. We do not often explore people's philosophical, theological, and anthropological assumptions about the world prior to being warm and friendly to them. If we did, we would likely always find that their assumptions do not perfectly match ours and do not always manifest in behaviors that we approve of. Nevertheless, we can lay a foundation for an interaction where we are not too scandalized by a person's story to ask about it, genuinely wanting to learn in the process.

Mutuality

If you have gone on a mission trip, you may recall the hopes you and your teammates shared as you prepared: "I hope to bring the light of Christ to this group of people," or "I want to help others in need." And you may also remember the stories you and your teammates told afterward, about how you received much more than you could ever have given to the people you thought you were going to serve. As Christians, we want to be like Christ, who came not to be served but to serve. This is certainly a beautiful desire. Too quickly, though, we forget that even as Christ will serve *through* us, he will also serve *us* through the people we meet while serving. This is part of the beauty of Christian witness. It is not merely a venue for those who "have" to give to those who "have not." Insofar as it is that way—insofar as a relationship moves only in one direction—it can tend to dehumanize those being cared for.

No one appreciates being patronized or treated as a charity case, and Asa and her mom are no exception. Consider how differently your own life has been impacted by people who remained aloof and patronized you than by people who treated you with respect. When people have challenged you in the realms of your faith, sense of self, identity, behaviors, and sins, what approach was most effective? Was it the one where a person you barely knew called you out for being a gossiper and said you couldn't speak to them again until you had victory over that sin? Was it the one where a longtime friend challenged you to consider the impact of a toxic relationship on your health, but only after hearing you out about why you had been drawn back to an abusive partner and validating how difficult it is to set healthy boundaries? Was it the one where a coworker refused to talk to you because they saw your divorce as unbiblical? Or the one where they checked in with you after hearing about the divorce: "I'm sorry to hear about your divorce. I'd like to just check in with you and hear how you are doing"? What approach promoted spiritual growth and reflected God's posture toward you? What led to greater isolation, resistance, and resentment? Usually, when someone effectively speaks into our lives, it is from a place of knowing about our lives, understanding the complexities therein, and offering concrete accompaniment, empathy, and appreciation for the challenges, rather than trite answers.

If we see Christian witness as a way to give patronizingly from our perceived high status, the people we are engaging with—people like Asa—may very well feel devalued. People navigating sexuality and gender have often felt like the lepers of the church today. They have been looked at with pity, fear, and in some cases, outright disgust. Regardless of whether they see their own gender incongruence as sinful, as a consequence of the fall, or as an aspect of diversity, they have felt ostracized. If we are honest, we have spent a great deal more time speaking *about* them than *to* them, let alone hearing *from* them. Many of us may struggle to appreciate what it would be like to feel as if your body is alien to you, a shell that you live in but don't belong in. Our inability to appreciate the pain of others does not make that pain go away. Rather, it makes our care less effective.

We have learned that care for others is at its best when it is intentionally relational. Imagine you are sitting down for the first time with Asa, after inviting her over for tea, as you have with others who have offered to babysit. As you sit with Asa, you realize she is funny, smart, and thoughtful, and you click with her right off the bat. After spending some time getting to know her, you share that you have heard about transgender people in news and media, but most of the portrayals have been alienating or polarizing. You ask her if she minds sharing a bit of her story so that you can better understand who she is.

An aloof approach may involve condescendingly quoting scripture to Asa about male/female sexual difference and arguing that God does not bless a person who pursues any gender identity other than their birth-sex identity. You could lead with knowledge, facts, and Bible verses to defend your theological view and then ask Asa if she still wants to baby-sit, or you could confidently state that, because of her self-identification, you don't want to hire her. This is one possible strategy, although we suspect Asa would not hear within such a response how much value you see in her, in her humor, intellect, and conscientiousness. She may miss the fact that you really have loved getting to know her and could see her being an excellent babysitter to your newborn. This approach can preclude dialogue rather than facilitate it.

Building a relationship on mutuality does not mean that you have nothing to offer. You may actually, over the course of a relationship with Asa, say some things that challenge her perspective on gender identity, insofar as you think about it differently than she does. However, the conversations you have about gender will be heard far differently if they emerge within the context of a relationship than if they come from a place of superiority. None of us benefit from being mentored by someone who does not first seek to know us. This is why we would do well to listen to Asa first, not solely with pity but with curiosity.

Different parents will likely respond differently to Asa's offer. Some will accept her offer, in the hopes that forming an ongoing relationship will enrich their family life and provide teachable moments with their children about an experience of the world they might otherwise not have known. Given how little we currently know about gender atypi-cal experiences, other parents might understandably be hesitant about how inviting Asa to babysit might communicate approval of how she is currently navigating difficult decisions around gender. They might initially respectfully decline the offer for this reason. Still other parents will perhaps sit down with Asa and tell her how honored they are to get to know her and will open the door to an ongoing relationship over time that may help them decide whether they will take her up on the offer. They may prioritize becoming friends with Asa to better determine their comfort level with her babysitting through seeing her level of maturity, trustworthiness, and responsibility, which are not possibly known merely by knowing her gender identity. If they were to accept the babysitting offer, they might aim for mutual understanding of the way Asa might communicate about her transgender experience to their children. Insofar as common ground and mutual trust could be maintained in this regard, they may gain a mentee, a babysitter, and a friend for years to come.

Ultimately, what we need to avoid is the response of a parent who laughs in Asa's face and says, "Leave my kids with *you*?" Like every other teen, Asa undoubtedly has challenges, questions, and difficulties, including but not solely related to gender. Reducing her to that will not help anyone. You don't know all the answers, but you can still communicate your appreciation for her life and her presence in your life. As in any honest relationship, it is important to acknowledge that there are likely things that you will not see eye to eye on, and you might have questions about her thoughts, beliefs, and ways of being in the world. It is good to ask if a person is open to dialogue in this regard. But first and foremost, it is good for Asa to know that you want to get to know her and hear more of her story and that you also would love to share yours.

Private Identity

When we think of a private or personal gender identity, we picture individuals for whom questions around gender identity are pressing matters. Those exploring a private identity, whether this identity is captured by a particular label or only by a sense of confusion, often find that their exploration is a current source of significant pain. Like those with public identities whom we discussed in the previous section, a person navigating private gender identity could be anyone: a neighbor, a friend, a coworker, your child, your nephew, or a youth you are mentoring. Unlike those with public identities, however, these people are asking for help from you, hoping that you will speak into their experience or expression of gender identity.

In the beginning of this chapter, we mentioned Chris, a teen in your church's youth group who you learn has been struggling with questions of gender identity and faith. He was recently diagnosed with gender dysphoria and carries years of emotional turmoil that he hid with a smile and stylish haircut. He cares deeply about the decisions he is making to manage distress; that's why he is seeking your guidance on how to proceed and how God sees him within this current challenge. He is worried that his decisions in this area of life, or the fact that he is drawn to a label that isn't male or female, might preclude him from a relationship with God.

Chris, who has just confided to you that he has wondered about the use of cross-sex hormones, heard in a recent podcast by a prominent evangelical pastor that cross-sex hormone use is "obviously immoral." Thus, Chris wonders if he would need to stop considering this option in order to serve God or if his wondering about this option is itself a sin. From the pastor's point of view, the podcast offers necessary theological clarity. However, Chris now wonders if he can belong in an evangelical faith community when he is still wrestling with ethical questions that some fellow Christians believe have obvious answers. As we said earlier, getting theology about sex and gender "right" (correct thinking) is not the same thing as being effective ministers of the gospel (correct practice). Asserting a theology too often translates into a refusal to make room for individuals who have questions about theology to receive care while they are in a place of questioning.

Taking a Long-Term View

A guiding principle for accompanying Chris could be taking a long-term view. Taking a long-term view means recognizing that resolving these questions (or Christian discipleship more generally) does not typically take place in the span of a few days or weeks; rather, we walk with people in the time we have with them, however long that is, and we know that their journey will in all likelihood extend beyond our time together (and the same is true of parents, whose influence wanes as children grow into maturity). First, just as you might do with anyone who shares intimate information, it is good to thank Chris for sharing his story. When the intimate information you're hearing describes something you have not experienced yourself, it can be helpful to name your own lack of understanding and invite him to help you understand better what he has been through. If Chris's questions are ones that you share, it is best to take a posture of accompaniment, normalizing how hard these questions are to answer. Even if you feel that you have the answers to Chris's every question, distributing those answers like a PEZ dispenser will likely be unhelpful. Answers are not what humans need most during the agony of questioning; rather, we need a person who is not scandalized by or afraid of the hard questions, someone who models the presence of Jesus to us in our wonderings. Assuring Chris that Jesus can handle his tough questions and is not surprised by them or scrambling to find answers can be a source of relief. This approach humanizes his questions and points him to Jesus for guidance.

Taking the Body Seriously

In his thoughtful exploration of the spiritual life, *Soulful Spirituality,* David Benner highlights the importance of reflecting on our body-soul unity. We must strike a balance in which we value a person's body without reducing the person to their body. He cautions that "spirituality moves us away from life whenever it distances us from our bodies. . . . Whenever our ties to our body are tenuous, our ties to reality are equally fragile." He goes on to say that "to be human is to be embodied, so any spirituality that fails to take the body seriously necessarily diminishes our humanity."[8]

In applying this principle to Chris's gender dysphoria, we ought to honor the depth of pain that exists when someone sees their physical body as alien to them. We pause here to consider the agony Chris must feel when he looks in the mirror and feels like a stranger in his body. Without discounting the body as something to be annihilated or altered in some way, we must all recognize the significance and scope of

Chris's suffering. This includes understanding the common triggers of his distress and the particular way gender dysphoria impacts his spiritual life and social connections. The pain in his embodied experience ought not be taken lightly. One of the most helpful means of coping that transgender Christians have shared with us is when people close to them believe them about the depth of their pain.[9]

Taking the body seriously could also mean shifting attention from disgust for aspects of one's body to valuing and discovering the way their body is a temple of the Holy Spirit. Some people have found it helpful to explore how their unique humanity can be expressed in and through their body, albeit a body stricken with the pain of gender dysphoria. They ask themselves, "What are the aspects of my embodied existence that I can appreciate?" "How can this particular body bring glory to God, even if I choose not to take steps through medical interventions?" This approach is not always possible with severe gender dysphoria, and what is possible varies from person to person. Still, it can be a valuable way of honoring that God is not scrambling for a "plan B" for their life in light of their difficulties. It can also create some distance for a person to appreciate their body, even while there are aspects of it that trouble them.

Developing a Theology of Suffering

Another guiding principle for engagement is developing a robust theology of suffering that Chris can enter into. Christianity has throughout its history offered a substantial theology of suffering. Yet many Christians have struggled to be present with people who are suffering. Perhaps we struggle to be in touch with our own poverty and lack, despite Jesus's blessing the poor in spirit, the mourning, and the meek in the Sermon on the Mount (Matt. 5–7). It is hard enough for us to sit with the questions that arise from our own pain, let alone the questions of those we care about.[10] Many of us try to resolve and dismiss pain quickly by offering premature solutions and trite answers, proof texting from Scripture passages taken out of context, or highlighting the silver lining instead of admitting to real and enduring difficulty.

We have to be careful here, though. A Christian view of suffering does not mean radical asceticism. Such a portrayal is depressing and devoid of the meaning-making structures necessary to avoid despair. Said another way, a theology of suffering is not the same thing as saying we ought not take reasonable steps to alleviate human suffering. Rather, it is balanced with the real understanding that suffering cannot be absolutely avoided. So when it cannot be avoided—and it is worth noting that even a social or medical transition does not eradicate all suffering—the question is, What then? Regardless of steps a person like Chris takes around gender identity, the reality is that he suffers. It is not so much for us to "diagnose" the cause of the suffering as it is for us to learn to help him discover the fullness of life. We have much to learn in this regard.

If you try to respond to Chris with easy answers that overlook suffering, you might say something like, "Well, remember that God created male and female in Genesis. God doesn't make mistakes." To this, we imagine Chris might ask, "Then what am I? Did God make a mistake on me? Because I feel a lot like a mistake." Even more likely, instead of verbalizing these questions, Chris might nod and remain silent, his deeper questions going unanswered. He might also feel missed by the rush to course correct. Course correction does little to acknowledge and take seriously the pain he feels or to consider whether Scripture can make sense of the ache he feels internally.

Another common but insufficient response to Chris could be, "Well, you should pray more about it. Jesus will help you pick up your cross and follow him." This isn't untrue, but it is an oversimplification. A statement like this often translates into, "Pray more about it (alone, because I don't know what to say). Jesus will help you pick up your cross and follow him (I hope, because I don't have a clue how to help)."

Before we throw in the towel, we must ask what the Christian tradition *can* offer to this conversation about dealing daily with gender dysphoria. We know that, for religious/spiritual people, coping with distress can be effective when it is religiously congruent, meaning that it draws from their faith and spirituality and sees these things as resources. We need not foreclose on religious resources, although we must be cognizant that they can be used poorly or in a manipulative way. That is not our intent.

There are resources that we can turn to for help with an applied theology of suffering.[11] Scripture itself "is a great book about suffering."[12] We will return below to the question of how we as Christians respond to suffering, including what it means to enter into Christ's suffering.

Praying Together

The psalms teach us how to pray by modeling such honesty. A third of the 150 psalms are prayers of lament, calling to God's attention the injustices and pains of this life. Many Christians feel ashamed and afraid to express their own lament to God, feeling as if they are sinning merely by articulating the doubts, anger, and angst they may feel. Care that affirms and encourages rugged honesty in prayer, including the fervor and agony with which Jesus prayed in the garden of Gethsemane, moves us away from the habit of restricting ourselves in our communal times of prayer to pleasant-sounding prayers of thanksgiving and polite requests.

Fruitful accompaniment can encourage those navigating gender dysphoria or considering emerging gender identities to ask Christ their questions in prayer and listen for his answer. As Pope Francis writes, God "does not get upset if you share your questions with him. He is concerned when you *don't* talk to him, when you are not open to dialogue with him. The Bible tells us that Jacob fought with God (cf. *Gen.* 32:25–31), but that did not keep him from persevering in his journey. The Lord himself urges us: 'Come, let us argue it out' (*Is.* 1:18). His love is so real, so true, so concrete, that it invites us to a relationship of openness and fruitful dialogue."[13] Christ is certainly not alien to suffering and to the human feeling of being forsaken by God. At the same time, he did not reject his Father or deny his existence. He called out to God in prayer from the cross. When we pray, we can echo his words, honestly and with the weight of our every emotion: "My God, my God, why have you forsaken me?" (Matt. 27:46). Those wrestling with a personal identity who subscribe to a traditional theology of gender can bring to

God the confusion about whether their own theology can account for their experience of gender. This wrestling may also be an opportunity for a deeper encounter with God, which opens up the doors to serve others more authentically.

Serving Together

In our research on the experiences of transgender Christians, we have found that service is an outlet to cope with the ache of distress. One transgender biological female said that she responded to her dysphoria by "helping other people—focusing on the problems of others." She reflected, "I was created to love God and love people. God made me generous and empathic and that's what matters."[14] This testimony confirms the many scriptural references indicating that we receive from God by giving of ourselves (Prov. 11:25; Matt. 10:8; Luke 6:38; 2 Cor. 9:11; Gal. 5:13). Many of us find that when we wrestle in our relationship with God, we can enter more fully into the wrestling of others that is inherent to the spiritual life, becoming more driven to serve them and to find transcendent meaning in the process.

In our previous discussion of how to approach those with a public transgender or emerging gender identity, we described the common pitfall of engaging from a place of superiority, thus pitying the person we approach or even infantilizing them. The same can be said for accompanying those wrestling with a private identity. Seeing them as people to be looked at condescendingly is not helpful here. Experiencing pain and suffering in the realm of gender identity is not necessarily a sign of deficit. We must push back on the narrative that those who suffer are lesser Christians. Jesus's entire ministry was dedicated to revealing the profound truth that suffering and sonship are not mutually exclusive: "Son though he was, he learned obedience from what he suffered" (Heb. 5:8). The Son of God did not stop being a son when he suffered. Neither do we. If anything, we are confirmed in our identity as children of God when we find ourselves in the crucible. It is out of the crucible that the suffering servant made an offering to God and the world unlike anything we have ever known. How might the suffering produced in obedience to Jesus prepare his followers to serve the world like he did?

We are told that the greatest among us will be servants to others (Matt. 23:11) and that the mission of Jesus was "to serve, and to give his life as a ransom for many" (Matt. 20:27–28; Mark 10:45). In generously giving of time and talents to the church, especially for those wrestling with gender identity, Christians offer a beautiful model of responding to Christ's call to service in this sacrificial and humble way. The future of the church hinges on how we serve, but especially on how we serve those whom we have marginalized historically. We have heard from some people navigating gender identity questions that other Christians can serve them by calling them after an event that tends to trigger gender-related distress and inviting them to share about the ongoing challenges they face. Other Christians can serve through moving gender-identity-related distress out of the category of sin and prioritizing learning about and taking seriously the experiential reality of gender dysphoria. Perhaps the largest act of service to these Christians, though, is not reducing them to their gender identity questions.

At the risk of reducing those with gender dysphoria to mere recipients of Christian service, we must recognize that we as a body suffer when we forget to consider the breadth of ways they can be participants in service. There are many roles within the church that those navigating gender identity questions can occupy and uniquely serve out of. Those navigating gender identity have much to teach us. For starters, they are well-equipped to model how to accompany others who are navigating similar challenges. While it is important not to think of them as the "resident experts" on gender dysphoria, they certainly could contribute particular insights into dialogues around gender identity, pastoral-care questions, and ways to make churches more prepared to care effectively. They can often be adeptly attuned to the damaging theological and pastoral-care narratives around gender identity that have wreaked havoc on the Christian church and led to a great deal of oppression over the centuries. Their service to the church can come in the form of highlighting the ways that rigid stereotyping is a disservice to all Christians and a poor reflection of the heart of God for each unique soul.

Beyond the realm of gender identity, those wrestling with personal identity bring a range of talents, personalities, and experiences, as well as unique perspectives on faith. Many have wrestled deeply through prayer and Scripture to come to know the person of Jesus and seek his insight in their life. This is often a result of the way gender identity concerns can lead people to lean into spiritual questions with a rigor that many Christians could learn from. We must not underestimate the level of spiritual maturity that we will glean when we invite those navigating gender identity questions to share and speak to the ways God has revealed himself in their lives. Even while having their own ongoing spiritual questions, they may have many spiritual answers to contribute in the midst of their wrestling. We have been moved to tears by the beauty that is evident in the lives, reflections, and wisdom of those wrestling with personal identity. The church suffers a lack insofar as we do not invite these individuals to be leaders, guides, and resources to us on matters of faith.

Suffering Together

A third pathway forward is in following Christ's model of how to suffer.[15] A couple came to see us for a consultation and shared their distress about the wife's long-standing experience of gender dysphoria. She was not sure about how she might cope with it and shared reservations about pursuing hormones and surgery. She had gone to her pastor for support, and the pastor responded with, "Just pick up your cross and follow Jesus. We all have to." The wife looked at us and said, "I actually believe that. The problem is, I have no clue what that means. What does that look like here? And to be honest, I am pretty sure our pastor had no clue either."

The comment from the pastor got him off the hook of trying to figure out what embracing the cross looked like in this specific case. Similar to telling a person who is grieving, "Don't cry; your family member is in heaven," her pastor's response, even if true, didn't alleviate the pain of the moment. This is not nearly as problematic as the fact that the response alone fails to offer a model for how to navigate grieving virtuously. If we quote Romans 5:3–5, which highlights the valuable fruit that can come of suffering, but leave this as the end of the conversation, the person is still there, left to suffer alone.

In the case of the pastor, it is possible that the discomfort of seeing the pain and entering into the confusion of gender dysphoria was too overwhelming. So he punted the issue, quoted some Scripture, and ended the meeting (as many other well-meaning pastors also do). The burden, then, was placed back on this spouse to translate the scriptural principle of embracing suffering into real life. She was left feeling as if the pastor failed to appreciate the depth of her pain or to take seriously just how weighty the cross was that he encouraged her to carry. This is precisely the realm of pastoral care. If pastoral care stops at quoting Scripture, the quality of the support is hindered. A robust theology of suffering is meant to be lived by all of us, not just applied as a blanket statement when some among us are trying to discern how to pursue holiness in the midst of ongoing pain. Having the right answer and offering it is not care. Accompaniment is. This involves praying with, serving with, and suffering with those who struggle with enduring realities like gender dysphoria.

Indeed, suffering may be an entryway into some of the elements of identity and community that have thus far been the more emotionally satisfying domain of the diversity framework. But suffering can be an especially difficult topic with youth. This does not mean we avoid helping teens make meaning out of their pain, but rather, we do so discerningly and only after truly appreciating the pain itself. We suspect that, when done correctly, engagement that *takes seriously* questions of suffering, lament, and soul care can lead to more meaning-making and sense-making that over time informs a young person's experience of themselves and of others, including God.[16]

In *The Way of Trust and Love*, Jacques Philippe suggests that Christians who are suffering first come to terms with the reality of their trial. This in itself will take time. Then, they can gradually move into asking the sorts of questions that uncover the meaning in the trial: "What attitude does God want me to have toward this situation? The point is to move from 'Why?' to 'How?' The real question isn't 'Why is this happening to me?' but 'How should I live through these things?' How am I called to face this situation? What call to growth is being made to me through this? That question will always get an answer."[17]

This strikes us as exactly right. How am I called to face this situation? is the question that every young person navigating gender identity concerns is going to need assistance exploring. Keep in mind that the ultraconservative/fundamentalist and liberal theological voices will offer their own account for how a young person should face their situation. Keep in mind, too, that these youth receive emotionally compelling answers to this question from peers, entertainment, and media. A compelling cultural story is being written for how to face any gender identity question. It is all the more valuable to explore the question of how they are called to face questions surrounding gender identity, as young people may foreclose prematurely on answers that simply reflect the prevailing cultural narrative, one that is increasingly applied to anyone who reflects any variation from a traditional gender identity.

Likewise, identity and community may be found on the other side of the question, What call to growth is being made to me through this? Our experience as psychologists is that there is an expanse that opens up on the other side of enduring suffering, a way forward through hardship that leads to a community of people who have traversed that difficult terrain. There is both identity and community to be found, but it requires a kind of openness and maturity that many people may struggle to see as viable given the current cultural context, both within and outside of our church doors. We are not saying to the youth suffering from gender dysphoria that all they must do is endure it; rather, we are exploring with them the question about growth within it. Growth may be related to decisions about how to manage gender dysphoria, but growth can also be explored in ways that may be at least to some degree independent of the discussion about management strategies.

One of the most important topics to address in any discussion of enduring suffering is fear. The fear is that God is not there with us in our suffering. Does God really love us? Or, since suffering does not always seem tied to any readily apparent purpose or meaning in the midst of it, are we possibly forsaken? Is God actually with us? One theological guide through the questions associated with fear and God's love for us is *Forsaken* by Thomas McCall.[18] Read resources that help you prepare to be present in ways that reflect the truths explored in Scripture.

Christians are charged with preparing ourselves to walk with people in their fears about God's love for them and to have a fixed point or "true north" that we move toward. In the case of suffering, that true north is through the love of God for us and his "holy love against sin" that is the "source of atonement"[19] for us. McCall offers us the following: "God is for us. It is not *part* of God that is for us—as if some divine persons or some divine attributes were opposed to me while others are for me—it is just *God* who is, in the impassible simplicity of the trinitarian life, radically *for us*. The death of Jesus does not make it possible for God to love us. The death of Jesus makes it possible for us truly to know God's love, makes it possible for us to love God."[20] After all, it is an encounter with the God who is love that changes all of us for the better, no matter the particular circumstances we find ourselves in.

Seeking a Narrative of Hope

Returning to the example of Chris, we want to think about what it looks like to codiscover a narrative of hope in the midst of his suffering. Too often, the narrative from Christians for the person with gender dysphoria has been one titled "sinful" or "disordered." Even well-meaning Christians can communicate this, unfortunately perpetuating what we hear in John's Gospel about the man who was born blind—that is, it was his or his family's sins that were to blame for his pain. Chris likely has wondered if he caused his suffering in some way or if it is a sign of his own sinfulness or irreparable brokenness. Who can thrive if their personal narrative stays there? We recall the words of Jesus to the crowd: "Neither this man nor his parents sinned, . . . but this happened so that the works of God might be displayed in him" (John 9:3). What if this was the more consistent pastoral response to the person with gender dysphoria? What if the couple we met with who were wanting to understand God's plan in their suffering had heard this from their pastor: "This happened so that the works of God might be displayed in you."

For Chris, who may have prayed for healing of his gender dysphoria to no avail, there is hope of ultimate healing. "It is not by sidestepping or fleeing from suffering that we are healed, but rather by our capacity for accepting it, maturing through it and finding meaning through union with Christ, who suffered with infinite love."[21] What, then, is the hope for Chris insofar as he increases his capacity to accept suffering?

> According to the Christian faith, "redemption"—salvation—is not simply a given. Redemption is offered to us in the sense that we have been given hope, trustworthy hope, by virtue of which we can face our present: the present, even if it is arduous, can be lived and accepted if it leads towards a goal, if we can be sure of this goal, and if this goal is great enough to justify the effort of the journey. . . . Here too we see as a distinguishing mark of Christians the fact that they have a future: it is not that they know the details of what awaits them, but they know in general terms that their life will not end in emptiness. Only when the future is certain as a positive reality does it become possible to live the present as well.[22]

Within this vision of hope comes an invitation for Chris into a community to suffer imperfectly with, structures to develop meaning-making in suffering, and opportunities to reflect on his suffering in light of the cross of Christ: "What do the scars of Christ teach us? They teach us that life is a struggle: that our condition of a final resurrection is exactly the same as His; that unless there is a cross in our lives, there will never be an empty tomb; that unless there is a Good Friday, there will never be an Easter Sunday; that unless there is a crown of thorns, there will never be a halo of light; and that unless we suffer with Him, we shall not rise with Him."[23]

When we suffer with Christ, and with his body of believers, even the deepest agony can be meaningful in light of the glory that is to come. Meaning-making does not take away pain, but it does foster intimacy in the midst of it. In casting a new vision with Chris, we can also highlight his virtues and strengths that are evident in and through this difficult experience. It takes great courage to share his story, and he ought to be lauded for his honorable desire to seek God's guidance in a realm of such complexity and social tension. Highlighting his spiritual maturity as he shares his thoughtful questions may come as a pleasant surprise to him when he might expect to be shamed for not having this all figured out. Assurance that God is with him and will help him become a godly person more and more each day can put him at ease when he wonders if he could ever be Christlike.

In fact, we would move toward highlighting for Chris that he is a lot more like Christ than he realizes. He is not only valuable but a necessary member of the body of Christ and a unique reflection of God. In his suffering with an enduring struggle of the human condition, limited by the human body he has, he is a witness to the God who embraced suffering and offered it as a profound lesson in the spiritual life. This could offer transcendent meaning to his life and transform his experience of his own gender incongruence, seeing it less as a sign of personal deficit and more as an opportunity for witness.

We can also explore with Chris how Jesus's own suffering is tied to the triune God's love for him. McCall reflects on Jesus's cry from the cross: "The cry of dereliction means that the Father abandoned the Son to this death at the hands of these sinful people, for us and our salvation. It means that the triune God is *for* us—and he is for us in a way that is beyond our wildest hopes or dreams."[24] As we quoted above (and it seems worth restating here), McCall goes on: "The death of Jesus does not make it possible for God to love us. The death of Jesus makes it possible for us truly to know God's love, makes it possible for us to love God."[25] These are such important themes in the story of hope Chris or any young person is invited into. That story is one in which a young person, as with all of us who are Christians, is called to a life characterized not by "moralistic effort" but by the "utter and complete renovation of the human person."[26] What young people will benefit from is a deeper, more personal experience of these theological truths, lived in close fellowship with other Christians who have a deep and personal experience of these truths and who can pray with them through how their questions and concerns surrounding gender identity might be understood and explored. We can also join them in the journey of sanctification, which can be confusing at times when also trying to figure out gender identity questions: "So when we are threatened with confusion about the way of holiness, we look to Jesus."[27] We can be confident that sanctification or the way of holiness, "the work of the triune God for us, is the will of the Father, who gives his Son and

Spirit to us; it is the provision of the Mediator, who gave himself for our cleansing and renewal; and it is the gracious operation of the Holy Spirit, who comes as the other comforter."[28]

We may not fully understand how all of these questions will be answered and what may be best moving forward. In our experience, the answers have varied from person to person. The seeking teen is different from the teen who suffers from gender dysphoria, and the teen with mild dysphoria differs from the teen with moderate or severe dysphoria. We remain hopeful because we know that the triune God is at work in the life of every young person who knows Christ and that no answer renders them unredeemable.

Many people with gender dysphoria are never told that they are particularly chosen to reflect God in a way no one else can and that he is at work in them too. This does not soften the blow of suffering, but it may be transformative just the same. Who of us would turn down the gift it is to discover that we are chosen by God, uniquely, to reveal his works in and through the experiences we endure? Who will remind young people of this fundamental truth?

This is where the body of Christ comes in. When it comes to gender dysphoria, carrying the burden within Christian communities is long overdue. Maybe when we embrace it in community, the meaning of it all will become more evident than ever.

As we bring this chapter to a close, we note that we have outlined three different types of people who are navigating gender identity and that not every Christian will be called to engage in all three areas. What we want to invite you to consider is whether you are called to engage with those with a political identity, a public identity, or a private identity. We also invite you to reflect on some of the suggestions for engaging differently with different people, and how each of these ways requires all of us to pray for wisdom as we consider a more nuanced approach.

CHAPTER 6

Locating the Person

A Relational-Narrative Approach

This chapter lays the foundation for approaches rooted in relationship. In relationships with a person navigating gender identity, connection makes all the difference. Yet forging this connection can be challenging because of the disparity in our experiences: many of us do not know what it is like to experience an internal sense of self that contrasts with our physical body. Although our differences in experience can make connection more difficult, it's not impossible. We just need to begin by listening.

We hope that an intentional movement toward listening will communicate "an openness of heart which makes possible that closeness without which genuine spiritual encounter cannot occur."[1] The reality is that, even after a great deal of listening, we may not know all of what we would like to know in order to feel adequate in this sphere. We are called to engage nonetheless. We recommend that, rather than responding to internal and external pressures to have everything figured out, you invest all your energy into truly listening. Hearing another person's story is a critical starting point for any intimate relationship, and it is intimate and vulnerable relationships that bear the most fruit.

As you prepare to listen thoughtfully in pursuit of relationship, it may be helpful to know some of the common life "chapters" transgender people experience so that you can ask questions relevant to their stories as you build relationships over time. In identifying these key life experiences, we will draw on recent research among younger transgender Christians who were asked to break down the chapters in their lives as those chapters pertained to gender identity development and personal faith.

A Narrative-Developmental Perspective

We often use the analogy that the person you are accompanying is like a book with many chapters. Indeed, when we have interviewed transgender persons of faith about their lives, they have often spoken of common experiences in different chapters, outlining a sort of blueprint. Let's summarize what we have found as frequently cited chapters and then discuss how those chapters can inform our approach.

A person's gender identity typically forms between ages two and four. That is, a person is aware of themselves as a boy or a girl (or they have a different experience of themselves that they may not be able to put into words) at a fairly young age. So the earliest chapter (chapter 1) within this blueprint centers around childhood and gender expressions perceived to be outside the norm. For example, in an interview a biological male who identifies as female titled this chapter of her life "Ignorance Is Bliss," stating, "I knew something wasn't quite right. [During] preschool I had a connection to dolls occasionally. Like playing house and pretend games. Lots of unexplained anxiety and outbursts of crying, but generally concerned with playing."[2]

The next chapter (chapter 2) is typically about the conflict that can be experienced as parents or others set limits on a child who behaves in ways outside of gender norms. Whereas the first chapters recounted by transgender persons we have interviewed were typically characterized by "ignorance" or "innocence," their second chapters were often defined by conflict over what felt like a normal way of being in the world. Conflicts could occur at any time, but they tended to be reported during late childhood and adolescence. For example, one biological male indicated that between twelve and eighteen years of age, he "felt shame at having to hide something and suppress it, started to be depressed but at the same time my faith became real and gave me a purpose in life."[3]

Chapter 3 addressed a shift in focus to their identity and faith as followers of Christ; often, they hoped that this conflict around gender identity would go away if they drew near to Christ and sought out spiritual resources. This turn often occurred during late adolescence or emerging adulthood. The way that people we interviewed engaged their faith often reflected a number of assumptions about what their faith said about sex and gender, as well as about what was possible or desirable in terms of outcomes.

The chapter about turning to one's religious faith was often followed by a chapter (chapter 4) that meant returning to gender identity concerns. In other words, attending to faith proved not to resolve the conflict around gender identity.

The final chapter (chapter 5) addressed how transgender persons had learned to cope with their experiences of gender identity. One biological female who identifies as transgender shared, "I dress a certain way to manage my dysphoria. Dressing as a tomboy helps. It's easier for female-to-male. I avoid situations when I would be expected to wear a dress—situations with heightened gender expectations. Black tie events. I understand which situations push my buttons and avoid them."[4]

How a Narrative-Developmental Perspective Informs Our Approach

How can the narrative-developmental perspective we have seen illustrated in these "chapters" inform your approach? You can begin by identifying the age range you tend to minister to. If you are a parent or work with children, you are likely to bear witness to chapters 1 and 2 described above. If you work with teens, you are more likely to see chapters 3 and 4. You could use your knowledge of these chapters as a starting point for conversation, allowing it to inform the questions you ask instead of feeling like you don't know where to begin when you are accompanying someone who has just shared about their gender identity. Parents can reflect back on these chapters and may find that their loved one has a different recollection of those key chapters. This should not be an interrogation of chapters; rather, the tone should be that of curiosity, so that one's loved one is not set on the defensive. For all of us, when we engage with a person in the context of a later chapter, we will hopefully get the opportunity to learn about a person's earlier chapters. They will not be identical to what we have described here—after all, everyone has their own story—but these chapters can be rough guides for what you might hear more about should the person you are in relationship with care to open up further about prior chapters.

Common Considerations in Chapter 1: Early Childhood

If you are outside the child's nuclear family, you likely won't be personally involved in chapter 1. A family member might bring concerns to your attention at this stage, as when a parent who is a close friend shares a concern with you or asks you for prayer about what they are seeing or hearing at home. In our experience, most parents see gender-atypical expression as a phase and do not reach out. Of course, they are often right, since such play, dress, and expression fall within the expected range of what children do to explore their sense of identity. If you are a parent of a young child who is displaying gender atypical interests, these are not things to overreact to, but it can be helpful to have a close friend who can "hold" your concerns in their care for you. When gender dysphoria is present, however, the play may look the same as it would otherwise, but it takes on a different meaning (that is, the child processes it differently), does not pass as a phase (in a few weeks or months), and can lead to chapter 2, a conflict with parents or other observing adults. It is still likely that gender dysphoria will abate on its own in most cases of childhood gender dysphoria, but even if it does, it is not the short-term phase many parents hope for.

The care you offer in this chapter will likely take the form of parental support. When bearing witness to this chapter in a child's life, it can be helpful to ask questions about how the child is behaving, what the child is saying about gender, and what the child has been asking about gender. Parents may need a sounding board in this uncertain time, allowing them to voice their fears and musings. We should hold in mind that gender identity is just one aspect of a child's experience about which parents may be concerned or may project fears of the future. In this way, it is not unlike other aspects of a child's experience that a parent may feel worried about: whether the child will grow up to be self-assured and self-confident, have supportive friends, and so forth. Parents need encouragement to be proactive about supporting their child's *current* healthy development without spending a great deal of energy catastrophizing the possible outcomes if their child's gender challenges continue into the future. Acceptance of the current reality does not mean a laissez-faire approach to parenting. It is important for parents to actively protect their child from mocking comments, whether these comments come from the other parent, the child's siblings, or peers. One thing we hope to all agree on is that bullying should never be tolerated, especially bullying toward vulnerable children.

For those who are parents, you can normalize a child's exploration of gender in this chapter when your child demonstrates preferences for certain toys, activities, or interests, without imbuing greater meaning or moral significance to such preferences. From a ministry perspective, we who support these parents can gently reassure them that these variations are common, especially if parents are prone to overreact to their child or blame themselves or their child for the child's gender-atypical interests, mannerisms, or activities. We can also assuage the sense of urgency they may feel to course correct their child. Not only is there nothing to be ashamed of if a child is interested in gender-atypical play, interests, or dress, but overreacting to such behavior is unlikely to serve as a course correction. Rather, parental attempts at course correction often feel punitive and shaming to children, leading some children to withdraw. Children who withdraw tend to receive the message that their expression of gender identity is something to hide or, worse, a sign of their fundamental inadequacy. This belief leads to great confusion for the child about their desires and subsequent shame. It also results in confusion for the parents when, years down the line, such behaviors or expressions reemerge, seemingly out of nowhere.

Common Considerations in Chapter 2: Subsequent Conflict

Chapter 2 will likely bring more direct considerations of questions and a sense of conflict around gender. The conflicts we have observed range from limit-setting by parents in the realms of clothing, behavior, and other gender atypical interests to "bigger issue" considerations such as participation in elementary school athletic teams, bathroom use, and more. Parents may wonder what to do in such scenarios.

A place to begin is to listen. For parents, this will mean listening to your child's yearnings that are manifest in gender atypicality. Again, resisting the urge to panic will be important here. A majority of young children with gender dysphoria do not experience this into adulthood. Regardless of whether your child does or does not, they will be positively impacted by your willingness to hear them out and consider the tensions they face.

A second consideration is the feedback the child may receive from others about their behaviors. Children with gender identity concerns tend to isolate from others out of fear of being "discovered" for their gender atypical interests. Especially if they have been noticed by parents, siblings, or others, they may act in accordance with rigid stereotypes in order to quell parental anxieties and avoid bullying. Demanding gender-compliant behaviors—insofar as they reflect rigid gender stereotypes—is tricky because it can undermine the capacity for authenticity in the parent-child relationship. A child may also refrain from looking to parents to speak into the child's wrestling if they are made to feel that gender atypicality is intolerable in the home.

In this chapter, it becomes increasingly important to check in with the child about bullying in other settings, including school and church. Parents will probably learn most honestly from your children if you avoid the word *bullying*, since many kids fail to identify the way they are treated with that word. Instead, parents could check in on the child by using words like *teasing* or even by giving descriptive examples of how a kid might respond to them because of their interests. If bullying is occurring, parents can give your child suggestions for responding to such comments, fostering the child's resilience and sense of autonomy in the face of harmful peer reactions.

Peer support is also important for these children. We often advise parents to help a child access strong peer support through mutual hobbies, even if these hobbies mean interacting with one sex more than the other. Encouraging the child to develop valuable community through these interactions is far more constructive than forcing a child to participate in activities stereotypically ascribed to boys or girls. It is also important to seek out options for play and peer interactions that increase a child's sense of self-worth and that are not reliant on their sense of gender identity being stable. Some parents have reported that as children discovered their talents in these formative years, their stress around gender identity became less overwhelming, even if it was still present. Attending to these other pieces of the child's identity can give parents a sense of empowerment and direction to act on behalf of your child's well-being, regardless of where the gender identity journey leads.

For those who are supporting parents, invite them to share with you what they have been seeing at home and how it impacts them. You can get a sense for the timeline and key events, themes, and so on. Resist the impulse to give direct advice. Listen. The opportunity to listen can be framed around three areas: behavior, meaning, and response.

- *Behavior.* What are they seeing? Are both parents (or other caregivers) seeing the same kinds of behaviors, or do behaviors vary based on who is interacting with the child? How long have they been seeing the behaviors?
- *Meaning.* What have these behaviors meant to each of them (or how have they been thinking about what they have seen)?
- *Response.* How have they each responded? Are the parents on the same page, or are they responding differently to what they

FOR PARENTS: **REFLECTING ON MESSAGES**

Parents, what we recommend you do at this point is to pay attention to what you are seeing and how you have responded. It can be helpful to discuss what you are seeing with your spouse, or with a close friend if you are a single parent. Are you seeing the same things that others do? What do you make of what you are noticing? Is the behavior a continuation of what you saw in chapter 1, or is it a new behavior? How have you been responding so far? What do you think you are doing that is helpful, and what makes it helpful? What do you think you are doing that is unhelpful, and what makes it unhelpful? In other words, take the three areas of behavior, meaning, and response and reflect on these areas in terms of whether they are a continuation from chapter 1 or a new behavior, imbued with the same or different meaning, and how you are coming to understand helpful versus unhelpful responses. How you determine "helpfulness" is likely tied to what messages you want to communicate to your child about their sense of self and gender identity. This is a good time to reflect on what you communicate with your responses. In doing so, you are reflecting on past messages, current messages, and potential future messages about your child's worth, your love for them, the love that God has for them, and so on. We also recommend seeking support from other parents who are navigating or have navigated similar dynamics. They may be a resource to you at this time to shed light on what they learned in their own process.

see because of a different set of assumptions, beliefs, or values? What limits (if any) have been set on gender expression, roles, behavior, and identity?

Common Considerations in Chapter 3: Christian Faith

In chapter 3, which typically occurs in adolescence or emerging adulthood, young people raised in Christian homes often turn to their faith with questions about their gender identity. They might explore at an intellectual level what their faith teaches about sex and gender. This turning to their faith could also be applied and practical. They might pray to God for their gender dysphoria to resolve, or they might ask God questions about how God sees them and about their worth to him.

These intellectual questions and their applied dimensions might come directly to you. Whether you are a pastor, mentor, or Christian parent, you may be asked about what Christianity has to contribute to the transgender discussion. If someone is in prayer about their gender identity or if they are asking for prayer, you might unpack with them what they are praying for and the way they hope you will pray for them in the process.

FOR PARENTS: FOSTERING COMMUNICATION

Parents, what seems important during this chapter of turning to one's faith is considering how your faith responds to complicated topics and how you communicate this to your teen. Your teen will likely already have made a number of assumptions about what you believe as a Christian about complicated matters, based on topics discussed at home or in church. In the area of gender identity, this may include what has been said about a Christian response to people who identify as transgender, various political issues tied to this topic (for example, "bathroom bills" and related legislation), what constitutes sin or disobedience and why, and so on. Assumptions may also be made about whether Christians love transgender persons, whether the topic of gender identity is welcome in church or essentially taboo, and how to respond to complex personal and social issues, including how to response when God does not answer a prayer for healing or resolution of an enduring reality in one's life. Finally, the way you personally talk about transgender people will absolutely inform your teen's level of comfort in sharing their journey with you. If you talk in a way that is mocking, condemning, or dismissive, your child will likely expect the same from you about their story. In many cases, they will refrain from asking you their questions or sharing that they wrestle with gender identity questions at all. If you talk in a way that is thoughtful, curious, honoring of the dignity of people, and dispassionate, you may find that they will trust you as a guided resource in their own questions.

In our previous study and in our clinical experience and consultations, we commonly see people turn to their Christian faith in an attempt to resolve their gender identity concerns. This turning often takes the form of Bible study and/or prayer. You may be asked to join someone's study of Scripture as they discern how the Bible responds to their experiences. Please keep in mind that this is an especially vulnerable time for a young person in terms of the weight that they, their parents, and their community may give to what God thinks about their experiences and their gender identity questions.

We have asked people navigating gender identity and faith what advice they would give to someone in youth ministry who is helping a young person navigate gender identity questions. Here are a few responses we received:

- "[Have] empathy toward gender dysphoria, regardless of personal morality."
- "They don't even talk about it. They dance around it. At least engage the topic. Talk—not in a condemning way, but talk about it."
- "Even if you don't feel it is morally right to be transgender, [there's] no need to judge us. You can still love us."
- "I did not decide this out of the blue. God created me this way just as he has created people who are blind or with allergies; this is . . . just a challenge."

We can see in these quotes an array of assumptions a teen might have about how Christianity addresses gender. These assumptions might be helpful to identify. Once identified, we might ask how these assumptions came about—perhaps they are based on interactions the teen has had with Christians, things they have read, or other sources. The line of questioning could progress this way:

- What assumptions does the teen have about how Christianity addresses sex and gender?

- What are their assumptions based on?
- What has been communicated to the teen about expectations for gender roles and identity?
- What do they understand about what contributes to their current gender identity?

If you haven't given gender identity much thought or you don't have much experience in this area, it's okay to say that. The most valuable thing you can provide is a willingness to engage, to learn together what God has to say, and to assure the teen that God has enough experience loving each person to make up for human deficits in our knowledge of this area. We also encourage you to not limit your conversations only to gender. Check in with the teen about a range of aspects of their life where they want to seek God's perspective. This moves the conversation away from always hyperfocusing on gender identity concerns. Teens with gender identity concerns are much more than these concerns, although the concerns are certainly relevant. Many teens have shared that when a relationship hyperfocuses on one piece of their story—for example, if a teen is compulsively watching pornography and every mentoring conversation centers around this—it can lead to an identification with that behavior as defining of their personhood in unhelpful ways.

Mentoring is incredibly valuable at this time. Youth are much more likely to turn to respected adults other than their parents for guidance. Support teens in finding mentors whom they respect and connect with; such relationships could help shape the teens' own identity exploration in meaningful ways. We have spoken a great deal about the sociocultural factors at play that are loudly speaking into adolescent identity development. Adult mentors can be a valuable voice to add to the discussion, though the fruit of these conversations may be hard to appreciate until years later. Effective mentorship gives space for young people to share about their daily challenges in an ongoing way. Over time, mentors can assist young people in critically thinking about the messages they have received concerning identity, meaning, and purpose without being immediately hostile to or dismissive of these messages. Once youth are able to honor and explore what is so appealing about the current gender identity landscape, they will be better equipped to engage critically with the parts of this landscape that they may not want to accept.

As we've said above, relationship with and care for someone cannot focus solely on their gender identity. Additionally, if we gauge fruitfulness based on specific gender identity outcomes or gauge a person's holiness based on their current desires or questions, we imagine more teens will turn elsewhere for companions as they explore gender identity. If a teen gets the sense that they are being patronized or seen as a project to be worked on or a problem to be solved, they will likely withdraw from relationship, just as many of us would, even if they really want someone to walk with them. It is no wonder that many teens are drawn to the openness and relativism of society at large when their alternative appears to be an environment of scrutiny and dismissal that condemns them for "liv[ing] in delusion."[5] Even if this accusation were true, no effective care has emerged from such a framework. Effective engagement conveys the message that questions about faith are expected throughout life and that these questions need not preclude a teen from the life of faith or a robust spiritual journey.

It has been said that when a young person comes out, their Christian parents often go into the closet. Parents also need support in this chapter. We have found that many parents feel that discussing their teens' gender identity is taboo, especially with pastors or small groups, where they might normally turn. Reducing stigma for the parents of teens navigating these questions would serve the church well. Having challenging conversations about gender identity is essential. But how we engage in these conversations also matters a great deal.

When gender identity is discussed in Christian spaces, parents are often blamed for their child's experience. We have heard of parents being told everything from "You should have stayed home instead of working when he was younger" to "Just take her to get her nails done, and maybe dress a bit more femininely yourself." These responses are not helpful; many parents have already blamed themselves and are racking their brains for ways they may have contributed to their child's

FOR PARENTS: TAKING A LONG-TERM VIEW

Parents, there are a couple of other things in this chapter that we want to highlight for you. First, we want you to be able to find and confide in people you can trust with what you are facing as a family. We don't want you to feel you have to go "into the closet" because a loved one has shared their experience of gender identity with you or with others in your community. Second, we don't want you to blame yourself for your loved one's questions surrounding gender identity. We really do not understand the origins of diverse gender identities, but that has not kept people from laying blame on parents. We do not see questions about gender identity as a reflection on you as parents or on your faith or walk with Christ. That's not how this works. Take the long view with your teen. They are going to be facing difficult decisions, and it would be better if they had you as a resource to them in the years to come, so let's try to stay in a relationship with them that demonstrates respect for them but also is the kind of relationship where you can ask honest questions and seek answers together, if possible.

experience, trying to decide where to go from here. These parents have probably already tried the strategies others are suggesting as quick fixes and have found these strategies wanting. The best way for others to avoid making unhelpful suggestions is by asking questions and listening carefully before beginning to make suggestions. One helpful approach is to ask the parents how they have responded so far, what unique challenges are at play, and how they might respond to their child's future decisions.

As teens grow, they become increasingly developmentally able to make decisions for themselves, and parents' efforts to course correct at this time may do little to direct their children's decisions about identity, dress, and behavior. Peer influences are usually much more powerful at this stage of life. Thus, support given to parents during this chapter will not necessarily have substantial direct impact on a teen's decisions, and teens should be receiving direct support of their own. Still, parents also need support in what can be an isolating time. They can

BECOME A BETTER TRAIL GUIDE

We have found the analogy of hiking helpful to describe coming alongside teens, whether you are a parent, a friend, or serving in formal youth ministry. When hiking, there is no shortage of challenges that can arise. Youth are navigating difficult terrain. A trail guide aids in making difficult terrain less daunting, expecially when it is full of twists and turns and moments where even the guide seems lost. A guide is patient, gentle, and oriented toward helping the one they guide take in the beauty all around them, even at the parts of the trail that are particularly difficult. A guide narrates what is seen but does not obstruct the view or manipulate what those they guide look at. They are there to point out aspects of the view that might be less visible and to broaden people's understanding of what they are seeing on the trek. The guide may provide tools that will be helpful, such as a map or a compass, but they can also tolerate when the person being guided refuses to use these tools. They know good spots to stop and rest, are able to identify the fatigue of the hiker, and are willing to pause and rest for the sake of others even if they feel personally equipped to forge ahead.

A good trail guide leaves no one behind. Thus, a trail guide may have to take it slowly, pacing the information they give hikers so as not to overwhelm them. The guide would not jump ahead to describe the next challenging part of the hike if the person they are guiding hasn't even made it through the first trying part.

be tempted to throw up their hands and give up, but the stress of this experience and its daily challenges will continue whether they actively engage in dialogue with their teen or not. It can be helpful to hear from parents what is most scary and frustrating and to encourage them to find ways to connect with their child over other commonalities to foster an open relationship over time. Offering places for the parent and young person to dialogue, whether through mediated conversations or through family therapy, can capitalize on these formative years to understand family dynamics better and help families experience greater cohesion.

Parents, friends, and those in formal youth ministry can use this metaphor as a helpful reference in coming alongside teenagers navigating gender identity. There will be many difficulties ahead. Our experience of gender is a complex and multifaceted reality, impacted by and impacting so many other areas of our life. None of us can leave our sense of gender identity aside, just like we can't escape our overall experience as a sexual being. Our sense of our gender identity is an important aspect of us, even if it is not the only or most important one. Thus, the difficult terrain of adolescence, and of exploring sexuality and gender, is more manageable when youth have guides along the way. Having a guide may not make the terrain any less terrifying, but it certainly does make it less lonely. Parents may feel like more of a trail guide when their child is younger and less so as their loved one enters adolescence and the parents' own influence gives way to peers and mentors. That's understandable. You can still gain something from the analogy that your teen is hiking difficult terrain, as it can pull you toward compassion and emphasize the need for reliable guides, even if you no longer feel like the primary ones.

For any of us who are invited into this discussion about gender identity with a teen, you might balk here, saying, "I am not a reliable guide!" We can appreciate your fear. If you don't feel well-equipped, imagine how a teenager feels. Remember, as in any form of accompaniment, you need not have all the answers. Any of us being cared for knows that we're not always best served by the person who thinks they have all the answers for our difficulties. We often prefer the person who is reflective with us about the journey. Thus, simply describing what you notice about the journey your youth are on can be a great help to them.

Common Considerations in Chapter 4: Revisiting Gender Identity

Chapter 4 of a young person's story may be a time to help them with the disappointment they may feel if their expectations have not been met for what Christianity could offer to their gender identity concerns. They may have been shamed by Christians or told that their questions about gender identity preclude them from a relationship with God. They may endure slights and mockery in youth group or from their family because they are not "man enough" or fall short of the "Proverbs 31 woman."[6] They may have been told that their interests, dress, or preferences mean they are under some spiritual oppression and that their desires to cross-dress ought to be prayed away. They may have tried this kind of prayer without success.

In our previous study and in our clinical experience and consultations, we have not heard of a person's turn to Christian faith resolving all of their gender identity concerns, nor does faith seem to resolve gender dysphoria if that is present. At the same time, people come to meet with us when gender identity concerns have not resolved, and there may be testimonies of different experiences for Christians than those we have seen. Still, it is not helpful to absolutely and confidently promise one outcome for every person, such as stating that Christian obedience will resolutely resolve gender concerns. We must consider the spiritual implications and the pain that results when gender dysphoria persists despite extensive prayer and spiritual pursuit. Many we have met with wonder if the lack of resolution is their fault, as if unanswered prayers solely indicate a spiritual deficit in the one praying or in a lack of love from God or care for their particular pain.

For someone who is wrestling with unmet expectations of resolution as they turned toward faith, helpful questions could include the following:

- What hopes or expectations did the person have when they focused on their faith as a guide?
- How does the person feel today about their Christian faith as a result of their previous expectations?
- What resources does their faith bring to the discussion of gender identity, interests, and expression? What have they been drawn to? What have they tried and found wanting?
- How is their relationship with Jesus impacted by their gender identity? And how is their experience of gender identity influenced by their relationship with Jesus?
- Where have they encountered Jesus in their difficulties? How do they imagine Jesus sees them today and responds to them insofar as they blame themselves for their ongoing distress?

Teens often overemphasize one aspect of identity to the exclusion of others. As they revisit gender identity, this could easily become the foreground of your conversations with them, whether you are a parent, mentor, youth minister, or friend. There is value in zooming out and asking about their overall connection with Jesus, personal prayer life, friendships, and interests. Zooming out in this way can help broaden their self-concept and increase their appreciation for the complex person they are. One critique often expressed in Christian circles is that broader LGBTQ+ cultural narratives perpetuate the idea that one aspect of identity should become the most important and definitive feature of a young person's life. It is a point well taken, and one that those within the LGBTQ+ community also have spoken about. LGBTQ+ Christians in particular have struggled with assumptions made by secular LGBTQ+ culture that they ought to look, dress, and act in certain ways because of their sexual desires or preferred gender expressions. One friend has shared that he struggled for many years with knowing if he was "gay enough," feeling pressured to comfort himself and his interests to a stereotype that was reductive and inauthentic.

Very often, though, Christian parents, mentors, and ministers who care for youth can become consumed with attending to a teen's gender identity, as if that is the only aspect of the person worth engaging with. Lesbian Christian writer Eve Tushnet has reflected on how often Christian people approach her as if lust is her "biggest and even only spiritual concern," reducing her to her attractions.[7] She reminds us that she is celibate and has gained significant self-mastery with regard to her sexuality, yet she has other ongoing spiritual concerns that must not be ignored for the sake of attending to her sexuality. Similarly, we could easily miss aspects of a teen's spiritual life that desperately need support if we gauge their spirituality exclusively by their sense of their own gender.

If a teen has not been able to tell their parents about their gender identity concerns, one consideration as they continue to experience these concerns is how to aid them in thinking through the decision of whether to talk to their parents and, if so, how. We mentioned earlier that the quality of the parent-teen relationship is one of the best predictors of a teen's well-being over time. We want to stress the importance of that relationship. Under no circumstances should you tell the teen's parents for them; rather, you could help prepare the teen to talk to their parents. Telling this information to parents prematurely can create a dynamic where the teen feels exposed and infantilized, as if they are being told on. It also signals a sense of urgency that can put undue pressure on the teen to address gender identity. Empowering them to talk to their parents is much more fruitful, honoring both their privacy and their capacity to share their story. It can also build intimacy and trust between the parent and child, as the child entrusts this aspect of their experience to their parents. Here are a few tips mentors and friends can offer teens for those conversations with their parents:

- *Be descriptive*. Share what you are experiencing without drawing only from the words or labels that might be unfamiliar to your parents. There is a big difference between telling your parents a label they may or may not understand and telling them about the painful daily experience that has drawn you to a label. In our experience, the more you can share in ways that spark your parents' empathy, the better off you are. For example, as opposed to saying, "I am bigender," a more fruitful approach may be, "This is really difficult and scary to tell you, but I also want to share this experience with you so that we can have a more honest relationship. I experience my gender differently than most people. Most people experience themselves as a boy or girl, a man or a woman. I experience myself as both, and there are a number of challenges that come with that, including how to even talk with you about it." Naming your parents' particular fears can also be helpful to shape the conversation: "I have not told you yet because I have been so worried that this will change things and that you will reject me or be ashamed of me, but I know it's important because I love you and want you in my life, even the parts that might be difficult to talk about." This can help your parents draw from the love and protection they have for you in that moment rather than acting out of fear and shock in a way that can be harmful.

- *Ask for what you need*. Let your parents know what you need at the moment. Maybe the most helpful thing would be a hug. Maybe you could ask to do something light and fun together as a family after your conversation is over, with everyone agreeing not to focus on gender identity for the rest of the evening, to help relieve your fear that everything will be different once you share this experience. Maybe you don't have the energy to explain it all right away, or maybe it would help to have them ask more about the details of your experience. Maybe you need time to think through your own theology of gender and you want to be freed from the expectation to answer every concern your parents may have at the moment.

- *Give parents time and space to respond*. If you have been navigating gender identity questions for some time, consider that your parents may need time and space to sort out their own response. This conversation may not be new to you, but for many parents it is altogether different from what they would expect. Culturally, theologically, and politically, these are challenging times for parents to discern how to respond without rejection while also honestly acknowledging the pain they may be feeling. Trust their love for you, even if their initial reaction does not adequately voice the love they have shown you at many other times in your life.

- *Follow up*. Great damage can happen if, after you disclose your gender identity concerns to your parents, the topic is never talked about again. This silence signals that gender identity questions are taboo and threatening. Everyone may contribute to this silence, hoping that if they don't talk about your concerns, they will go away. You may have to bring this topic up again with your parents and family, since many parents may fear that you don't want to talk about it, assuming that you would initiate if you did. Remember that your parents may not bring the topic up out of a desire to respect your privacy, or they may be concerned that they do not know how to support you or will offend you by their lack of understanding.

You can help the teen come to a more accurate understanding of how a parent could react to disclosure so that they know what to expect. As much as you know this to be true, assure the teen that their parents love them, but acknowledge that their parents may also struggle to convey their love during this conversation. This warning can help the teen resist internalizing initial reactions from their parents as reflective of how the parents, the faith community, or God truly see the teen. Perhaps those in mentoring relationships can offer to be present to talk to the parents as well, especially if the situation has the potential to escalate or be unsafe for the teen. This gives the parents another person to express their reactions to, without the teen receiving the brunt of the reaction. These are critical moments that can set a trajectory for communication moving forward. At the same time, even if the initial disclosure is characterized by hurt and perceived rejection, this does not mean there is no hope. Commit to journeying with the teen through this time so they know that, no matter the reaction they experience from their parents, they are not alone.

Common Considerations in Chapter 5: Learning to Cope

Recall that chapter 5 is typically experienced at some point in adolescence or early adulthood. We are thinking here of a time after initial attempts to experience a resolution of gender incongruence through prayer for healing or other faith-based strategies have been unsuccessful. There may be a time of coming to terms with the enduring reality of gender identity experiences that are different from those of others around them.

What is the teen (or young adult) coping with? That is, what triggers gender-related distress? Maybe it is sitting in the classic "guys' talk" at a youth conference. Maybe it is the "women's book club" at church, where female stereotypes are offered as the epitome of Christian holiness. Maybe it is attending particular events where the teen would be expected to dress in a gender-typical way, such as a wedding. One way you can be supportive of those coping with gender dysphoria is to take time to understand what people, places, things, and events are particularly challenging for them.

What has the teen tried in terms of coping strategies? Listen to their answers. Let the teen tell you how this has been for them and the steps they have taken to cope with what is likely an ongoing and difficult situation. Coping strategies vary from person to person, and this person may have tried different strategies months or years ago. It is good to have a better sense for what they have tried, what has worked, and what has not worked, especially before suggesting that they do more of the same. Offering trite solutions before listening could signal that you are not interested in wrestling with the complexity of their experience.

Once you have listened, it can be helpful to work with the teen to develop strategies for managing these difficulties. Do they have people they can talk to or give a knowing look to when they hear an attacking comment at their expense or at the expense of someone who looks or dresses like them? Whom can they ask to check in on them before, during, and after difficult events, to give them space to debrief, to pray with them, and to offer comfort through a hug? Who can help them figure out how to respond when they are feeling misunderstood by others or when others misread their gender atypicality as a sign of willful disobedience to God and his plan for gender identity?

It may be helpful to keep in mind that some of what you might consider gender-atypical behavior, and some of what has been imbued with moral significance in Christian circles, can function as a coping strategy. For example, you may have several adolescent females in your youth group who choose to keep a shorter haircut, but for the person with gender dysphoria, the decision is likely less about fashion or style and more about management of dysphoria. Even a nickname can function in this way. This is important to keep in mind when teens begin to share coping strategies you would not have thought of. Asking more

FOR PARENTS: A MEASURED RESPONSE

Parents, what we recommend for you during this chapter is to offer a measured response to steps your loved one may take to manage their gender dysphoria, if gender dysphoria is in fact present. It can be easy to interpret gender atypical expression as pushing back against established norms for gender and sex in society, including Christian settings, where such pushback may be thought of in terms of "right" and "wrong" behavior (i.e., sin).

We encourage a measured response for a couple reasons. First, when teenagers make decisions about gender expression, they are often still asking the question, Do you love me? We want to be sure they know that they are loved. Second, your loved one may be managing their dysphoria rather than intending to reject social norms or specific teachings of a faith community. We have found it is better to recognize strategies for what they are and to honor their function, before inviting a person to consider any alternatives. If you begin to think about gender atypical expressions as strategies for managing dysphoria, for instance, does that make sense of your teenager's behavior? Does it begin to make sense to you, at least in terms of coping with distress? Even if you aren't "for" the behavior or expression, can you appreciate how it may function in your loved one's life before responding to it? Can your response be informed by an appreciation for the way the strategies "help" when little else has?

about what is helpful about these strategies, and discussing questions or concerns the teen has had about their moral significance, opens up meaningful dialogue about coping as well as about the messaging a teen has received about these behaviors.

The desperation a teen may feel, as well as feelings of powerlessness and frustration about their experience, cannot be underestimated. Beneath the façade of confidence some teens demonstrate about their beliefs on sex and gender, about labels that resonate with their experience, or the like, each teen is facing enduring suffering in this fallen world. We do well to connect them to spiritual resources that can help them make meaning out of their experiences of being "different." A powerful reminder comes in assuring a teen who feels marginalized and alone that Jesus came for the one and would leave the ninety-nine on their behalf. He cares deeply about their story, about their decisions, and about how they manage their life moving forward. He is ready to help them figure out these challenging circumstances, and you are too. We believe that if our youth hear this message, they will be encouraged and much more eager to seek out Jesus's will for their lives.

Current and Future Chapters

We have been discussing how a person's life can be framed as a book with many chapters. If this language resonates with the person who is struggling with gender identity questions, you might also ask them what chapter they are currently writing, as well as the titles and themes of chapters they hope to write in the future.

If the teen is considering more invasive procedures—medical interventions such as hormonal treatment or surgical procedures—it would be helpful for them to be familiar with not only the potential benefits and risks of such steps but also the implications of such steps within the community of which they are a part. While friends are often the most powerful voice, parents, mentors, and youth ministers also provide critical perspectives when it comes to these considerations.

These questions may be helpful in framing your relationship with and care for a teenager:

- Is the teen willing to allow me to accompany them? Does the image of walking alongside them resonate?
- In the spirit of walking alongside, what does the teen need to know for the future?
- As I walk with the teen, how can the teen be best prepared for the future?
- Who might they also talk to? Who has information or experiences that this teen might benefit from listening to? If I am

a parent, who can I offer as other resources if my teen is not ready, or I am not ready, to consider these things?

- If I am not a parent, have the parents been brought into the discussion? If they have not, can I be a resource in shaping that conversation?

Similar questions can guide those of us seeking to support and care for parents (although much will depend on what future pathways a teenager is exploring):

- Can I come alongside the parents on this difficult journey?
- If I am walking alongside the parents, do the parents believe they are walking together or walking "away" or "apart" from one another on this topic?
- As I walk with the parents, what do the parents need to know for the future? Where can they turn for support?
- Do the parents believe they are walking together with their loved one, or do they see the loved one walking in a different direction?
- How can the parents be best prepared for the future? Who has information or experiences that the parents might benefit from listening to?

The relational-narrative perspective, which is informed by a developmental understanding of gender identity, depicts experiences of gender incongruence. The chapters we have described show what we could call "classic" or "traditional" experiences of gender incongruence, in which the incongruence is experienced earlier in life and is what clinicians refer to as "early onset" gender dysphoria.

Historically, it has been less common for a person to report gender dysphoria that develops after puberty, in late adolescence, or in adulthood ("late onset" gender dysphoria).[8] We do know of cases that are truly late onset. However, such cases have been rare until recently, and it was especially uncommon for biological females to present with

RECOGNIZING THE TIMING OF ENGAGEMENT

Engagement changes based on when you encounter another person. We recall consulting with a church facing the question of how to respond to a family whose child had transitioned one summer and who was now informing the church of the gender identity the child would use in the coming school year. The church was not ministering on the front end in the decision-making process. Nor was the church ministering ten or fifteen years after a transition had taken place. They were being notified during the transition process.

Given how different needs can be depending on the time at which they occur, it is important to take stock of where in the process of gender identity decision-making you are with the person you accompany. We can think of timing roughly along these lines:

1. *Prior* to a gender identity trajectory being decided
2. *At the time* the gender identity trajectory is being decided
3. *After* a gender identity trajectory has been realized for any length of time

Prior

Prior to gender identity decisions, it is often only family and close friends who are aware of the questions about gender identity. Others may be privy to some of the actual information-gathering that occurs prior to the decision-making process, and you may be invited to pray for them and speak into some of the fears and anxieties they share.

If you are not a parent or family member, it will be important to listen to the person or family as they share with you the nature of their concern, the information they are obtaining, and the decisions they are facing as they have come to frame them. This is also an opportunity to recognize how these decisions are affecting them and what they have considered in terms of different possible outcomes related to each path they are evaluating.

With a child, keep in mind that people may be weighing whether to take a "wait and see" approach with the child, whether to try to manage the child's environment, whether to consider a social transition for the child, whether to consider puberty blockers, and so on.

With an adolescent, the person may be weighing whether to live according to their birth sex and find ways to cope with gender dysphoria, whether to explore other avenues for identity and community if there is no dysphoria present, whether to consider a social transition, whether to use cross-sex hormones, and so on.

At the Time

If a person or family is asking for your assistance, you may be praying for them for wisdom—that is, a broad sense of the big picture—or for prudence—guidance in a specific here-and-now decision. In addition to prayers for ongoing wisdom and prudence for future decisions, you may also be praying for them to have peace about decisions already made.

Will there be consequences for the decisions the person or family is making at this moment? Is your role one in which you have been asked to discuss with the individual or family the concerns of a particular church setting? Do you believe you have sufficient information about the decisions the person or family has been facing, the different options they have been weighing, and their understanding of possible outcomes as they have explored different trajectories? If you want to know whether you have listened well enough to weigh in, a good rule of thumb is to ask whether you would be able to explain the journey and corresponding decision-making process to someone else in front of the person you've been listening to. If they would feel that you have accurately captured what decisions they faced, how they weighed different options, and what life has been like for them since, then you've truly listened well.

After

Engagement after is about how you relate to people whom you are meeting now but who have already faced these difficult decisions perhaps five or ten or fifteen years ago. The initial approach may tend to take the form of hospitality, as well as possibly listening to the person's journey if they care to share with you what that process was like. It is important to listen to the person and to suspend judgment as you try to understand the logic of the decisions they made from their point of view. As with engagement at the time of decision-making, an indication that you have listened well to the person or family is that you could share their journey and the decisions they have faced with another person (and in the presence of the person or family making the decisions) and they would say that you have understood them, the decisions they faced, what they weighed, and how they understood the steps they were taking.

late-onset gender dysphoria. This is not the case today. One of the most significant shifts we are witnessing in culture in recent years is the dramatic increase in cases of biological females reporting gender dysphoria. Many of these are late-onset cases that are particularly challenging for families and clinicians alike. These experiences do not fit the narrative-developmental perspective that we shared at the outset of this chapter, which is in part what makes them so challenging.

There is today such a wide array of gender identity options for young people whose experience of their gender is different from what they take to be the norm. As with any buffet, the more options there are, the more likely we are to pick from a wider range of choices. How the buffet is stocked will set the parameters for the options that lay before the consumer. We have seen a proliferation of emerging gender identities that are available to youth today—gender expansive, gender creative, bigender, and so on. Yet we have few clinicians or Christian persons who function as reliable guides on this new terrain. Who can function like nutritionists guiding people to healthier and more sustainable options from the buffet? If gender identity exploration remains like a buffet, this will present unique challenges. We must think through how to meet the needs of young people spiritually as they are navigating such a vital stage of identity development.

CHAPTER 7

Engaging Youth

Looking beneath the Surface

Christian discipleship, which attends to the whole person, is meant to draw human beings closer to Christ. In him, we more fully come to know our supreme identity and calling. Our spiritual lives, then, "can and should be in the service of becoming more deeply human" and more fully alive.[1] Ministry, in both formal and informal contexts, offers the opportunity for the church to bring the message of Christ to everyone without exception. There is no shortage of obstacles to this pursuit. However, the experience of alternative gender identities places teens and those who minister to them in a uniquely challenging position. Cultural narratives have identified Christianity as the source of an oppressive narrative against authentic gender identity and against young people realizing their authentic selves. Christians have often misidentified transgender people as the source of an aggressive movement away from "biblical values." Our youth are stuck in the crossfire, and the need to minister precisely in this area is as important today as ever before.

The challenge we have seen for engaging questions around gender identity is the way in which those who are engaging youth can be reactive and miss the chance to be a powerful witness to Christ today. This is a dilemma we will examine more closely now.

We want to remind the reader to distinguish *gender theory* from *the people navigating* gender identity concerns. When we think of gender theory, we are thinking of the movement toward deconstructing sex and gender norms and seeing biological realities as no longer instructive about one's sense of self as male/female or masculine/feminine. Although Christian engagement around this theoretical development is only beginning, much more has been written on how to think about gender theory as Christians than on how to support people navigating gender identity concerns.

Although we do not intend to offer a fully developed repudiation of gender theory here, we do wish to offer a few thoughts on the topic. A recent article by Janet Hyde and colleagues serves as a good prototypical account advocating for gender theory in the field of psychology.[2] In it the authors reach the conclusion that a gender binary has been undermined by research in several areas, such as studies that show brain structures where there is significant overlap between men and women, the presence in both men and women of those hormones understood as "male hormones" and "female hormones," and so on. When we think through the article's account of gender theory, it is not so much that the research cited is inaccurate as it is that the underlying assumptions about what these findings mean reflect a commitment to the view that the sex/gender binary is itself "culturally determined" and "malleable."[3] Others have criticized those conclusions and identified overlooked areas of research that challenge both the assumptions and the conclusions.[4] Further, it is important to consider how, for many people the binary is instructive and a reliable guide into a sense of identity that is anchoring.

Perhaps the greatest omission in the account of Hyde and her colleagues is the failure to discuss human reproductive capacity as a function of sexual dimorphism and clear evidence for some level of meaningful distinction between men and women. To discount the binary because there is significant overlap and meaningful similarities between men and women does little to account for anatomical and reproductive distinctions that reflect a binary. Although there are certainly important exceptions to the binary that research and theology must appreciate and account for, to eradicate the binary because of exceptions seems hasty and driven more by sociocultural movements than by obvious scientific data.

Some readers may feel they have greater clarity about how to think about and engage with gender theory than about how to respond to a person navigating gender identity. We also want to hold in mind the reality that we may not yet know whether the person we are ministering to suffers from gender dysphoria or is searching for identity and community and is finding these things in transgender or emerging gender identities. Nuance is critical here, as it will absolutely inform our approach.

Locating Youth Navigating Gender Identity

As we outline our approach to youth, we begin with an illustration (figure 4) intended to help you locate youth navigating gender identity questions. Though the questions they have about gender identity are their own, you can see in the illustration that they explore these questions with reference to many other people in their lives: their local faith community, of which you may be a part; their family, whom you may or may not know; their school; their friends; the mental health community; and the transgender and broader LGBTQ+ community.

Each of these individuals, groups, or institutions may be intentionally or unintentionally speaking into the youth's experience as they navigate these important questions. You, too, will want to be cognizant and intentional about the messages you communicate and sensitive to the messages youth are receiving from others. You will also want to appreciate what is compelling about the various messages, even if they are ones you find problematic.

Consider all the different points of reference in figure 4. These can be angles of entry into a constructive discussion with a young person, inviting them to reflect on how they are navigating gender identity in light of their personal faith, their local faith community, their family, their peers and friendships, their local school system, their exposure

Figure 4

Locating Youth Navigating Gender Identity

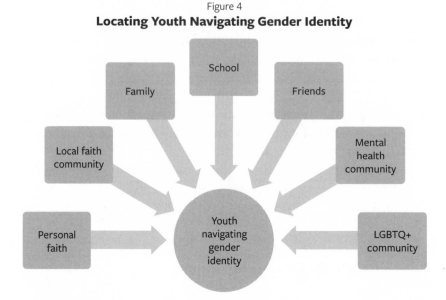

to mental health care and potential work with a mental health profession, and their experiences with the LGBTQ+ community (if they are connected to the community at this time).

To get more specific, you could ask the following questions:

- How has it been for you at our/your church as you've been exploring questions about your gender identity?
- Who have you been able to share your story with? What are some of the burning questions you have when you think about our/your church?
- How has it been for you at home as you've been exploring gender identity?
- How have the conversations with your parents gone? What was the best conversation you've had so far? What made that conversation good? What was the most difficult conversation? What made that conversation especially challenging?
- How has it been for you at school as you've been sorting out these questions about gender identity there?

- Who have you been able to share your story with? What are some of the questions you have when you think about school?
- Have you had the opportunity to share some of your experiences with your friends? If so, how have these conversations gone? What have been some of the best experiences? What made those conversations good? What have been some of the more challenging conversations? What made those conversations especially challenging?
- I know that other people navigating questions around gender identity have sometimes spoken with a counselor or psychologist. Is that something you've had the opportunity to do? If so, how has that been for you?
- If you have been to counseling, what's been most helpful for you? What do you hope to explore down the road? What remaining questions do you have for your work there?
- People may be plugged in to the transgender or LGBTQ+ community to different degrees. Is that something you've explored? If so, how has that been for you?

These are intended to be primarily open-ended questions that allow you to engage a youth by inviting them to have an encounter with an adult who is sincere in asking good questions and listening to the answers. Such an encounter should encourage the youth to share their experiences, offer their thoughts regarding what they've experienced and how it has been for them, and gain insight in the process.

We cannot emphasize enough that asking these questions requires a genuine desire to understand how the youth thinks about the variety of people and perspectives weighing in on their gender identity. We emphasize this because some people in Christian circles have turned questions like these into opportunities to tell the youth how misguided they are. Instead of listening for understanding, these people interrupt as soon as a youth says something they disagree with, responding with uninvited, oversimplified statements such as "I'll tell you what God thinks about transgender!" or with antagonistic questions such as "Don't you see that this transgender business is all delusional?" These statements, clear efforts to challenge the youth's thinking, do not reflect a discipleship heart toward the youth. For any of us, being challenged in our perspective is most effective when it is done by those we trust, in relationships founded on mutual respect, where our thoughts and feelings are appreciated, heard out, and validated, even if they are not agreed with. Disputation is a limiting gesture, especially if we use it prematurely.

A young person's answers to the above questions could shape the direction we take with them. Their answers may signal to you which questions the teen has already wrestled with, which questions they still have, and the current challenges they are facing. Knowing these things, you can make informed, prayerful decisions about what approaches to take. For instance, if a youth is wrestling with personal faith and what God thinks about their gender identity struggles, the conversation will likely take a different direction than if the youth is wrestling with mental health concerns, has not yet sought out care, and wants to know where to turn for resources. If they are wrestling with how to talk to their parents about their difficulties, they will need a different kind of support than if they are out to their parents but struggling with bullying from their peers. As with any other relationship, we must patiently withhold solutions until we hear the whole story.

Responding to Gender Atypicality

In chapter 3 we mentioned the iceberg as a useful analogy to remind us that people have different motivations for gender-atypical expression. In this chapter we want to extend the iceberg analogy as an effective strategy in journeying with transgender youth. Let us explain more about icebergs as we begin. An iceberg is part of a glacier that breaks off and floats at the surface of the water because it's lower in density than the water around it. About 90 percent of an iceberg is submerged under the surface of the water. What is above the surface, the tip, is what is visible to most observers and what any of us would react to if we saw one approaching on the water.

Gender atypical expression—often but not exclusively cross-dressing—can be thought of as what occurs *above the surface* of the water. Examples could include a teen's hairstyle, dress, makeup, jewelry, and grooming techniques (or lack thereof). Increasingly, teens are exploring self-expression through these means in ways that are gender atypical. If you respond only to what is above the surface, your approach will be severely limited. In our experience, you will tend to overreact to behaviors you find provocative, missing an opportunity to minister to the deeper needs and desires motivating these behaviors. This is why we recommend that Christians who wish to engage with young people not be overly reactive to the various gender-atypical expressions happening above the surface. When we are reactive, we can unintentionally communicate to youth that they are unacceptable and that their questions will not be tolerated but rather squashed immediately.

Take Teddy, for example, a teen who shows up to youth group with rainbow-painted nails and clothing that makes it difficult to determine if he is a boy or girl. The youth worker, Nancy, tries to meet Teddy where he's at, but ultimately cannot resist the impulse to question Teddy about his clothing and nails, suggesting that it promotes a message contrary to the church's conservative values around marriage and sexuality.

We can understand why people react strongly to what they see at the tip of the iceberg. However, we caution Christians against reacting only to the tip of the iceberg while ignoring the much larger realities that lie beneath the surface. We want to highlight the value of becoming aware of our gut reactions and tempering them to effectively care for someone like Teddy, sacrificing expediency for the sake of the person.

We want to remind Nancy that Teddy's painted nails and clothing are the tip of an iceberg. In reacting to the tip, Nancy may achieve behavioral compliance: Teddy may no longer wear the same clothes or present that way at youth group. However, this kind of response may be a missed opportunity to understand what is beneath the surface. Perhaps Teddy will simply bide his time, his unresolved questions festering, until he leaves the church and is free of the restrictions he currently lives within. Either way, we cannot truly teach Teddy or learn from him if we only respond to the tip of the iceberg.

What is at stake? This is an important question. What message does it send if Nancy's sole response to Teddy is to lecture him about his style choices, demanding that he wear male-typical clothing and clean his nails to be welcomed back at youth group? A teen like Teddy might be testing the waters of his own exploration with gender identity by presenting this way. He may be attempting to disclose that he or people he cares about have questions about Christian values of sex and gender. He may be a committed Christian who is wrestling with how his Christian faith applies to his life in the areas of sex and gender. Teddy walks into that church with a history, a unique story, thoughts, feelings, desires, and needs that far exceed the question of whether his clothing and painted nails are "acceptable" at youth group. He may take away from this interaction that his thoughts, feelings, and underlying questions are not tolerated by or of interest to the Christians in his life. This could lead to isolation, feeling "othered," and assuming that Christians are hostile toward anything that challenges their way of thinking.

If you are engaging beneath the surface, you may or may not discuss with a teen whether a particular way of dressing is acceptable, but your conversation certainly cannot stop there. Effective engagement will not only notice what is above the surface but will also focus on and begin attending to what may be happening below the surface. This new approach, you will find, is less efficient. But we believe that much is at stake if we compromise relationships for the sake of efficiency.

Think of how often youth engage in behaviors to get attention. When they try to get attention, even through less effective strategies, youth are signaling that they have care needs. If we react to youth behaviors only reflexively, we can unknowingly communicate messages that our youth misunderstand and feel shamed by. And even when we do reflexively react, apologies will go a long way toward repairing relationships. Unless we ask, youth may never tell us what underlying factors are motivating their behaviors. (They are great at poker faces, aren't they?) Because of this, we will never get to know what, if anything, lies

ADDRESSING NAMES AND PRONOUNS

Gender identity labels represent yet another possibility for what lies at the tip of the iceberg and what can be seen above water. Julia spent one year coleading a ministry group for sexual- and gender-minority Christian young adults. At the end of one fellowship dinner, another leader approached her and asked to talk with her and a young person, Jay, who had been attending the group for some time. The young person initiated the conversation, stating that they no longer went by male pronouns. They were hoping to be addressed at the next group meeting by female pronouns. Rather than reactively shutting Jay down, Julia assured Jay she wanted to think through this together, as it seemed really important. Julia asked what prompted this shift for Jay and said that she hoped there could be more conversation to understand more.

As they talked, Jay shared that she wanted to "try this" and see how it was, but also was not sure if it would be permanent. At this point, Julia and Jay talked about the implications of sharing something publicly, as in some sort of announcement at the start of the next meeting, versus introducing herself one-on-one to people as a way to share her story more personally with others. Julia named that this was not a consideration the group had faced before, and she highlighted the importance of finding a solution that wouldn't subject Jay to undue hurt from others but also would take into account the impact of different solutions on Jay and other members of the group.

Julia wondered with Jay about the impact of having to make a public statement and the benefits and drawbacks of this. Julia shared the value of vulnerability in community and conveyed the possibility that Jay may like to invite other people into her story without the level of attention that would come from a public announcement to the group. Julia expressed to Jay the possibility of continuing this discussion and taking some time to think about the options, rather than resolving the discussion and making a decision right then about how she wanted to approach this at the next meeting. Julia thought about her fears related to different approaches and shared a few concerns with Jay. Ultimately, they decided that Jay would practice sharing this with close friends and peers first, given the way a public announcement could be confusing to others, could be solidifying in a way that might make it hard for Jay to make a different decision in the future, and could subject Jay to hurtful reactions from those in the group who don't know Jay personally and may have concerns about Jay's adoption of female pronouns.

It is important, and certainly complex, to think through how we will address this increasingly likely experience. We have erred on the side of practicing hospitality by honoring the name and pronouns that a person introduces as without feeling as if we are making an anthropological statement by honoring the name they are known as. In doing so, we have found that young people appreciate the gesture, even while being able to hear the questions that we might have about the reason for this decision on the part of the young person. The youth we have met with rarely adopt a name and pronouns to make a statement about their theology of gender. Rather, they are most often seeking to find a name that does not heighten gender-related distress.

Even if you agree to honor the name and pronouns a person identifies with, this still leaves room for dialogue with the young person and their peers about the shift in pronouns. It is important to normalize that different Christians will have different levels of comfort with addressing a person by a name and pronouns that conveys an alternate gender identity. This is another important thing to think through with a young person like Jay. Even if a minister is open to adopting this name, there will likely be those who have discomfort with this or concerns about it. It will also be important to consider how Jay might handle and process those interactions, helping Jay protect against internalizing such concerns as rejection.

beneath the surface. Attending to what is beneath the surface, though, is the heart of effective care.

Learning not to overreact is probably a familiar skill for those involved in effective engagement. Especially if we work with or are parents of youth, we are used to teens exploring their different identities in ways that on the surface may seem peculiar, random, or shocking (as when a teen changes their hairstyle, "best friends," or preferences for hobbies several times within a year). Our hope is that, instead of being reactive to a teen's search for identity and the way it manifests, we begin attending to what is beneath the surface of these external expressions of self. Simply acknowledging the motivations of the teen engaged in gender-atypical behavior does not yet take account of the deeper emotional and spiritual factors informing the teen's conscious motivations.

Beneath the Surface

We turn our attention now to what emotional and spiritual needs reside beneath the surface of gender-atypical expressions and labels. Beneath the surface are the thoughts, emotions, strivings, longings, and needs that each human person, Teddy included, experiences. There are also

Figure 5
Iceberg Metaphor

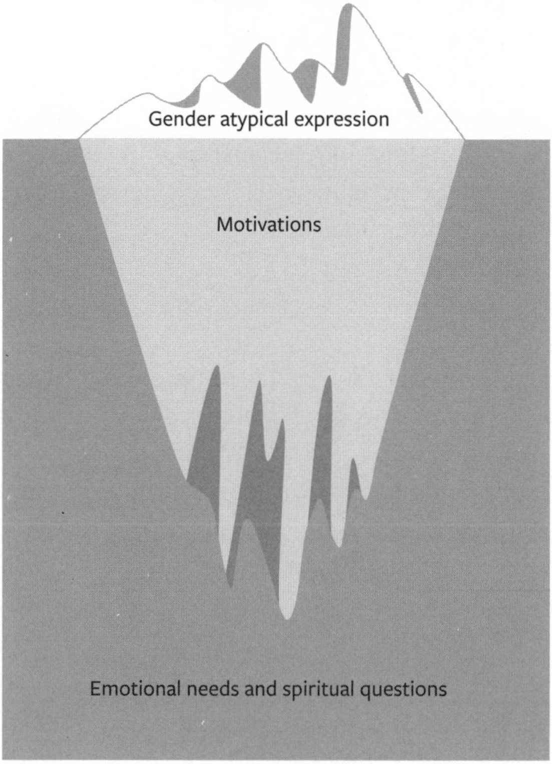

Gender atypical expression

Motivations

Emotional needs and spiritual questions

questions beneath the surface. These questions are oriented around a search for identity (Who am I?), community (Where do I belong?), meaning (What is the reason for my life and experiences?), and purpose (What do I offer the world?), as well as spiritual questions (Where is God in all of this?) and questions about the capacity to find fellowship in the broader Christian faith community (Am I wanted here?). Effective engagement with Teddy and others must address such questions.

As a starting point, we benefit from holding in mind that a youth's questions will not be resolutely answered in one interaction. Those in ministry can often feel the burden of presenting teens as perfected creatures after one conversation or even one year of mentoring (and parents often feel the burden to do the same). The reality of ministry (in all forms) that takes a long-term view is that it requires great patience, especially given how our teens also feel internal and external pressures to find resolution quickly. We must relieve ourselves and our youth of this burden. The task of answering such important and deep questions as those listed above is a lifelong one. At the same time, adolescence is a time when questions of identity and community are front and center. In this season of life, those in relationship with teens can speak into their lives powerfully, especially when our engagement occurs within a consistent, caring relationship.

Valuing Stories

Teens today are driven by stories and testimonies. They are captivated by the lived experience of people. Phenomenology rather than theology drives their considerations of truth. Knowing this is essential as we engage effectively. Building relationships, sharing personal stories, and honoring testimonies from people who represent diverse experiences are critical steps in transmitting the gospel narrative. If our engagement with these questions stops at passing comments such as "You are not trans" or "Being transgender is a grave sin," many teens will likely assume that those speaking are out of touch with the reality they live every day. Teddy, for instance, may be considering identifying as trans because of the kind and welcoming trans people he has met and who he feels a sense of comradery with. In these encounters, he may have concluded that God couldn't possibly hate him or condemn him for identifying as trans, given the goodness he sees in other transgender people. Thus, he could benefit from being accompanied on his search for identity, community, meaning, and purpose by people who appreciate the depth of his questions and the stories of people's lives that have shaped his consideration thus far.

Teens are in a phase of life that includes many shifts, unexpected turns, and mistakes. The ways teens seek to answer their questions about identity, community, meaning, and purpose are certainly not always healthy. Yet healthy or not, teens need mentors who are along for the ride and willing to have nuanced thinking, even about influences that might be cause for concern. Most of us remember that, in our youth, being told what to do and what not to do often led to acts of rebellion. Parents blacklisting that "bad seed" we had been hanging out with often only inclined us toward them more. All-good or all-bad categories being assigned to groups of people will not compel the youth today either. If anything, it will leave them feeling alienated for caring about the people some Christians seem to hate, or it will leave them with a sense that Christians don't love everyone after all. They may disidentify with their faith as a way to resolve the tension they feel.

Fostering Discernment

Many parents, people in formal youth ministry, and others who accompany teens informally have asked whether it is better to be prescriptive with teens, taking certain options for resolving gender identity off the table for the sake of clarity. As with anything, when it comes to considerations of gender, we would caution against a prescriptive approach. In such complicated territory, we do well to be guides rather than dictators.

We want to draw from what we know in the realm of effective parenting to illustrate this point. It is well understood that authoritarian models of relating to children are least effective and are often damaging. That is, a high level of demands and expectations paired with low warmth and low responsiveness does little for the healthy development of any of us. It often leads us either to internalize our difficulties or to externalize behaviors as a way of expressing unmet needs.[5]

Transposing this approach into the realm of gender identity exploration, some Christians might convey a more authoritarian approach through high demands and expectations around the behaviors, thoughts, and questions of teens. They might assert that a teen like Teddy must not dress, act, or explore gender identity in certain ways, taking some options off the table for him. We have found that this approach is ineffective. After all, an increasing number of options still exist for teens in the world today, whether or not we name and discuss them. Just because *we* take options off the table does not mean a teen will do so. If we refuse to discuss certain options, it may leave the teen feeling that their longing for these options cannot be addressed in a relationship with us or God. Thus, it encourages the teen to do some of their crucial thinking in isolation from both you and God. This can translate into low warmth and attendance to the questions beneath the surface for a teen, ultimately leaving the teen with little choice but to go underground with such questions or to act out all the more, causing much more conflict in the long run.

We want to offer another way to respond to Teddy that is more effective, modeled after healthy approaches to parenting. Rather than taking options off the table or only naming options that are in keeping with your values, it helps for a teen to be able to name and lay out all that is available, thinking critically about each possibility. This approach still holds out expectations and demands for a young person like Teddy, but it also offers warmth and responsiveness to his personal questions that could otherwise go unanswered.

Even if a teen forecloses on a pathway for a time or seems content with a more authoritarian model of engagement, many of these teens will find the blacklisted options reemerging later, perhaps as they move on to college. We would prefer that they wrestle through and discern the options with a mentor present rather than foreclosing, only to return to these options alone or solely with peers at a later time. To explore options and think critically about them builds the maturity of the individual to know why they pursue whichever path they choose, rather than temporarily foreclosing on a path only to later rediscover and move to it.

Returning to the example of Teddy, engagement is at its best when it invites ongoing conversation with him so that he has someone to turn to with his questions about gender and faith. Nancy could begin by asking Teddy to share a bit more about what he was drawn to in particular clothing and style and what he appreciates about the LGBTQ+ community as he is exploring it. If she instead said to Teddy, "Get your identity in Christ and not in the LGBTQ+ community," Teddy might feel as if he is being attacked and may assume that identification as transgender is a grave offense. This doesn't mean he won't do it; it just means he might no longer look to Nancy as a source of support as he considers this and other matters.

To combat cultural narratives that assert that Christians don't care about transgender people, Nancy could convey in words and actions, "I want to be here for you as you wrestle with these questions." This shows that she is willing to wrestle alongside Teddy, offering him a glimpse of tangible Christian community to process such important questions. Saying this is one thing, but follow-up through actions is critical. If Nancy never follows up or initiates a conversation again, her silence will speak volumes.

Assuming Nancy does follow up and she and Teddy end up developing a trusting relationship, Nancy could begin by inviting him to share what he was hoping to accomplish in presenting himself at youth group the way he did. Perhaps she would learn that he has been doing some research online and was encouraged to try it out to see what it felt like. Here, she can invite a conversation about his gender identity journey and what prompted the research in the first place. As they talk more, Teddy might share that his gender identity exploration raises questions for him about historic Christian sexual ethics, especially given the hurtful way fellow Christians have spoken about people who dress and present like him. If Nancy learns these things, she could affirm Teddy's desire for an answer to the question, Who am I? and could ask more about some of the research he has been turning to in answering this.

Investigating his sources of community, she could learn about the way he has experienced youth group in light of his presentation. She could also inquire about the ways he believes Christians in his peer group, in youth group, in his school, and in other areas of life have fallen short in their care for him and those who are exploring gender identity. Such conversations could include helping Teddy think through how to respond when he hears people being offensive to LGBTQ+ people, if his desire is to be an advocate in some way.

Maybe in doing so Nancy will learn that Teddy had been getting picked on by some of the guys long before he painted his nails and saw the behavior as a way to show them he isn't as insecure as they think he is. Certainly Nancy can also help him think through how his presentation might be received by others and consider what responses he could have when he is picked on for any number of things. This could be an important opportunity to speak into Teddy's exploration and support and empower him to advocate for himself in what can be painful interactions.

It is also important for Teddy to know that Jesus cared deeply for the marginalized in his community too. Teddy will benefit from hearing that his role in Christian community is essential in inviting others to care deeply. Empowering Teddy to find a sense of purpose in being a voice of assertion and compassion in youth group is important. This can communicate that his presence and perspective is valued and is an important asset to making the atmosphere more reflective of God's heart for all people.

It can be a gift for Nancy to offer to pray *with* Teddy and *for* Teddy as he explores his own and others' gender identity. She could put words to her own questions about God's plan and purpose in what can often be confusing considerations. In doing so, she can serve as a model for Teddy of gut-wrenching honesty before God in prayer and can normalize that a life of faith includes questioning. She can remind Teddy of the Psalms, where King David agonizingly and repeatedly brings his questions to God, in order to encourage Teddy to do the same.

With time Nancy could inquire about Teddy's strivings, hopes, dreams, and desires more broadly, always attending to both the ways these things seem to be satisfied in dominant cultural narratives about gender and the questions he has about those narratives. There is certainly room to challenge Teddy to think through how the dominant cultural narratives may or may not be helpful in casting a vision for gender identity that honors God. But if that challenge occurs outside of relationship, so much is missed. Within an intimate relationship, she can help him look more deeply into the underlying longings and strivings that are under the surface of his behaviors, conveying that these aspects of him are a valuable place of ongoing exploration.

Teddy's gender identity journey, like that of every other teen you encounter, will likely not end when he graduates high school. Nevertheless, this chapter of teens' lives is formative. Ultimately, the hope is that, in going beneath the surface, we can build relationships with youth that offer a resounding yes to their questions, Am I wanted here? and, Do I belong? In the midst of many questions without answers, we must answer these questions unwaveringly. Once we have offered convicted affirmation that these youth are wanted and belong, we can join with them in seeking out resources to guide a healthy development of self-understanding more broadly, with the most valuable resource being a personal relationship and ongoing encounter with the person of Jesus Christ. If they don't hear that the body of Christ wants them, it will be even more difficult for them to discover the fullness of life in Christ.

CHAPTER 8

Ministry Structures for Youth

Julia was sitting in a "girls' talk" at a youth conference, surrounded by five hundred youth, and she scanned the room. The speaker was naming a litany of "common" female experiences: "caking on make-up to hide a blemish, reading Cosmo *magazine and criticizing every girl based on that standard, taking an hour trying to get your hair perfect, spending hundreds of dollars getting your nails done, and obsessing over every guy that walks by." The speaker clearly thought everyone in the room could identify with these things. Based on the laughter, knowing glances, and periodic eruptions of applause, Julia could sense that the speaker was mostly right that her audience shared these experiences. Mostly.*

A teen in the row in front of Julia caught her eye. Andi was wearing a silly hat, as kids on retreats often do, which read, "Free hugs." But as Julia looked closer, she noticed Andi's disgruntled look. Something seemed off. (Julia assumed it was the lack of sleep, another common experience on these weekend trips.) After the talk, many of the girls lined up to take selfies with the speaker. Andi was there too, near the end of the line—but just before she reached the front, the speaker was rushed out of the room to get to her next talk. Andi walked away distraught, with tears suddenly streaming down her face. Julia approached her and asked, "Are free hugs still available?" Andi continued sobbing. Once she could catch her breath, she explained: "I hate girls' talks. There must be something wrong with me. Why can't I relate to any of the stories she tells? Why aren't I like everyone else? I know God loves me, and I'm grateful for that. But it's so hard to sit in that room and feel like an alien. Why don't I belong? I ask God why, why, why, and I don't have an answer."

Andi reminds us of what is at stake in pastoral care around gender identity. Here was a believer in Jesus, seeking him, wanting to know him, and beginning to receive his love into her heart. She knew he loved her. But she wasn't so sure about where she fit in the body of Christ. She was lonely, angry, and terrified that she would never find her place in the church. She was asking fundamental questions that we all ask about identity and community, meaning, and purpose, though these questions lay beneath the surface. She was sitting in a girls' talk, in a community that says she too is a child of God, and a girl. But the talk said nothing about her experience. This was a tragic loss of an opportunity to shape her future and the future of all those who would care for her in the coming years.

Youth ministry environments provide some of the most powerful and formative support for youth in America today. In a society where the nuclear family has weakened and many teens are actively seeking mentors and sources of support outside the home, youth ministry offers a haven. This chapter is directed at formal youth ministry structures for this reason, and it will present a narrower focus than our previous chapters. But we invite family members and other Christians interested in accompaniment to listen in and to begin to think of ways this information can be useful for you. Parents, for instance, can think about how their church's ministry structures may be playing a role in their own teen's journey.

Ministry to youth is a critical opportunity to offer resources, the primary one being a relationship with God that is mediated by authentic community. We must not underestimate the power of a personal relationship with Jesus in shaping individuals, cultures, and society as a whole. If those of us in ministry never build a relationship with Andi and others where they can ask their gender identity questions, as the last chapter articulated, she will likely conclude that she can't ask those questions in church and go elsewhere. Of equal importance, though, is how we "talk" to Andi through the structures we create in ministry to address her questions and those of the people who love her. We must equip ourselves to talk explicitly about the gender concerns our teens face, so that they don't feel like it is scandalous to have such questions or that we have nothing to offer them when they ask us. How we answer Andi with our words and deeds matters.

If we do not use the forum of ministry talks, speaker series, and trainings to talk about gender identity and engage in this and other current cultural discussions effectively, such conversations will occur, and are occurring, at the peer level without more mature voices speaking into them. Conversely, if we are part of these conversations, and especially if we initiate them, we will be better able to shape them in keeping with a Christian worldview. We have too long left youth like Andi to navigate gender identity questions in silence, because the way we talk about gender comes more often from stereotyping or even from a place of fear and damage control rather than from active and eager readiness to wrestle with these challenging topics.

Names Create Realities

Moving beyond committing to having the conversation about gender identity, it is worth considering how we will approach these conversations. When it comes to broad ministry structures, if we care about communicating well to people like Andi, we need to think carefully about the language we use to describe people navigating emerging gender identities. It's often the names we give to people that shape and reflect our model of ministry. How we name and think about people, even when we think they are not in the room, certainly also shapes how we interact with them. As Jenell Paris puts it, "Names create realities."[1] If we think about someone in certain terms, we will relate to them differently than if we think about them in other terms. For example, if we reduce a person to a word like *abomination*, we contribute to a reality and way of relating that is quite different than if we think about them as someone God wants to have a relationship with as his "beloved."

We mentioned in chapter 1 that there was a point in history when *transgender* was the term chosen by those advocating for a public and political identity that exceeded medical and psychiatric categories. Up until that time, people navigating gender identity were often thought of as "sick" or "mentally ill." Christian communities have also called them "abominations" and "sinful." Our culture is rapidly moving to a place of celebration in which we call transgender identity an expression of diversity. In other cultures, diverse gender identities have been celebrated and revered or demonized and criminalized. In each case, the language used to reference and describe gender identity experiences matters.

Names have important implications for ministry, and we want to think about the names we use and the realities we declare when we think about transgender youth and teens who adopt various emerging gender identities. Some readers will seek to apply this principle by arguing that using the language of gender identity is itself bad because it creates new gender realities: for example, the fact that a biological female teen refers to herself as "gender nonbinary" creates a reality that should be avoided. We agree that those in ministry to teens should be thoughtful about the power of the gender labels teens adopt, and we have addressed that concern already. We can often get caught in arguing about gender identity labels without ever being reflective about the labels we draw from and their power. In that spirit, instead of solely having a discussion of what language *other* people should use, we want to look at how the names we adopt in ministry create realities for our ministry. In other words, how we think about youth navigating gender identity questions will shape our approach to ministry.

As a Christian who wishes to minister to young people navigating gender identity in our present culture, what name will you use to shape your approach to ministry? As you recall the words that have historically been used to name transgender and emerging gender identities—such as *sick, mentally ill, abomination, sinful, revered,* and *celebrated*—you might have been drawn to one or another word. Any one of these words will frame your encounters with transgender teens and shape your ministry approach. We are concerned that many Christian ministers tend to adopt the label "sinful" to describe diverging gender identities, which limits their approach to ministry insofar as it means they view emerging gender identities as simply "willful disobedience."

Consider this example: Audrey came with her mother for a consultation about her gender identity. She was seventeen and in her senior year of high school. She was a biological female who presented as a young woman, but it was clear throughout our time together that she experienced gender dysphoria. She was not turning to transgender as an identity to find social connections that she could not achieve otherwise. No, she was in great pain, and that pain had been exacerbated by meetings with three separate pastors in the preceding six months. Each pastor had told her mother that Audrey was simply "willfully disobedient" for having gender identity questions. Their pastoral care took the form of disputation: "God made you a girl, and you have to renounce any other thought, turn from the sin of gender confusion, and seek God." Each pastor offered a slight variation on this pastoral advice.

The names "sin" and "willful disobedience" limit options for ministry precisely because they offer a narrow conceptualization of causal pathways and subsequent pastoral solutions. Such names can lead to tragic outcomes because they lay blame upon a person who did not choose to experience their gender identity as they currently experience it. We believe that limiting your ministry model in this way will drive people from your community (and rightly so). Who can thrive within that framework? Regardless of the word you are drawn to, the lens through which you see a person matters in ministry; and frankly, they will probably get a sense of the word you are working from whether or not you are aware of it and whether or not you share it with them.

Offering a New Name

The word we are drawn to when we think of teens navigating gender identity questions is *beloved*. We like this word because it has less to do with how we think about the emerging gender identity and more to do with how we think of the teen as a whole person. It reminds us of how God sees the people we minister to (regardless of the name and pronouns they use, the apparel they choose, etc.). Not only that, but it also offers an identity for the teen to live into, one that will likely inform every aspect of their life and open them up to life-giving community, meaning, and purpose.

We explored in chapter 4 how various lenses for perceiving gender incongruity result in particular ministry postures and how these postures determine the subsequent gestures available in pastoral care. Pastoral care moves beyond the theoretical and into the lived experiences of people. Regardless of where we land concerning the morality of gender-atypical expressions and cross-sex identification, we must still understand and come alongside the real people who experience (and sometimes act on) desires to live outside, beyond, or between the gender binary. Many of these young people feel as if they do not belong in their bodies. This feeling can translate into a global perceived lack of belonging; Christians with gender incongruity may sense this lack of belonging in the Christian communities they are part of as well. We cannot fully appreciate the isolation, loneliness, grief, anger, and angst that come from experiencing this "otherness" until we hear someone's story. Feelings of otherness can make the questions every youth asks—about identity, community, meaning, and purpose—even harder to answer; or worse, youth adopt a name that alienates them further from others and leads to great shame and despair.

What a gift it could be then if "beloved" becomes the name we offer to Andi and other youth feeling this aching sense that they do not belong. Offering this name to Andi would mean that, no matter how much she suffers, she can be assured that she is delighted in and sought after by God. We can imagine the power of sharing in a talk on gender identity the lesson of the prodigal son and reminding Andi that she too is accounted for in the story. Henri Nouwen, in *The Return of the Prodigal Son: A Story of Homecoming*, notes,

> All this time God has been trying to find me, to know me, and to love me. The question is not "How am I to find God?" but "How am I to let myself be found by him?" The question is not "How am I to know God?" but "How am I to let myself be known by God?" And, finally, the question is not "How am I to love God?" but "How am I to let myself be loved by God?" God is looking into the distance for me, trying to find me, and longing to bring me home.[2]

What if Andi could be assured that she is not alone in asking God and the church the questions she has? Nouwen and other spiritual masters have asked the same questions. In asking these questions, Andi belongs and is wanted desperately, so much so that God is looking into the distance, trying to find her, and longing to bring her home to a relationship with him. Flowing from Nouwen's reflection, we can remind Andi that God wants to find her even more than she wants to be found, wants to know her even more than she wants to be known, and wants her to let him love her even more than she wants to be loved. She need not earn his love, but only receive it. This love changes everything. And this love is not conditioned on her resolving gender identity.

At a practical level, could we in ministry say to Andi some of the following statements?

- "Girls' talks, boys' talks—I know they don't do justice to everyone's experience. When you were sitting in on the girls' talk, what did you hear?"
- "I think you are asking good and important questions, and these are the questions that belong in the church and in our youth group. You, and the questions you are raising, are wanted here."
- "My understanding is that for most people, gender identity is not experienced as very complicated. At the same time, for others, gender identity can be an area of questioning or concern. It's not uncommon when you have a different experience to wonder whether you belong, what can be asked, and so on. Well, let me assure you, you belong. We want you here."
- "As you are working with others, maybe a counselor or a physician, on questions you have about your gender or gender identity, I'd like to be a source of support to you, too, a resource, someone who you can share as much (or as little) as you want to and who can remember you in prayer, or even join you in prayer, as you sort out what you think about everything, as well as where to go from here."

- "I don't know all of the answers either, but I do know that God loves you, and I'm glad you know that and are leaning into that relationship. I'm also glad to help you make connections in the church, including with me, so that you can experience the love that God has for you through real people who care about you too."

Surely it is true that God is seeking each youth we meet even more than we have sought them, and God loves each youth more profoundly than we can fathom. Yet many youth struggle to receive this love. So we move now to discussing the barriers we see to transgender youth encountering love within Christian youth ministry structures. Shame, often perpetuated by rigid stereotyping, is the first barrier we will explore. We will then explore how rigid stereotyping must be challenged in ministry to alleviate an undue burden on our youth.

Overcoming Shame

Shame differs from guilt in an important way. A feeling of guilt leads to remorse about a particular action; shame tells us that we are to blame for our actions. Guilt says, "That thing I did was bad," whereas shame says, "I am bad." Shame emerges from a host of negative beliefs that influence a person's ability to perceive themselves as good and worthy of love.[3] Shame is a paralyzing feeling that does not motivate us to make changes. As a result, people who feel shame likely hold others at arm's length for fear of being rejected by others just as they have come to reject themselves.

It is important to think through which particular structures perpetuate the belief among Christian youth that "I am bad and must keep people and God at a distance for fear of rejection." What could reinforce this belief, especially for gender nonconforming youth? Any time common experiences of gender are assumed to apply to everyone and taken for granted, those with a different experience can feel excluded. For example, if puberty is talked about as nothing more than a rite of passage for young people, this leaves little room for a transgender teen like Andi to share about what for her may be a horrifyingly shameful experience. We cannot fully appreciate the shame attached to being the brunt of degrading comments about gender from other youth, such as "Man up" or "Don't be such a girl." This language lacks charity and silences those among us who may be already wondering if we are "good enough" as a man or woman. Thus, youth ministers can encourage youth and those in leadership to be attuned to the way these comments can be hurtful to others and intervene appropriately when such statements are made.

For all of us, our sense of masculinity or femininity is touched in varying degrees by the fall. One does not have to struggle with gender identity concerns to feel ashamed from time to time for not being "man enough" or "woman enough." We can likely all think back to times when we hid aspects of ourselves because we feared rejection and felt that we didn't "measure up." Imagine, then, the difficulties of those who have always felt ostracized for gender-related reasons insofar as they do not fit rigid sex and gender stereotypes. While some people are quick to blame Western culture for this state of affairs, it may be worth asking what part our Christian communities have played in ostracizing people who don't fit within gendered expectations and moving them to a place where they feel the need to occupy an emerging gender identity to capture their experience. In what way do we set standards in ministry for what is "man enough" or "woman enough" that some people can't meet without being inauthentic?

Even the formation of things like same-sex small groups can be challenging for some youth today. When you think of your youth group's same-sex small groups, how often would a person with gender identity concerns feel "othered" by comments, topics of conversation, or jokes? How often is your programming guided by narrow stereotypes about what boys and girls like? Who are the people chosen to lead programming, give the "guys' and girls' talks," and serve as mentors of authentic masculinity and femininity?

We would propose a level of awareness that some youth will be negatively impacted by group structures, interactions, and programs and may even need to be checked in with after things like a same-sex talk or small-group discussion. According to the leading shame researcher, Brené Brown, if we do not talk about shame, it will have much more power over dictating our lives.[4] Youth will likely feel "seen" in a powerful way if, after a youth event that focuses on gender-related concerns, ministers named the shame the youth may feel. We can also help our youth identify triggers of shame, and ways they can manage such moments as they arise. Cognizance of our youth for whom gender identity is conflicted speaks volumes about the fact that they are not alone in this experience and that they are cared for on their gender identity journey. This allows for intimacy in moments that would otherwise lead to isolation and, in some cases, the depths of despair.

Challenging Stereotypes in Word and Deed

We want to revisit the recipe for shame. There are significant ways we all can contribute to shame by holding up standards and expectations of masculinity and femininity that are rooted not in biblical truths but in American cultural norms. Norms are not bad in and of themselves, but when they become the standard by which we gauge authentic masculinity and femininity—or when we moralize these norms and accuse people of sinfulness for failing to fit within them—there is cause for concern.

If we dig in our heels and perpetuate rigid stereotypes of masculinity and femininity in ministry structures, we will also perpetuate the sense that there is no place for those who don't see themselves within these categories. Again, this is not to say there is no value in talking about masculinity and femininity or that these norms should be discarded altogether. However, we must think through what we are communicating in ministry about these aspects of identity that could be harmful to some youth over time.

One important way that youth ministries can come alongside youth who experience gender incongruity is to be proactive in addressing and debunking these stereotypes whenever we have the chance. You may be familiar with the typical guys' and girls' talks at youth events, similar to what Andi experienced in the story at the start of this chapter. As we hear more from Andi and other transgender youth after such talks, we can recognize the way these venues tend to perpetuate stereotypes that can be isolating for some. Even if these stereotypes negatively impacted only one person, addressing them would have value. After all, Jesus's ministry model is one that leaves behind ninety-nine sheep to seek out the forgotten one.

Those who structure youth talks could benefit from being intentional with how we talk about men and women, particularly in the examples we use. We cannot underestimate the power of the examples we give (and the examples we don't give) in communicating tacit messages to youth. Our examples communicate to the teens we think are in the room. If we only ever talk about men as stoic beings unwilling to discuss their emotions, we should not be surprised to discover a generation of young men who gauge their masculine identity and their access to male community according to their lack of emotionality. If our primary examples of "real men" are football players and lumberjacks, those in the room who can't relate to such men will wonder if they are really men after all. Likewise, stereotypically feminine notions of passivity, hyperemotionality, and hypersensitivity offer few women a dignified path into adulthood. We wonder if some youth might feel less inclined to move beyond the male/female binary if they didn't experience only stifling and restrictive models of masculinity and femininity.

It may be somewhat counterintuitive in ministry, but it is more helpful to expand (rather than constrict) what it means to be a man or a woman in terms of gendered interests, activities, and appearance. In some sense, we all suffer if we continue reinforcing expectations for maleness and femaleness that the majority of us will never meet. Christian thinker Edith Stein offers this reflection on men and women: "Indeed, no woman is only woman; like a man, each has her individual specialty and talent, and this talent gives her the capability of doing professional work, be it artistic, scientific, technical, etc."[5] In other words, Stein proposes (and subsequent research has confirmed) that men and women have more variability within their gender group than people tend to expect when it comes to traits and aspects of personality, even while there do appear to be, on average, differences between men and women.[6]

What would it look like to adjust the way we speak about masculinity and femininity in light of Stein's reflection? What would it look like to allow for young people to discover their unique sense of being a gendered child of God and the purpose God has in their particular traits, personality, interests, and talents? What would it look like to take seriously the barriers to discovering their dignity in and through their unique selves?

There is value in honoring men with interests stereotypically considered feminine, such as art and music, by naming such men in our talks and examples. How quickly we forget about the men who created the beautiful music and churches of historic Christianity, including Michelangelo, Mozart, and Beethoven. Were they lesser men because their creativity was manifest in their art form? Did they glorify God in a less admirable way because their interests did not find them being cheered for at the football game? We can also draw from the rich portrayal of men throughout Scripture, especially Christ himself, who was anything but the macho, pompous, hypersexual, and emotionally devoid models sometimes presented for men today. Young people will gauge their sense of manliness from what is talked about at youth group and in other settings, or they will push back against those notions and identify elsewhere.

Young girls benefit from being encouraged to foster self-confidence and self-assertion as well as meekness and humility. Some youth with gender identity concerns have referenced their desire for greater confidence and strength and lower emotionality as evidence that they ought to adopt a male identity. There are certainly cultural pressures, as well as historic oppression and stigmatization, that factor into this. For the church, though, it might be helpful to draw from more constructive and complex representations of women through Christian history that allow young people to rethink what it means to be a godly woman. (If all they imagine is a woman who is passively submitting to everyone else's needs, we have failed them!) We have a multitude of Christian women in Scripture, including Ruth, Esther, Deborah, Priscilla, Huldah, Junia, and Mary, who represent anything but the rigid stereotypes women are often presented with.

When it comes to specific structuring of things like small groups, we wonder what it would look like to balance between separating youth by gender and making space for fostering relationships and interactions that are not gender-specific. All young people also benefit from building relationships beyond same-gender ones. We have found in other settings, such as ministries and therapy groups, that there is a great value in opportunities that don't separate men and women or don't draw from stereotypically male or female interests in developing activities for gendered small groups. This will be especially helpful for those young people who find such moments painful.

When it comes to discipling and mentoring youth, can we delight in the interests of a variety of youth, even if these interests are not our own? What would it be like to model for those you mentor that you as a minister are just as curious to hear about the piano piece one young man is learning as the basketball game another played in? Or that you are just as excited for one young woman's softball triumphs as for another's stylish outfit? If we do not take delight in our teens' interests and talents, they may stop sharing them. Offering examples of men and women with a wide variety of roles and gifts expands our teens' imaginations for how they can use their talents to glorify God and build up the church. We do well when we anticipate a range of experiences and speak to them, inviting the youth to speak to their unique experiences as well.

Offering a Path to Thrive In

Eve Tushnet, writing in the realm of sexuality, says, "Right now gay teens hear a robust 'Yes!' from the mainstream media and gay culture. From the Church, they hear only a 'No.' And you can't have a vocation of not-gay-marrying and not-having-sex. You can't have a vocation of No."[7] The same could be said about gender identity. If youth only hear a no to their wrestling with gender identity or that of their friends, they will struggle to find a path that offers meaning and purpose in the church. They will leave and will likely discover meaning and purpose elsewhere, even if that meaning and purpose departs greatly from the Christian vision.

Carol, a Christian-ministry leader, was seeking to understand more deeply the experience of Sam, a transgender college student in her women's Bible study. In a consultation with Julia, Carol spoke about the complications that arose when Sam joined the Bible study. Carol met with Sam to discuss these complications, and Sam shared that she identifies privately as genderqueer. She confided in Carol that she was considering taking hormones to manage her gender dysphoria but would not pursue surgery for religious reasons. Sam was seeking a community of believers to connect with. She had gone to the LGBTQ+ group on campus, but that group was dismissive of her reservations about surgery, so she wanted to be among people with similar religious values. Sam wanted to share her private identity and wrestling with the small group but was afraid of how she might do so. She had many questions. She wondered if she would be allowed to stay in the Bible study if she transitioned. What did the Bible say about transitioning? Could she share with the group her experience of gender dysphoria? Would she go to hell if she took hormones? She had struggled for five years with this distress and wondered if she could ever be "normal."

Julia encouraged Carol to foster a trusting relationship that allowed Sam to ask hard questions, to explore possibilities, and most importantly, to deepen her faith. In Carol's mentoring relationship with Sam, creating space to discuss questions about gender identity was important, but so too was seeing Sam as a whole person, someone who could be discipled into greater maturity of faith. Julia reminded Carol that Sam was a person seeking Jesus, someone eager to discover again and again his invitation to know, love, and serve him, receive his love, and discern the particular ways her life could bear witness to his glory. Julia encouraged Carol to assure Sam that she was wanted and that no one else could fulfill the mission that God had placed on her life.

Carol became troubled as Julia spoke. She was increasingly overwhelmed by the many variables to consider and the variety of dilemmas to solve when working with individuals like Sam. In exasperation, she said what many others before her have asked us: "Isn't this a minority of people? Why must we shape everything for the sake of one or two people?" In response, Julia highlighted the importance of being honest. If we say Sam is wanted, our actions must follow. If we say she is not wanted because she makes our ministry complicated, we need to reflect on whether our ministry is revealing the heart of Christ.

Carol's question was an important one, as it points to a challenging reality. When we consider Jesus's shepherding model of seeking out the one rather than staying with the ninety-nine, we soon find that it is inconvenient to pursue the one. As a result, we might be tempted to believe that the one is negligible and not worth leaving the ninety-nine for. This is part of what makes the teaching of Christ radical, challenging, and ever relevant. It is corrective of our human tendency to neglect the minority. Jesus's call to follow him pushes us to consider how much energy we are willing to expend on behalf of the one. This dilemma is not new, although the stakes are particularly high in our current cultural climate. Our youth are watching. Will we seek out the one, even if it means complicating things for the ninety-nine? Or will we protect the comfort of the ninety-nine at the expense of the one? Before we say all are wanted and all belong, we must reflect on whether we truly mean it. If we do, we can trust that God will help us navigate the complications along the way. And if we don't, we need to ask whether we are actually following Jesus.

Perhaps the most critical reality Carol must face is the challenge of offering Sam a path to thrive in. If a person like Sam does not seek to transition, Carol and the church as a whole must reflect on what message of hope we can offer, particularly if Sam suffers from gender dysphoria, since this may be a painful experience of incongruence that is unlikely to abate. If Sam does transition, even if Carol believes this is not God's best for her, what message can Carol offer to Sam on the other side of transition? Keep in mind that the decision to transition may have been viewed as an attempt to manage a painful experience of gender dysphoria or it could be presented as the path toward authenticity; in either instance, such a decision is increasingly supported by the broader culture. This means that some youth we minister to will come to us on the other side of transition. We must remember, too, that the dominant narrative of gender identity today is compelling because it offers a path youth believe they can thrive in. What is the counter-narrative Christianity can offer young people like Sam?

The vision Christianity offers each person is distinct from the vision of the culture in a powerful way. Jesus's model for life is rooted in the belief that we are made by love and for love. Encountering God's sacrificial and unconditional love initiates a life of prayer and intimacy with God, seeking knowledge of God, service to God and his people, and community on this side of eternity. It is important for Sam to hear that she is invited into this life of love and is capable of loving with this love. Carol can help Sam consider the unique ways she could foster a life of prayer, come to know God more, encounter and serve his people through her particular giftings, and form and maintain a vibrant community of believers who can journey with her through this life.

In and through the Christian life, Christ offers even more than fellow believers to journey with us. He offers himself, and he is worth pursuing as the source and summit of our identity. Sam is his "beloved." Gender identity questions do not preclude Sam from this fundamental identity and source of her dignity. If nothing else, our ministry ought to communicate this truth anew.

Engaging Culture

Christianity is countercultural, but it need not despise culture in the process. Rather, connecting with youth in the current culture requires being creative, both in engaging what is so compelling about the current narratives they are offered and in helping youth think through the holes in a postmodern vision for humanity. We can explore the ways a self-seeking vision guided solely by our desires is found wanting. We can offer examples of holy people who reveal the truths of Christian faith in captivating ways. We can use current events as a starting point for dialogue around the questions youth are asking anyway. We can prioritize relationships with people we disagree with, in the hopes that modeling convicted civility will compel our youth to do the same, but without abandoning convictions in the process. Ultimately, we can assure youth that, regardless of where they go in life, Jesus is eager to go with them, to speak into their story, and to accompany them on the journey home.

As this chapter comes to a close, we want to leave you with some final reflections to focus your ministry approach with today's youth.

- *Stay attuned.* Just as we accompany the person, we stay engaged with the culture. As people are navigating gender identity questions, it is important to stay attuned to the culture itself. Expose yourself to, and listen to, what emerges in culture through media, music, and politics rather than rolling your eyes or merely refuting what is happening in culture because, at face value, it seems flawed in some way.

- *Honor strategies.* As we stay attuned to the cultural context in which people explore their options around gender identity and expression, honor the strategies that are emerging as more appealing than others. This includes reframing the way we talk about cultural norms and resisting the temptation to blacklist certain people or certain messages, unless we also appreciate what about those people or messages would draw our youth to them. To honor is not to agree with or endorse—although you might—but is to appreciate how those decisions made sense to the person (and to a changing culture) in the decision-making process. Recognize that individual strategies reflect cultural strategies. Learn what you can about what the culture sees in those strategies and why they are so compelling.

- *Expand horizons.* Ask questions that expand horizons, open up possibilities, and illuminate assumptions, expectations, and dreams for the future. Ultimately, the primary horizon for those who do not know Christ is to trust Christ with their life. A secondary horizon in the context of this discussion is to begin to trust Christ with their gender identity and expression. Foster curiosity about what could be possible for young people within a life in Christ rather than only offering a theology of "nos" around gender exploration.

As cultural norms for sex and gender shift, as culture embraces and celebrates emerging and expanding gender identities, the Christian engages that same culture in specific and personal acts of love, a love that God has for the people who compose that society.

Whether we are engaged in formal youth ministry or are otherwise simply coming alongside youth today, Christians engage culture to offer anew the gospel in all its beauty, goodness, and truth. This is the ultimate answer for young people today, as for people of every age. We can do this insofar as we meet the youth where they are and listen to them there, as we help them reflect on the very culture that shapes them. We can then begin to appreciate the competing visions they are offered. We must lead with mercy and great humility, acknowledging what we know and don't know about gender identity and the way some of our own structures have perpetuated the isolation some of our youth feel. We must ask forgiveness for the ways we and other Christians have failed and continue to fail in love. We cannot underestimate the importance of setting an example, even in acknowledging our weaknesses. Young people today are desperately seeking models of authentic, vibrant, and passionate life. Humility, grace, mercy, and joy will draw them to the source. Culture need not prevent them.

CHAPTER 9

Recovering a Hermeneutic of Christian Hope

The invitation to enter God's story of redemption entails tension in the present, with our hope set fully on Christ's return, when he will make all things new. The church is currently grappling with how to respond to gender theory and eroding sex and gender norms, as well as how to respond to youth navigating gender identity concerns that may sometimes coincide with mental health concerns. In light of this grappling, we want to close our book with Christian hope, which we believe can inform a Christ-centered response to each of these challenges.

There is certainly a place to more deeply explore what sanctification could look like in the lives of Christians navigating gender identity questions—and in the lives of all Christians, for that matter. But this does not mean that Christians navigating gender identity questions require a new or separate path to sanctification. On the contrary, the path of sanctification remains the same for us all: prayer, service, and embracing suffering, even as it relates to the unknown territory of gender identity. We are reminded not to be afraid, for our God, who will never leave or forsake us, has called us each by name (Deut. 31:6). In answering his call, we will find him whom our soul has longed for since the day we were born.

We are reminded that God is not surprised by any of this. He knew we would find ourselves in our present circumstances, where sex and gender norms are challenged at every turn. God knows what he is doing and how he will bring glory and beautiful redemption out of every age of human existence. He has not abandoned his church at this critical time, nor will he do so. The Christian God is not a deist God who stands far off and watches humanity's destruction. Rather, this God we profess is an incarnational God who has taken on our fleshly existence and redeemed it through his own suffering, death, and resurrection. Even if we do not yet understand what he is doing, we will. The essence of hope is this: "Hope that is seen is no hope at all. Who hopes for what they already have? But if we hope for what we do not yet have, we wait for it patiently" (Rom. 8:24–25).

What is it that we await? "The God of all grace, who called you to his eternal glory in Christ, after you have suffered a little while, will himself restore you and make you strong, firm and steadfast" (1 Pet. 5:10). This anticipation of restoration is the fundamental hope offered in Christianity:

> Praise be to the God and Father of our Lord Jesus Christ! In his great mercy he has given us new birth into a living hope through the resurrection of Jesus Christ from the dead, and into an inheritance that can never perish, spoil or fade. This inheritance is kept in heaven for you, who through faith are shielded by God's power until the coming of the salvation that is ready to be revealed in the last time. In all this you greatly rejoice, though now for a little while you may have had to suffer grief in all kinds of trials. (1 Pet. 1:3–6)

Our Savior promises the restoration of all that was lost in the fall and the arrival of a fullness we cannot begin to fathom. This glorification— our glorification—will bring the resurrection of our bodies. With our eyes fixed on this, we are invited to greatly rejoice!

Thomas Dubay challenges us to wrestle with the way our belief translates, or doesn't, into our daily lives: "If we wonder why, despite the millions of us who follow Christ, the world has not long ago been converted, we need not look far for one solution. We are not perceived as [people] on fire. We look too much like everyone else. We appear to be compromisers, people who say that they believe in everlasting life but actually live as though this life is the only one we have."[1]

There is often a spirit of defensiveness, panic, and despair among Christians today. I think of the grandmother who sighs, clinging to her Bible, and says to her grandchild, "I feel sorry that you are alive at this time. I am glad that I am on my way out." This pessimism in the face of our current culture is a hindrance to the gospel, in that it can keep us from engaging culture in meaningful ways. It also is an unfortunate departure from the conviction that God never ceases to pursue humanity, even when humanity seems to stop pursuing God. God loves those we love more than we do. To let that truth penetrate our hearts is to be steadfast in hope, so that all of us can enter into the glory prepared for us.

The fall touches everything. It touches our sexuality, the congruence between sex and gender, our self-worth, our capacity to trust instead of doubting God's love for us, our bodies, and our lives. The Christian teachings of redemption and glorification challenge us to recall the age-old profession of faith, "I believe in the resurrection of the body, and life everlasting." Christians may disagree about the bodies we will have at the resurrection, whether our bodies will have scars like Christ's did, what life will be like in the world to come, how quickly we will experience this life after death, and who will be beside us there. But Christians can agree about the fundamental reality of eternal life and the radical hope it offers those who claim Christ.

Christian pastor and writer Father Jacques Philippe highlights the fruits that flow when we make an offering of what we experience in the fallen world we live in. What we first see as an oppressive force can be transformed by God's grace. This is redemption at work, and through redemption, we can discover in the most painful of circumstances the meaning and purpose we all so desperately seek.

Our freedom always has this marvelous power to make what is taken from us—by life, events, or other people—into something offered. Externally there is no visible difference, but internally everything is transfigured; fate into free choice, constraint into love, loss into fruitfulness. Human freedom is of absolutely unheard-of greatness. It does not confer the power to change everything, but it does empower us to give a meaning to everything, even meaningless things; and that is much better. We are not always masters of the unfolding of our lives, but we can always be masters of the meaning we give them. Our freedom can transform any event in our lives into an expression of love, abandonment, trust, hope, and offering.[2]

We want to remind people suffering with gender dysphoria that even the seemingly meaningless reality of gender incongruence, the deep pain it causes, and the critical decisions it puts before you can be an offering that carries great meaning. If you have not transitioned and carry unique challenges in wrestling with gender identity on a daily basis, your story is important. If you have transitioned and found it wanting, your story is also important. If you have transitioned and continue to bear the weight of ongoing hormonal treatments, disgusted looks from Christians at the grocery store, and pointed fingers, remember that God is not disgusted by you. God is not scandalized by your existence. It is good that you are alive.

No matter your story, we hope to extend the words of Henri Nouwen: "We may be little, insignificant servants in the eyes of a world motivated by efficiency, control, and success. But when we realize that God has chosen us from all eternity, sent us into the world as the blessed ones, handed us over to suffering, can't we, then, also trust that our little lives will multiply themselves and be able to fulfill the needs of countless people?"[3] This is the message of hope for those navigating gender identity questions. You belong, and you have much to offer the church. You are chosen by God with a purpose that no one else can fulfill. You are beloved. You can trust that he will use your story uniquely to build up his kingdom. He is not surprised by your story but is ever ready to speak through it to a world desperately in need of him.

The Christian message of hope must acknowledge the heavy weight of the cross being carried by those who are navigating gender identity concerns. We must not invalidate this pain by saying, "I didn't like Barbies either as a kid, so I get it," or "You look handsome as a guy. Why would you want to be anything else?" No, our hope must both radically confront the pain of the cross of gender dysphoria and radically assert God's help, manifest in human form through our help.

In accepting the depths of this difficult reality, we can offer the encouragement that, with the help of God and one another, we can learn to thrive in this life and the life to come. Together we can embrace the painful and allow it to be transformed by God's grace, in and through a relationship with Christ that is deep, intimate, and authentic. This means bringing to God the pain of gender dysphoria, knowing that he is not surprised by it, scandalized by it, or disgusted by those who experience it. God is not scrambling to find a plan B, even if we are. His plan A is unique to each human soul, regardless of our sensed gender identity.

For those seeking identity and community through emerging gender identities, we invite you to consider how culture may be shaping your language and gender identity options in unprecedented ways. Some of the management strategies that may help a person suffering from gender dysphoria may not produce the same kind of results for you. There may be other avenues for you to consider, other options for identity and community that may be more satisfying over time.

For those who are fearful of the range of gender identity options available to young people today, there is also hope. The Christian doctrine of free will highlights God's capacity to tolerate and honor human choices. God places all options on the table, and he always reminds us that fullness of life flows from uniting to his will. He wills that we choose the good, yet he does not want us to be motivated by compulsion or by fear of the consequences of choosing something else. C. S. Lewis's book *Mere Christianity* echoes this case:

> A world of automata—of creatures that worked like machines—would hardly be worth creating. The happiness which God designs for His higher creatures is the happiness of being freely, voluntarily united to Him and to each other in an ecstasy of love and delight compared with

which the most rapturous love between a man and a woman on this earth is mere milk and water. And for that they've got to be free.

Of course God knew what would happen if they used their freedom the wrong way: apparently, He thought it worth the risk.[4]

Some of us may wish God had not given us, or our loved ones, this freedom. And yet here we are. We live at a time of radical choices. We can make choices to change and control our bodies in radical ways, and many of us take advantage of these choices to one degree or another. When we choose, we endure the implications of our choices. Still, we can take courage in remembering that God remains on the other side of every choice, ready to accompany us on the next leg of the journey. We have all made choices that are sinful, immoral, or wrong. These choices may hinder our ability to see our dignity and to be seen as dignified. Yet no choice, however grave it may be, makes a person irredeemable.

To those who have experienced hatred from Christians for your questions, experiences, or expressions of gender identity, we pray that you will forgive us. We have imperfectly shown the radical love our God has for you. He is pursuing you even when we have failed you. We have been Pharisees when we were called to be disciples. Do not let our weaknesses hinder your encounter with God, who is love and who never ceases to offer you fullness of life in him.

To families navigating the challenges of gender identity, we echo these words of encouragement from a Christian pastor: "Jesus has a plan for your family and His purposes will not be thwarted by sin and brokenness—if you but surrender your hurts to Him in love and trust. . . . In times when you may feel that your family is not a perfect icon of the Trinity, take comfort in knowing that there are many ways to image the love of God. Sometimes, that image is the Cross of Christ."[5] Thank you for your witness as you have wrestled with the tension of truth and mercy. We pray that you continue to enter into the messiness of it all, and we pray that the church can help you along the way.

To those who are struggling in this cultural climate to find your bearings, know that you are not alone. We too are wrestling with these tensions and hoping to work together to discover God's calling for us in the current state of affairs. All of us, as we carry the crosses of this life, can cling to the words of Christ, who promised, "I am with you always" (Matt. 28:20). He did not leave us to our own devices after the ascension but sent his Holy Spirit to guide us to the fullness of truth. This is a blessing and a challenge. A blessing, because our trustworthy God will provide us with wisdom, understanding, knowledge, and all the other fruits of the Spirit for this journey toward eternity. A challenge, because he does so in his own timing, in his own way.

We are sure the first disciples of Jesus were much like we are today. They would have liked Jesus to rise after one day, not three, and to tell them what he was up to long before he revealed his plans and fulfilled his promises. The waiting is painful as we seek answers to many questions that are not easy to resolve. We need discernment, certainly. We need faith in God's provision of timely help. We desperately need to cling to the hope of Christ's presence here and the home he has prepared for us after all is laid to rest. This is the gospel.

But most importantly, we must remember that while faith, hope, and love reflect the Christian witness, among these, love is the greatest (1 Cor. 13:13). Sharing this charity with others hinges on our own encounter with a loving God. In the words of the apostle Paul, let us be "convinced that neither death nor life, neither angels nor demons, neither the present nor the future, nor any powers, neither height nor depth, nor anything else in all creation, will be able to separate us from the love of God that is in Christ Jesus our Lord" (Rom. 8:38–39). Let us turn to our Lord in prayer, asking him to help us grow in charity for ourselves and one another each day, trusting in his mercy and asking forgiveness when we fail, ever seeking to see the face of Christ in and reflect his love to each person we meet, without exception.

NOTES

Chapter 1 Transgender Experiences and Emerging Gender Identities

1. *Gender Revolution: A Journey with Katie Couric*, aired February 6, 2017, on National Geographic, http://natgeotv.com/ca/gender-revolution.

2. Steven Dryden, "A Short History of LGBT Rights in the UK," British Library, accessed December 3, 2019, https://www.bl.uk/lgbtq-histories/articles/a-short-history -of-lgbt-rights-in-the-uk.

3. Stephen Whittle, "A Brief History of Transgender Issues," *Guardian*, June 2, 2010, https://www.theguardian.com/lifeandstyle/2010/jun/02/brief-history-transgender-issues. See also Susan Stryker, *Transgender History: The Roots of Today's Revolution*, 2nd ed. (New York: Seal Press, 2017), 46.

4. Whittle, "A Brief History of Transgender Issues."

5. Whittle, "A Brief History of Transgender Issues."

6. Tey Meadow, *Trans Kids: Being Gendered in the Twenty-First Century* (Oakland: University of California Press, 2018), 17.

7. Whittle, "A Brief History of Transgender Issues." The report goes on to note additional milestones in the relatively recent history of care for people navigating gender identity conflicts: "In the UK, Michael (formerly Laura) Dillon managed to obtain gender reassignment treatment during the war. In the late 1940s he even had a penis constructed by the plastic surgeon Sir Harold Gilles, who later became famous for his work with burns victims. Michael Dillon trained and worked as a ship's doctor until he was outed by the Sunday Express in 1958. He withdrew to India where he became a Buddhist monk and writer until his death in 1962."

8. Jun Koh, "The History of the Concept of Gender Identity Disorder" [in Japanese], *Seishin Shinkeigaku Zasshi* 114, no. 6 (2012): 673.

9. Harry Benjamin, *The Transsexual Phenomenon: A Scientific Report on Transsexualism and Sex Conversion in the Human Male and Female* (New York: Julian, 1966).

10. Stryker, *Transgender History*, 96.

11. Stryker, *Transgender History*, 97.

12. Stryker, *Transgender History*, 118.

13. American Psychiatric Association, *Diagnostic and Statistical Manual of Mental Disorders: DSM-III* (Arlington, VA: American Psychiatric Association, 1980).

14. American Psychiatric Association, *Diagnostic and Statistical Manual of Mental Disorders: DSM-III-R* (Arlington, VA: American Psychiatric Association, 1987); American Psychiatric Association, *Diagnostic and Statistical Manual of Mental Disorders: DSM-IV* (Arlington, VA: American Psychiatric Association, 1994); see also Koh, "The History of the Concept of Gender Identity Disorder."

15. Jack Drescher, "Queer Diagnoses: Parallels and Contrasts in the History of Homosexuality, Gender Variance, and the Diagnostic and Statistical Manual," *Archives of Sexual Behavior* 39 (2010): 427–60.

16. Stryker, *Transgender History*, 139.

17. American Psychiatric Association, *Diagnostic and Statistical Manual of Mental Disorders: DSM-5* (Arlington, VA: American Psychiatric Association, 2013).

18. Roy Richard Grinker, "Being Trans Is Not a Mental Disorder: When Will the American Psychiatric Association Finally Stop Treating It Like It Is?," *New York Times*, December 6, 2018, https://www.nytimes.com/2018/12/06/opinion/trans-gender-dysphoria-mental-disorder.html.

19. American Psychiatric Association, *DSM-5*, 452.

20. Julie Greenberg, "Legal Aspects of Gender Assignment," *Endocrinologist* 13, no. 3 (2003): 277–86; American Psychiatric Association, *DSM-5*, 452.

21. Meadow, *Trans Kids*, 17–18; Drescher, "Queer Diagnoses," 439.

22. Drescher, "Queer Diagnoses," 438.

23. Drescher, "Queer Diagnoses," 438.

24. Ray Blanchard, "Nonhomosexual Gender Dysphoria," *Journal of Sex Research* 24, no. 1 (1988): 188–93; see also Blanchard, "The Concept of Autogynephilia and the Typology of Male Gender Dysphoria," *Journal of Nervous and Mental Disease* 177, no. 10 (1989): 616–23; Blanchard, "The Classification and Labeling of Nonhomosexual Gender Dysphorias," *Archives of Sexual Behavior* 18, no. 4 (1989): 315–34; Blanchard, "Early History of the Concept of Autogynephilia," *Archives of Sexual Behavior* 34, no. 4 (2005): 439–46; Blanchard, "Clinical Observations and Systematic Studies of Autogynephilia," *Journal of Sex & Marital Therapy* 17, no. 4 (1991): 235–51; Ray Blanchard, Leonard Clemmensen, and Betty Steiner, "Heterosexual and Homosexual Gender Dysphoria," *Archives of Sexual Behavior* 16, no. 2 (1987): 139–52.

25. Anne A. Lawrence, "Sexual Orientation versus Age of Onset as Bases for Typologies (Subtypes) for Gender Identity Disorder in Adolescents and Adults," *Archives of Sexual Behavior* 39 (2010): 514–45; see also Lynn Conway, "Rogue Theories of Transsexualism: By Seeing a Collection of Such Theories Side-By-Side, We Grasp the Strangeness of Them All," *Lynn Conway*, June 18, 2006, http://ai.eecs.umich.edu/people/conway/TS/Rogue%20Theories/Rogue%20Theories.html.

26. Charles Moser, "Blanchard's Autogynephilia Theory: A Critique," *Journal of Homosexuality* 50, no. 6 (2010): 790–809.

27. Zein Murib, "Transgender: Examining an Emerging Political Identity Using Three Political Processes," *Politics, Groups, and Identities* 3, no. 3 (2015): 381–97; we introduced an abbreviated historical account in Mark Yarhouse and Julia Sadusky, "The Complexities of Gender Identity: Toward a More Nuanced Approach to the Transgender Experience," in *Understanding Transgender Identities: Four Views*, ed. James K. Beilby and Paul R. Eddy, 101–30 (Grand Rapids: Baker Academic, 2019).

28. Murib, "Transgender," 384.

29. Murib, "Transgender," 384.

30. Murib, "Transgender," 387. Stryker, *Transgender History*, 36–37, observes that "*transgender* entered widespread use in the early 1990s, although the word has a longer history that stretches back to the mid-1960s and has meant many contradictory things at different times" (italics in original).

31. Stryker, *Transgender History*, 16.

32. Meadow, *Trans Kids*, 3.

33. Stryker, *Transgender History*, 16.

34. Stryker, *Transgender History*, 16.

35. Drescher, "Queer Diagnoses," 444.

36. Stryker, *Transgender History*, 19.

37. Stryker, *Transgender History*, 19–20.

38. Murib, "Transgender."

Chapter 2 How Language and Categories Shape Gender Identities

1. Jon Brooks, "A New Generation Overthrows Gender," *MPR News*, May 2, 2017, https://www.mprnews.org/story/2017/05/02/npr-new-generation-overthrows-gender. We originally discussed this report and emerging gender identities in a short booklet titled *Approaching Gender Dysphoria* (Cambridge: Grove Ethics, 2018), https://grove books.co.uk/products/e-188-approaching-gender-dysphoria.

2. Kerith Conron et al., "Transgender Health in Massachusetts: Results from a Household Probability Sample of Adults," *American Journal of Public Health* 102, no. 1 (2012): 118–22; Gary Gates, "How Many People Are Gay, Bisexual, and Transgender?," Williams Institute, April 2011, http://williamsinstitute.law.ucla.edu/wp-con tent/uploads/Gates-How-Many-People-LGBT-Apr-2011.pdf.

3. For example, the Williams Institute estimates that 0.6 percent of adults in the United States identify as transgender. Andrew R. Flores et al., "How Many Adults Identify as Transgender in the United States?," Williams Institute, June 2016, https:// williamsinstitute.law.ucla.edu/wp-content/uploads/How-Many-Adults-Identify-as -Transgender-in-the-United-States.pdf.

4. Another 1.6 percent indicated "I am not sure if I am transgender." Michelle Johns et al., "Transgender Identity and Experiences of Violence Victimization, Substance Use, Suicide Risk, and Sexual Risk Behaviors among High School Students—19 States and Large Urban School Districts, 2017," *Morbidity and Mortality Weekly Report*, January 25, 2019, https://www.cdc.gov/mmwr/volumes/68/wr/pdfs/mm6803a3-H.pdf.

5. GLAAD, "New GLAAD Study Reveals Twenty Percent of Millennials Identify as LGBTQ," GLAAD, March 30, 2017, https://www.glaad.org/blog/new-glaad-study -reveals-twenty-percent-millennials-identify-lgbtq.

6. Kate Lyons, "Gender Identity Clinic Services under Strain as Referral Rates Soar," *Guardian*, July 10, 2016, https://www.theguardian.com/society/2016/jul/10/transgender -clinic-waiting-times-patient-numbers-soar-gender-identity-services.

7. William J. Malone, "No Child Is Born in the Wrong Body . . . and Other Thoughts on the Concept of Gender Identity," *4thWaveNow*, August 19, 2019, https://4thwave now.com/2019/08/19/no-child-is-born-in-the-wrong-body-and-other-thoughts-on-the -concept-of-gender-identity/.

8. Paul Marsden, "Memetics and Social Contagion: Two Sides of the Same Coin?," in *A Memetics Compendium*, ed. Robert Finkelstein, 1145–60 (self-pub., 2008), http://citeseerx.ist.psu.edu/viewdoc/download?doi=10.1.1.731.4497&rep=rep1&type=pdf #page=1145.

9. As an example, the landing page for the survey itself appears to risk "priming the pump" by describing the phenomenon the researcher was looking for rather than allowing for the possibility of the phenomenon (or other accounts) to be reported in a more open-ended manner.

10. Lisa Littman, "Parent Reports of Adolescents and Young Adults Perceived to Show Signs of a Rapid Onset of Gender Dysphoria," *PLOS ONE*, August 16, 2018, http://journals.plos.org/plosone/article?id=10.1371/journal.pone.0202330. The post-publication "reassessment of the article" can be found here: https://journals.plos.org/plosone/article?id=10.1371/journal.pone.0214157.

11. American Psychiatric Association, *Diagnostic and Statistical Manual of Mental Disorders: DSM-5* (Arlington, VA: American Psychiatric Association, 2013), 456–57.

12. Ryan T. Anderson, *When Harry Became Sally: Responding to the Transgender Moment* (New York: Encounter Books, 2018).

13. Shulamith Firestone, *The Dialectic of Sex: The Case for Feminist Revolution* (New York: William Morrow, 1971), 8, https://teoriaevolutiva.files.wordpress.com/2013/10/firestone-shulamith-dialectic-sex-case-feminist-revolution.pdf.

14. Firestone, *The Dialectic of Sex*, 10.

15. Firestone, *The Dialectic of Sex*, 11.

16. Interestingly, the American Psychological Association recently published guidelines for clinical practice with men and boys: American Psychological Association, Boys and Men Guidelines Group, "APA Guidelines for Psychological Practice with Boys and Men," August 2018, https://www.apa.org/about/policy/boys-men-practice-guidelines.pdf. These guidelines have been criticized for their denunciation of "traditional masculinity." Angela Chen, "New Therapist Guidelines Receive Criticism for Claim That Traditional Masculinity Harms Men," *The Verge*, January 11, 2019, https://www.theverge.com/2019/1/11/18178346/masculinity-therapist-guidelines-american-psychological-association-apa-mental-health.

17. Ian Hacking, *The Social Construction of What?* (Cambridge, MA: Harvard University Press, 1999); Ian Hacking, "Making Up People," *London Review of Books* 28, no. 16 (2006): 23–26, https://www.lrb.co.uk/v28/n16/ian-hacking/making-up-people. Thank you to Mark Talbot who first suggested we consider Ian Hacking's work in our examination of trends in mental health. We originally discussed the looping effect and how it may relate to emerging gender identities in Mark A. Yarhouse and Julia Sadusky, "The Complexities of Gender Identity: Toward a More Nuanced Approach to the Transgender Experience," in *Understanding Transgender Identities: Four Views*, ed. James K. Beilby and Paul R. Eddy, 101–30 (Grand Rapids: Baker Academic, 2019).

18. Nick Haslam, "Looping Effects and the Expanding Concepts of Mental Disorder," *Journal of Psychopathology* 22 (2016): 4.

19. Ian Hacking, "Making Up People," in *Reconstructing Individualism: Autonomy, Individuality, and the Self in Western Thought*, ed. Thomas C. Heller, Morton Sosna, and David E. Wellbery (Stanford, CA: Stanford University Press, 1986), 223.

20. Hacking, "Making Up People" (1986), 226. Hacking traces the concern with labeling and naming to Foucault: "We should try to discover how it is that subjects are gradually, progressively, really and materially constituted through a multiplicity of organisms, forces, energies, and materials, desires, thoughts, etc." Hacking considers whether the more recent attempts at making people up are "linked to control" and reflect "a particular medico-forensic-political language of individual and social control."

21. Hacking, "Making Up People" (2006), 23–26.

22. Hacking, "Making Up People" (1986), 223.

23. Haslam, "Looping Effects and the Expanding Concepts of Mental Disorder," 4.

24. Hacking, "Making Up People" (2006), 23–26.

25. Hacking, *The Social Construction of What?*, 31.

26. Hacking, "Making Up People" (2006), 23–26.

27. Hacking, "Making Up People" (1986), 227.

28. Hacking, "Making Up People" (1986), 228.

29. Hacking, "Making Up People" (1986), 228.

30. Hacking, "Making Up People" (1986), 228.

31. American Psychiatric Association, *Diagnostic and Statistical Manual of Mental Disorders: DSM-IV-R* (Arlington, VA: American Psychiatric Association, 2000).

32. We anticipate that this diagnosis will not be in subsequent revisions of the *DSM*. Gender dysphoria is no longer listed in the chapter on mental and behavioral disorders in the *International Classification of Diseases*, 11th edition (*ICD-11*). It is now under "Conditions Related to Sexual Health." Dustin Graham, "Non-Conforming, Part 1: ICD-11," *Lancet* 6, no. 6 (June 2019), https://www.thelancet.com/journals/lanpsy/arti cle/PIIS2215-0366(19)30168-3/fulltext. See https://icd.who.int/en.

33. Debate about diagnosis can arise where it overlaps with requests for invasive procedures. For example, if a fifteen-year-old states that they are gender nonbinary and not distressed by their experience but they request chest reconstruction surgery to remove their breasts, will the request for such an invasive procedure be interpreted as evidence of distress? Some mental health professionals will view such a request as a sign of distress and warrant the diagnosis of gender dysphoria, while others may take the subjective self-report of no distress as clearing the teen from the diagnosis as such (unless the diagnosis is needed to secure the surgical intervention requested).

34. Tey Meadow, *Trans Kids: Being Gendered in the Twenty-First Century* (Oakland: University of California Press, 2018), 20.

35. Lindsey Tanner, "More U.S. Teens Identify as Transgender, Survey Finds," *USA Today*, February 5, 2018, https://www.usatoday.com/story/news/nation/2018/02/05/more -u-s-teens-identify-transgender-survey-finds/306357002/.

36. Hacking, *The Social Construction of What?*, 31.

37. Hacking, "Making Up People" (2006), 23–26.

38. The "gender unicorn" has become an increasingly common image used to educate people about gender identity. It is seen by some as an improvement on the "genderbread person" to allow for more dimensions to consider, remove the use of labels to anchor the scales provided to individuals, and change the language of "biological sex" to "sex assigned at birth." An article by Felicity Ho and Alexander Mussap seeks to use the gender unicorn to measure gender and emphasizes the importance of providing "no explicit anchors" or labels for locating oneself, departing from using *woman*

and *man* as the anchors for the continuum of gender identity. Their article asserts that providing an expanded "selection of gender categories and allowing participants to endorse any categories that apply to them" is also too limited, thus determining the need to remove language that could be experienced as excluding to some people. As a result of removing anchors, the 269 participants in the study utilized fifty-eight distinct labels or descriptions to convey their gender. When reflecting on the limitations of the study, the authors wondered about how to define *cisgender, transgender,* and other labels at all given this level of diversity when no framework was given, and concluded that there is a tension between being respectful of "self-determination and research categorization." See Ho and Mussap, "The Gender Identity Scale: Adapting the Gender Unicorn to Measure Gender Identity," *Psychology of Sexual Orientation & Gender Diversity* 6, no. 2 (2019): 217–31.

39. Meadow, *Trans Kids*, 5.

40. Antonio Guillamon, Carme Junque, and Esther Gómez-Gil, "A Review of the Status of Brain Structure Research in Transsexualism," *Archives of Sexual Behaviors* 45, no. 7 (October 2016): 1615–48; Milton Diamond, "Transsexualism as an Intersex Condition," Pacific Center for Sex and Society, last updated May 20, 2017, https://www.hawaii.edu/PCSS/biblio/articles/2015to2019/2016-transsexualism.html; Rosa Fernández et al., "Molecular Basis of Gender Dysphoria: Androgen and Estrogen Receptor Interaction," *Psychoneuroendocrinology* 98 (December 2018): 165.

41. Meadow, *Trans Kids*, 11.

42. Ian Hacking, "The Looping Effects of Human Kinds," in *Causal Cognition: A Multidisciplinary Debate*, ed. Dan Sperber, David Premack, and Ann James Premack (Oxford: Oxford University Press, 1995), 368.

43. Hacking, "The Looping Effects of Human Kinds," 368.

44. Alan Jacobs, "Children's Crusades," *Snakes and Ladders* (blog), March 28, 2018, https://blog.ayjay.org/childrens-crusades/; Jacobs quotes Diane Ehrensaft from Sara Solovitch, "When Kids Come in Saying They Are Transgender (or No Gender) These Doctors Try to Help," *Washington Post*, January 21, 2018, https://www.washington post.com/national/health-science/when-kids-come-in-saying-they-are-transgender-or -no-gender-these-doctors-try-to-help/2018/01/19/f635e5fa-dac0-11e7-a841-2066faf731 ef_story.html.

Chapter 3 Controversies in Care

1. Mark A. Yarhouse, *Understanding Gender Dysphoria: Navigating Transgender Issues in a Changing Culture* (Downers Grove, IL: InterVarsity, 2015), 101–7.

2. Diane Ehrensaft, "Gender Nonconforming Youth: Current Perspectives," *Adolescent Health, Medicine and Therapeutics* 8 (2017): 61.

3. Jason Rafferty, "Ensuring Comprehensive Care and Support for Transgender and Gender-Diverse Children and Adolescents," *Pediatrics* 142, no. 4 (October 2018), http://pediatrics.aappublications.org/content/142/4/e20182162.

4. Ehrensaft, "Gender Nonconforming Youth," 60.

5. Rafferty, "Ensuring Comprehensive Care."

6. Ehrensaft, "Gender Nonconforming Youth," 60.

7. Ehrensaft, "Gender Nonconforming Youth," 62.

8. Rafferty, "Ensuring Comprehensive Care."

9. Rafferty, "Ensuring Comprehensive Care."

10. James Cantor, "American Academy of Pediatrics Policy and Trans-Kids: Fact-Checking," *Sexology Today*, October 17, 2018, http://www.sexologytoday.org/2018/10/american-academy-of-pediatrics-policy.html.

11. Cantor, "American Academy of Pediatrics Policy" (italics in original).

12. Cantor, "American Academy of Pediatrics Policy." At the end of the article, Cantor lists the eleven outcome studies and provides the numbers of gender dysphoric children whose dysphoria desisted.

13. Cantor, "American Academy of Pediatrics Policy" (italics in original).

14. Priyanka Boghani, "When Transgender Kids Transition, Medical Risks Are Both Known and Unknown," *Frontline*, June 30, 2015, https://www.pbs.org/wgbh/front line/article/when-transgender-kids-transition-medical-risks-are-both-known-and-un known/.

15. *Frontline*, season 2015, episode 1, "Growing Up Trans," directed by Miri Navasky and Karen O'Connor, https://www.pbs.org/wgbh/frontline/film/growing-up-trans/.

16. Yarhouse, *Understanding Gender Dysphoria*, 107–9.

17. Maura Priest, "Transgender Children and the Right to Transition: Medical Ethics When Parents Mean Well but Cause Harm," *American Journal of Bioethics* 19, no. 2 (2019): 45.

18. Jacqueline Ruttimann, "Blocking Puberty in Transgender Youth," *Endocrine News*, January 2013, https://endocrinenews.endocrine.org/blocking-puberty-in-trans gender-youth/.

19. Annelou DeVries et al., "Puberty Suppression in Adolescents with Gender Identity Disorder: A Prospective Follow-Up," *Journal of Sexual Medicine* 8, no. 8 (2011): 2276–83.

20. Michael Biggs, "Tavistock's Experimentation with Puberty Blockers: Scrutinizing the Evidence," *Transgender Trend*, March 2, 2019, https://www.transgendertrend.com/tavistock-experiment-puberty-blockers/.

21. Biggs ends his article "Tavistock's Experimentation with Puberty Blockers" with several questions he posed to the director of the Tavistock Gender Identity Development Service (GIDS) clinic, which ran a clinical trial from 2010–14:

> On what evidence did you claim in 2014 that 'the results thus far have been positive'? When preliminary results in 2015 showed that children after a year on blockers showed a statistically significant increase in reported self-harm, was this ever investigated? Why did you never publish the negative results reported to Tavistock's Board of Directors in 2015 and to WPATH in 2016? Why did your only published article . . . using data from the study omit all the outcomes that were negative in the preliminary results . . . ? In your article, why did the abstract and conclusion not report the finding that there was no statistically significant difference between the group given GnRHa and the control group? In your article, what accounts for the reduction in the number of subjects from 201 to 71 over eighteen months? What steps have you taken to monitor the 'long-term safety and effectiveness of early intervention', as these experimental subjects become adults?

22. Navasky and O'Connor, "Growing Up Trans."

23. Navasky and O'Connor, "Growing Up Trans."

24. James Cantor, "Do Trans-Kids Stay Trans- When They Grow Up?," *Sexology Today*, January 11, 2016, http://www.sexologytoday.org/2016/01/do-trans-kids-stay -trans-when-they-grow_99.html.

25. Ruttimann, "Blocking Puberty in Transgender Youth."

26. In his review of the literature, Stephen M. Rosenthal writes, "Transgender adolescents may wish to preserve fertility, which may be otherwise compromised if puberty is suppressed at an early stage and the patient completes phenotypic transition with the use of cross-sex hormones." "Transgender Youth: Current Trends," *Annals of Pediatric Endocrinology and Metabolism* 21, no. 4 (December 2016): 185–92.

27. Ruttimann, "Blocking Puberty in Transgender Youth."

28. Lindsey Tanner, "More U.S. Teens Identify as Transgender, Survey Finds," *USA Today*, February 5, 2018, https://www.usatoday.com/story/news/nation/2018/02/05 /more-u-s-teens-identify-transgender-survey-finds/306357002/.

29. Ehrensaft, "Gender Nonconforming Youth," 57.

30. Lisa Littman, "Parent Reports of Adolescents and Young Adults Perceived to Show Signs of a Rapid Onset of Gender Dysphoria," *PLOS ONE*, August 16, 2018, https://journals.plos.org/plosone/article?id=10.1371/journal.pone.0202330.

31. Meredith Wadman, "New Paper Ignites Storm over Whether Teens Experience 'Rapid Onset' of Transgender Identity," *Science*, August 30, 2018, http://www.science mag.org/news/2018/08/new-paper-ignites-storm-over-whether-teens-experience-rapid -onset-transgender-identity.

32. Lisa Littman, "Correction: Parent Reports of Adolescents and Young Adults Perceived to Show Signs of a Rapid Onset of Gender Dysphoria," *PLOS ONE*, March 19, 2019, https://journals.plos.org/plosone/article?id=10.1371/journal.pone.0214157.

33. Tom Bartlett, "Journal Issues Revised Version of Controversial Paper That Questioned Why Some Teens Identify as Transgender," *Chronicle of Higher Education*, March 19, 2019, https://www.chronicle.com/article/Journal-Issues-Revised-Version/245928.

34. Wadman, "New Paper Ignites Storm."

35. Ellen Gamerman, "Everybody's an Art Curator: As More Art Institutions Outsource Exhibits to the Crowd, Is It Time to Rethink the Role of the Museum?" *Wall Street Journal*, October 23, 2014, https://www.wsj.com/articles/everybodys-an-art -curator-1414102402.

36. Gamerman, "Everybody's an Art Curator." This article has been cited in discussions of a few topics, and we want to consider how it is in some ways analogous to services to youth reporting any number of emerging gender identities.

37. Ehrensaft, "Gender Nonconforming Youth," 57–67.

38. Yarhouse, *Understanding Gender Dysphoria*.

39. Jamie Doward, "Gender Identity Clinic Accused of Fast-Tracking Young Adults," *Guardian*, November 3, 2018, https://www.theguardian.com/society/2018/nov/03/tavis tock-centre-gender-identity-clinic-accused-fast-tracking-young-adults.

40. Doward, "Gender Identity Clinic."

41. Doward, "Gender Identity Clinic."

42. American Psychiatric Association, *Diagnostic and Statistical Manual of Mental Disorders: DSM-5* (Arlington, VA: American Psychiatric Association, 2013).

43. Sabrina Barr, "Transgender No Longer Classified as 'Mental Disorder' by World Health Organisation," *Independent*, May 28, 2019, https://www.independent.co.uk

/life-style/transgender-world-health-organisation-mental-disorder-who-gender-icd11
-update-a8932786.html.

44. Andrea Long Chu, "My New Vagina Won't Make Me Happy: And It Shouldn't Have To," *New York Times*, November 24, 2018, https://www.nytimes.com/2018/11 /24/opinion/sunday/vaginoplasty-transgender-medicine.html.

45. Chu, "My New Vagina Won't Make Me Happy."

46. Chu, "My New Vagina Won't Make Me Happy."

47. Chu, "My New Vagina Won't Make Me Happy."

48. Chu, "My New Vagina Won't Make Me Happy."

49. Mark A. Yarhouse and Julia Sadusky, "A Christian Survey of Sex Reassignment Surgery and Hormone Therapy," *Center for Faith, Sexuality, and Gender*. https://www .centerforfaith.com.

Chapter 4 Foundations for Relationship

1. Richard Mouw, *Restless Faith: Holding Evangelical Beliefs in a World of Contested Labels* (Grand Rapids: Brazos, 2019).

2. Richard Mouw, *Consulting the Faithful: What Christian Intellectuals Can Learn from Popular Religion* (Grand Rapids: Eerdmans, 1994), 54.

3. Ian Hacking, "Representing and Intervening: Introductory Topics in the Philosophy of Natural Science," *Journal of the History of Science Society* 77, no. 1 (1986): 234.

4. Our thanks to Stanton L. Jones for his insights into how various theological positions can reflect each of the three lenses.

5. Randy White, *Encounter God in the City: Onramps to Personal and Community Transformation* (Downers Grove, IL: InterVarsity, 2009), 179.

6. Andy Crouch, *Culture Making: Recovering Our Creative Calling* (Downers Grove: InterVarsity, 2008); Jenell Paris, *The Good News about Conflict: Transforming Religious Struggle over Sexuality*, Fuller School of Psychology Integration Series (Eugene, OR: Cascade Books, 2016).

7. Thomas Merton, *No Man Is an Island* (New York: Harcourt, 1955), xvi.

8. Edward Sri, *Pope Francis and the Joy of the Gospel: Rediscovering the Heart of a Disciple* (Huntington, IN: Our Sunday Visitor, 2014), 66.

9. Sri, *Pope Francis*, 66.

10. Mother Mary Francis, *Come, Lord Jesus: Meditations on the Art of Waiting* (San Francisco: Ignatius, 2010).

11. C. S. Lewis, *A Grief Observed* (San Francisco: HarperCollins, 2001), 25.

12. Caleb Kaltenbach, *Messy Grace: How a Pastor with Gay Parents Learned to Love Others without Sacrificing Conviction* (Colorado Springs: Waterbrook, 2015), 158.

13. Kaltenbach, *Messy Grace*, 107.

14. Kaltenbach, *Messy Grace*, 31.

15. Kaltenbach, *Messy Grace*, 32.

Chapter 5 Locating Your Area of Engagement

1. We first introduced this distinction in Mark A. Yarhouse and Julia Sadusky, "The Complexities of Gender Identity: Toward a More Nuanced Approach to the

Transgender Experience," in *Understanding Transgender Identities: Four Views*, ed. James K. Beilby and Paul R. Eddy, 101–30 (Grand Rapids: Baker Academic, 2019).

2. Caleb Kaltenbach, *Messy Grace: How a Pastor with Gay Parents Learned to Love Others without Sacrificing Conviction* (Colorado Springs: Waterbrook, 2015), 50.

3. Kaltenbach, *Messy Grace*, 50–51.

4. Quoted in Mary Kuharski, *Prayers for Life: Forty Daily Devotions* (Notre Dame, IN: Ave Maria Press, 2014), 24.

5. Robert Barron, "How to Have a Good Religious Argument," *The Word on Fire Show*, episode 158, December 17, 2018.

6. Fulton J. Sheen, *The Power of Love* (New York: Image Books, 1968), 9.

7. Kaltenbach, *Messy Grace*.

8. David G. Benner, *Soulful Spirituality: Becoming Fully Alive and Deeply Human* (Grand Rapids: Brazos, 2011), 5.

9. Mark A. Yarhouse and Dara Houp, "Transgender Christians: Gender Identity, Family Relationships, and Religious Faith," in *Transgender Youth: Perceptions, Media Influences, and Social Challenges*, ed. Sheyma Vaughn, 51–65 (New York: Nova Science Publishers, 2016).

10. In one reflection by St. John Paul II on suffering, he illuminates the mysterious nature of suffering that can make it both worthy of great respect and also quite terrifying to approach: "Declaring the power of salvific suffering, the Apostle Paul says: 'In my flesh I complete what is lacking in Christ's afflictions for the sake of his body, that is, the Church.' . . . Human suffering evokes *compassion;* it also evokes *respect,* and in its own way *it intimidates.* For in suffering is contained the greatness of a specific mystery . . . for man, in his suffering, remains an intangible mystery." John Paul II, *Salvifici Doloris: Apostolic Letter on the Christian Meaning of Suffering* (Rome, Italy: Libreria Editrice Vaticana, 1984), http://w2.vatican.va/content/john-paul-ii/en/apost_letters/1984/documents/hf_jp-ii_apl_11021984_salvifici-doloris.html.

11. Thomas McCall, *Forsaken: The Trinity and the Cross, and Why It Matters* (Downers Grove, IL: IVP Academic, 2012); Peter Kreeft, *Making Sense out of Suffering* (Ann Arbor, MI: Servant Books, 1986); Jacques Philippe, *The Way of Trust and Love* (New York: Scepter Books, 2012); Arthur C. McGill, *Suffering: A Test of Theological Method* (Philadelphia: Geneva Press, 1968); John Stackhouse Jr., *Can God Be Trusted?*, 2nd ed. (Downers Grove, IL: InterVarsity, 2009); C. S. Lewis, *A Grief Observed* (San Francisco: HarperCollins, 2001); John Paul II, *Salvifici Doloris*.

12. John Paul II, *Salvifici Doloris*.

13. Francis, *Christus Vivit: To Young People and to the Entire People of God* (Huntington, IN: Our Sunday Visitor, 2019), 117, http://w2.vatican.va/content/francesco/en/apost_exhortations/documents/papa-francesco_esortazione-ap_20190325_christus-vivit.html.

14. Yarhouse and Houp, "Transgender Christians," 58.

15. We have previously written about developing a theology of suffering related to gender dysphoria and about the complexities therein. See Mark A. Yarhouse and Julia Sadusky, "Gender Dysphoria and the Question of Distinctively Christian Resources," *In All Things*, January 30, 2018, https://inallthings.org/tag/gender-dysphoria/.

16. John Paul II also highlights the importance of normalizing the inevitability of the questions that emerge in the midst of suffering rather than seeing them as a sign

of spiritual deficit: "Within each form of suffering endured by man, and at the same time at the basis of the whole world of suffering, there inevitably arises *the question: why?* It is a question about the cause, the reason, and equally, about the purpose of suffering, and, in brief, a question about its meaning." John Paul II, *Salvifici Doloris*.

17. Philippe, *Way of Trust and Love*, 129.

18. McCall, *Forsaken*. We also recommend Mark Talbot's new book series, Suffering and the Christian Life. The first book in that series is *When the Stars Disappear: Help and Hope from the Stories of Suffering in the Scripture* (Carol Stream, IL: Crossway, forthcoming). Likewise, Arthur McGill, in his book *Suffering*, argues that love is the intrinsic nature of God, and giving is intrinsic to love. Expending yourself for others and "self-denial is inseparable from such love" (50). This leads to an insightful account of the debate between Arius and Athanasius and McGill's position that "between the Father and the Son there exists a relationship of *total and mutual self-giving*" (70). The follower of Christ, then, is called to "dispossession" and "surrendering to another" (108). Although we do not desire suffering, we recognize that we are subject to both suffering and sorrow, that our own "existence reflects both the struggle and victory of Christ" (111). We can rest in the "almightiness" of the Father, who "confers all his own being and glory upon his Son" (113).

19. McCall, *Forsaken*, 89.

20. McCall, *Forsaken*, 91 (italics in original).

21. Benedict XVI, *Saved in Hope: Spe Salvi* (Rome, Italy: Libreria Editrice Vaticana, 2007), http://w2.vatican.va/content/benedict-xvi/en/encyclicals/documents/hf_ben-xvi_enc_20071130_spe-salvi.html.

22. Benedict XVI, *Saved in Hope*.

23. Diane L. Ruzicka, *Redemptive Suffering in the Life of the Church: Offering Up Your Daily Suffering to Cooperate with Christ in Redeeming the World* (self-pub., 2015), 94.

24. McCall, *Forsaken*, 47.

25. McCall, *Forsaken*, 91.

26. McCall, *Forsaken*, 139.

27. McCall, *Forsaken*, 141.

28. McCall, *Forsaken*, 143.

Chapter 6   Locating the Person

1. Francis, *Evangelii Gaudium: The Joy of the Gospel* (Dublin: Veritas Publications, 2013), 81–82.

2. Mark A. Yarhouse and Dara Houp, "Transgender Christians: Gender Identity, Family Relationships, and Religious Faith," in *Transgender Youth: Perceptions, Media Influences, and Social Challenges*, ed. Sheyma Vaughn (New York: Nova Science Publishers), 55.

3. Yarhouse and Houp, "Transgender Christians," 56.

4. Yarhouse and Houp, "Transgender Christians," 56.

5. Sky Cline, "The Transgender Delusion," EvangelicalBible.com, 2018, https://evangelicalbible.com/the-transgender-delusion/.

6. Brittany Ann, "6 Surprising Facts about the Proverbs 31 Woman (Virtuous Woman)," Equipping Godly Women, last modified October 7, 2018, https://equipping godlywomen.com/homemaking/the-proverbs-31-woman-shes-not-who-you-think/.

7. Eve Tushnet, "Pope Francis Wants the Church to Apologize to Gay People. Here's What That Could Look Like," Vox, July 1, 2016, https://www.vox.com/2016/7/1/1207 0954/pope-francis-lgbt-apology.

8. It should also be noted that sometimes gender dysphoria can develop out of other issues that the person has struggled with for some time, such as a fetish.

Chapter 7 Engaging Youth

1. David Benner, *Soulful Spirituality: Becoming Fully Alive and Deeply Human* (Grand Rapids: Brazos, 2011), 4.

2. Janet S. Hyde et al., "The Future of Sex and Gender in Psychology: Five Challenges to the Gender Binary," *American Psychologist* 74, no. 2 (2018): 171–93.

3. Hyde et al., "Future of Sex and Gender," 171.

4. See Michelle A. Cretella, Christopher H. Rosik, and A. A. Howsepian, "Sex and Gender Are Distinct Variables Critical to Health: Comment on Hyde, Bigler, Joel, Tate, and van Anders," *American Psychologist* 74, no. 7 (2019): 842–44.

5. Chaoyi He, "Authoritarian vs. Authoritative Parenting" (working paper, UCLA Center for MH in Schools, http://smhp.psych.ucla.edu/pdfdocs/parent.pdf).

Chapter 8 Ministry Structures for Youth

1. This is a phrase from Jenell Paris's book *The Good News about Conflict: Transforming Religious Struggle over Sexuality* (Eugene, OR: Wipf & Stock, 2016). She reminds us in her discussion that we have named same-sex sexuality in many ways and that we would do well to think about the names we use in ministry to describe people who are navigating same-sex sexuality.

2. Henri Nouwen, *The Return of the Prodigal Son: A Story of Homecoming* (New York: Doubleday Dell, 1994), 106.

3. Veronica Johnson and Mark A. Yarhouse, "Shame in Sexual Minorities: Stigma, Internal Cognitions, and Counseling Considerations," *Counseling & Values* 58, no. 1 (2013): 85–103.

4. Brené Brown, *Daring Greatly: How the Courage to Be Vulnerable Transforms the Way We Live, Love, Parent, and Lead* (New York: Gotham, 2012). See also Curt Thompson, *The Soul of Shame* (Downers Grove, IL: InterVarsity, 2015).

5. Edith Stein, *Essays on Woman*, trans. Freda Mary Oben, 2nd ed. (Washington, DC: ICS Publications, 1966), 50.

6. Quoted in Janet Hyde and Janet Mertz, "Gender, Culture, and Mathematics Performance," *Proceedings of the National Academy of Sciences* 106, no. 22 (2009): 8801–7; see also Daphna Joel et al., "Sex beyond the Genitalia: The Human Brain Mosaic," *Proceedings of the National Academy of Sciences* 112, no. 50 (2015): 15468–73; Susan South, Amber M. Jarnecke, and Colin E. Vize, "Sex Differences in the Big Five Model Personality Traits: A Behavior Genetics Exploration," *Journal of Research in Personality* 74 (2018): 158–65; Yanna Weisberg, Colin DeYoung, and Jacob Hirsh, "Gender Differences in Personality across the Ten Aspects of the Big Five," *Frontiers*

in Psychology 2, no. 178 (2011): 1–11, https://www.ncbi.nlm.nih.gov/pmc/articles/PM C3149680/pdf/fpsyg-02-00178.pdf.

7. Eve Tushnet, "The Botany Club: Gay Kids in Catholic Schools," *American Conservative*, May 30, 2012, https://www.theamericanconservative.com/2012/05/30/the -botany-club-gay-kids-in-catholic-schools/.

Chapter 9 Recovering a Hermeneutic of Christian Hope

1. Thomas Dubay, *Happy Are You Poor: The Simple Life and Spiritual Freedom* (San Francisco: Ignatius, 2003).

2. Jacques Philippe, *Interior Freedom* (New York: Scepter, 2002), 57.

3. Henri Nouwen, *The Life of the Beloved: Spiritual Living in a Secular World* (New York: Crossroad, 2002).

4. C. S. Lewis, *Mere Christianity*, in *The Complete C. S. Lewis Signature Classics* (San Francisco: HarperSanFrancisco, 2002), 34.

5. Thomas J. Olmsted, "Complete My Joy," Catholicculture.org, December 30, 2018, https://www.catholicculture.org/culture/library/view.cfm?recnum=12046.

BIBLIOGRAPHY

American Psychiatric Association. *Diagnostic and Statistical Manual of Mental Disorders: DSM-III*. Arlington, VA: American Psychiatric Association, 1980.

American Psychiatric Association. *Diagnostic and Statistical Manual of Mental Disorders: DSM-III-R*. Arlington, VA: American Psychiatric Association, 1987.

American Psychiatric Association. *Diagnostic and Statistical Manual of Mental Disorders: DSM-IV*. Arlington, VA: American Psychiatric Association, 1994.

American Psychiatric Association. *Diagnostic and Statistical Manual of Mental Disorders: DSM-IV-TR*. Arlington, VA: American Psychiatric Association, 2000.

American Psychiatric Association. *Diagnostic and Statistical Manual of Mental Disorders: DSM-5*. Arlington, VA: American Psychiatric Association, 2013.

American Psychological Association, Boys and Men Guidelines Group. "APA Guidelines for Psychological Practice with Boys and Men." August 2018. https://www.apa.org/about/policy/boys-men-practice-guidelines.pdf.

Anderson, Ryan T. *When Harry Became Sally: Responding to the Transgender Moment*. New York: Encounter Books, 2018.

Ann, Brittany. "6 Surprising Facts about the Proverbs 31 Woman (Virtuous Woman)." Equipping Godly Women. Last modified October 7, 2018. https://equippinggodlywomen.com/homemaking/the-proverbs-31-woman-shes-not-who-you-think/.

Barr, Sabrina. "Transgender No Longer Classified as 'Mental Disorder' by World Health Organisation." *Independent*, May 28, 2019. https://www.independent.co.uk/life-style/transgender-world-health-organisation-mental-disorder-who-gender-icd11-update-a8932786.html.

Barron, Robert. "How to Have a Good Religious Argument." *The Word on Fire Show*, episode 158, December 17, 2018. https://wordonfireshow.com/episode158/.

Bartlett, Tom. "Journal Issues Revised Version of Controversial Paper That Questioned Why Some Teens Identify as Transgender." *Chronicle of Higher Education*, March 19, 2019. https://www.chronicle.com/article/Journal-Issues-Revised-Version/245928.

Benedict XVI. *Saved in Hope: Spe Salvi*. Rome, Italy: Libreria Editrice Vaticana, 2007. http://w2.vatican.va/content/benedict-xvi/en/encyclicals/documents/hf_ben-xvi_enc_20071130_spe-salvi.html.

Benjamin, Harry. *The Transsexual Phenomenon: A Scientific Report on Transsexualism and Sex Conversion in the Human Male and Female*. New York: Julian, 1966.

Benner, David G. *Soulful Spirituality: Becoming Fully Alive and Deeply Human*. Grand Rapids: Brazos, 2011.

Biggs, Michael. "Tavistock's Experimentation with Puberty Blockers: Scrutinizing the Evidence." Transgender Trend, March 2, 2019. https://www.transgendertrend.com/tavistock-experiment-puberty-blockers/.

Blanchard, Ray. "The Classification and Labeling of Nonhomosexual Gender Dysphorias." *Archives of Sexual Behavior* 18, no. 4 (1989): 315–34.

———. "Clinical Observations and Systematic Studies of Autogynephilia." *Journal of Sex & Marital Therapy* 17, no. 4 (1991): 235–51.

———. "The Concept of Autogynephilia and the Typology of Male Gender Dysphoria." *Journal of Nervous and Mental Disease* 177, no. 10 (1989): 616–23.

———. "Early History of the Concept of Autogynephilia." *Archives of Sexual Behavior* 34, no. 4 (2005): 439–46.

———. "Nonhomosexual Gender Dysphoria." *Journal of Sex Research* 24, no. 1 (1988): 188–93.

Blanchard, Ray, Leonard Clemmensen, and Betty Steiner. "Heterosexual and Homosexual Gender Dysphoria." *Archives of Sexual Behavior* 16, no. 2 (1987): 139–52.

Boghani, Priyanka. "When Transgender Kids Transition, Medical Risks Are Both Known and Unknown." *Frontline*, June 30, 2015. https://www.pbs.org/wgbh/frontline/article/when-transgender-kids-transition-medical-risks-are-both-known-and-unknown/.

Brooks, Jon. "A New Generation Overthrows Gender." *MPR News*, May 2, 2017. https://www.mprnews.org/story/2017/05/02/npr-new-generation-over throws-gender.

Brown, Brené. *Daring Greatly: How the Courage to Be Vulnerable Transforms the Way We Live, Love, Parent, and Lead*. New York: Gotham, 2012.

Cantor, James. "American Academy of Pediatrics Policy and Trans-Kids: Fact-Checking." *Sexology Today*, October 17, 2018. http://www.sexologytoday .org/2018/10/american-academy-of-pediatrics-policy.html.

———. "Do Trans-Kids Stay Trans- When They Grow Up?" *Sexology Today*, January 11, 2016. http://www.sexologytoday.org/2016/01/do-trans-kids-stay -trans-when-they-grow_99.html.

Chen, Angela. "New Therapist Guidelines Receive Criticism for Claim That Traditional Masculinity Harms Men." *The Verge*, January 11, 2019. https:// www.theverge.com/2019/1/11/18178346/masculinity-therapist-guidelines -american-psychological-association-apa-mental-health.

Chu, Andrea Long. "My New Vagina Won't Make Me Happy: And It Shouldn't Have To." *New York Times*, November 24, 2018. https://www.nytimes.com /2018/11/24/opinion/sunday/vaginoplasty-transgender-medicine.html.

Cline, Sky. "The Transgender Delusion." EvangelicalBible.com. Accessed October 13, 2019. https://evangelicalbible.com/the-transgender-delusion/.

Conron, Kerith, Gunner Scott, Grace Sterling Stowell, and Stewart Landers. "Transgender Health in Massachusetts: Results from a Household Probability Sample of Adults." *American Journal of Public Health* 102, no. 1 (2012): 118–22.

Conway, Lynn. "Rogue Theories of Transsexualism: By Seeing a Collection of Such Theories Side-by-Side, We Grasp the Strangeness of Them All." Lynn Conway (personal website), June 18, 2006. http://ai.eecs.umich.edu/people /conway/TS/Rogue%20Theories/Rogue%20Theories.html.

Cretella, Michelle A., Christopher H. Rosik, and A. A. Howsepian. "Sex and Gender Are Distinct Variables Critical to Health: Comment on Hyde, Bigler, Joel, Tate, and van Anders." *American Psychologist* 74, no. 7 (2019): 842–44.

DeVries, Annelou, Thomas Steensma, Theo Doreleijers, and Peggy Cohen-Kettenis. "Puberty Suppression in Adolescents with Gender Identity Disorder: A Prospective Follow-Up." *Journal of Sexual Medicine* 8, no. 8 (2011): 2276–83.

Diamond, Milton. "Transsexualism as an Intersex Condition." Pacific Center for Sex and Society, last updated May 20, 2017. https://www.hawaii.edu/PC SS/biblio/articles/2015to2019/2016-transsexualism.html.

Doward, Jamie. "Gender Identity Clinic Accused of Fast-Tracking Young Adults." *Guardian*, November 3, 2018. https://www.theguardian.com/society /2018/nov/03/tavistock-centre-gender-identity-clinic-accused-fast-tracking -young-adults.

Drescher, Jack. "Queer Diagnoses: Parallels and Contrasts in the History of Homosexuality, Gender Variance, and the Diagnostic and Statistical Manual." *Archives of Sexual Behavior* 39 (2010): 427–60.

Dryden, Steven. "A Short History of LGBT Rights in the UK." British Library, accessed December 3, 2019. https://www.bl.uk/lgbtq-histories/articles/a -short-history-of-lgbt-rights-in-the-uk.

Dubay, Thomas. *Happy Are You Poor: The Simple Life and Spiritual Freedom.* San Francisco: Ignatius, 2003.

Ehrensaft, Diane. "Gender Nonconforming Youth: Current Perspectives." *Adolescent Health, Medicine and Therapeutics* 8 (2017): 57–67.

Fernández, Rosa, Antonio Guillamon, Joselyn Cortés-Cortés, Esther Gómez-Gil, Amalia Jácome, Isabel Esteva, MariCruz Almaraz, Mireia Mora, Gloria Aranada, and Eduardo Pásaro. "Molecular Basis of Gender Dysphoria: Androgen and Estrogen Receptor Interaction." *Psychoneuroendocrinology* 98 (December 2018): 161–67.

Firestone, Shulamith. *The Dialectic of Sex: The Case for Feminist Revolution.* New York: William Morrow, 1971. https://teoriaevolutiva.files.wordpress .com/2013/10/firestone-shulamith-dialectic-sex-case-feminist-revolution.pdf.

Flores, Andrew R., Jody L. Herman, Gary J. Gates, and Taylor N. T. Brown. "How Many Adults Identify as Transgender in the United States?" Williams Institute, June 2016. https://williamsinstitute.law.ucla.edu/wp-content/up loads/How-Many-Adults-Identify-as-Transgender-in-the-United-States.pdf.

Francis. *Christus Vivit: To Young People and to the Entire People of God.* Huntington, IN: Our Sunday Visitor, 2019. http://w2.vatican.va/content/francesco /en/apost_exhortations/documents/papa-francesco_esortazione-ap_20190325 _christus-vivit.html.

———. *Evangelii Gaudium: The Joy of the Gospel.* Dublin: Veritas Publications, 2013.

Gamerman, Ellen. "Everybody's an Art Curator: As More Art Institutions Outsource Exhibits to the Crowd, Is It Time to Rethink the Role of the Museum?" *Wall Street Journal*, October 23, 2014. https://www.wsj.com/articles /everybodys-an-art-curator-1414102402.

Gates, Gary. "How Many People Are Gay, Bisexual, and Transgender?" Williams Institute, April 2011. http://williamsinstitute.law.ucla.edu/wp-content /uploads/Gates-How-Many-People-LGBT-Apr-2011.pdf.

Gender Revolution: A Journey with Katie Couric. Aired February 6, 2017, on National Geographic. http://natgeotv.com/ca/gender-revolution.

Ghezzi, Bert, ed. *Think Right, Live Well: Daily Reflections with Archbishop Fulton J. Sheen*. Huntington, IN: Our Sunday Visitor, 2017.

GLAAD. "New GLAAD Study Reveals Twenty Percent of Millennials Identify as LGBTQ." GLAAD, March 30, 2017. https://www.glaad.org/blog/new -glaad-study-reveals-twenty-percent-millennials-identify-lgbtq.

Graham, Dustin. "Non-Conforming, Part 1: ICD-11." *Lancet* 6, no. 6 (June 2019). https://www.thelancet.com/journals/lanpsy/article/PIIS2215-0366(19)3 0168-3/fulltext.

Greenberg, Julie. "Legal Aspects of Gender Assignment." *Endocrinologist* 13, no. 3 (2003): 277–86.

Grinker, Roy Richard. "Being Trans Is Not a Mental Disorder: When Will the American Psychiatric Association Finally Stop Treating It Like It Is?" *New York Times*, December 6, 2018. https://www.nytimes.com/2018/12/06/opin ion/trans-gender-dysphoria-mental-disorder.html.

Guillamon, Antonio, Carme Junque, and Esther Gómez-Gil. "A Review of the Status of Brain Structure Research in Transsexualism." *Archives of Sexual Behaviors* 45, no. 7 (October 2016): 1615–48.

Hacking, Ian. "The Looping Effects of Human Kinds." In *Causal Cognition: A Multidisciplinary Debate*, ed. Dan Sperber, David Premack, and Ann James Premack, 351–83. Oxford: Oxford University Press, 1995.

———. "Making Up People." In *Reconstructing Individualism: Autonomy, Individuality, and the Self in Western Thought*, ed. Thomas C. Heller, Morton Sosna, and David E. Wellbery, 222–36. Stanford, CA: Stanford University Press, 1986.

———. "Making Up People." *London Review of Books* 28, no. 16 (2006): 23–26. https://www.lrb.co.uk/v28/n16/ian-hacking/making-up-people.

———. "Representing and Intervening: Introductory Topics in the Philosophy of Natural Science." *Journal of the History of Science Society* 77, no. 1 (1986): 234.

———. *The Social Construction of What?* Cambridge, MA: Harvard University Press, 1999.

Hahn, Scott. *The Fourth Cup: Unveiling the Mystery of the Last Supper and the Cross*. New York: Crown, 2018.

Haslam, Nick. "Looping Effects and the Expanding Concepts of Mental Disorder." *Journal of Psychopathology* 22 (2016): 4–9.

He, Chaoyi. "Authoritarian vs. Authoritative Parenting." Working paper, UCLA Center for MH in Schools. http://smhp.psych.ucla.edu/pdfdocs/parent.pdf.

Ho, Felicity, and Alexander Mussap. "The Gender Identity Scale: Adapting the Gender Unicorn to Measure Gender Identity." *Psychology of Sexual Orientation & Gender Diversity* 6, no. 2 (2019): 217–31.

Hyde, Janet S., Rebecca S. Bigler, Daphna Joel, Charlotte C. Tate, and Sari M. van Anders. "The Future of Sex and Gender in Psychology: Five Challenges to the Gender Binary." *American Psychologist* 74, no. 2 (2018): 171–93.

Hyde, Janet, and Janet Mertz. "Gender, Culture, and Mathematics Performance." *Proceedings of the National Academy of Sciences* 106, no. 22 (2009): 8801–7.

Jacobs, Alan. "Children's Crusades." *Snakes and Ladders* (blog), March 28, 2018. https://blog.ayjay.org/childrens-crusades/.

Joel, Daphna, Zohar Berman, Ido Tavor, Nadav Wexler, Osama Gaber, Yaniv Stein, Nisan Shefi, et al. "Sex beyond the Genitalia: The Human Brain Mosaic." *Proceedings of the National Academy of Sciences* 112, no. 50 (2015): 15468–73.

John Paul II. *Salvifici Doloris: Apostolic Letter on the Christian Meaning of Suffering*. Rome, Italy: Libreria Editrice Vaticana, 1984. http://w2.vatican.va/content/john-paul-ii/en/apost_letters/1984/documents/hf_jp-ii_apl_11021984_salvifici-doloris.html.

Johns, Michelle M., Richard Lowry, Jack Andrzejewski, Lisa C. Barrios, Zewditu Demissie, Timothy McManus, Catherine N. Rasberry, Leah Robin, and Michael Underwood. "Transgender Identity and Experiences of Violence Victimization, Substance Use, Suicide Risk, and Sexual Risk Behaviors among High School Students—19 States and Large Urban School Districts, 2017." *Morbidity and Mortality Weekly Report*, January 25, 2019. https://www.cdc.gov/mmwr/volumes/68/wr/pdfs/mm6803a3-H.pdf.

Johnson, Veronica, and Mark A. Yarhouse. "Shame in Sexual Minorities: Stigma, Internal Cognitions, and Counseling Considerations." *Counseling & Values* 58, no. 1 (2013): 85–103.

Kaltenbach, Caleb. *Messy Grace: How a Pastor with Gay Parents Learned to Love Others without Sacrificing Conviction*. Colorado Springs: Waterbrook, 2015.

Koh, Jun. "The History of the Concept of Gender Identity Disorder" [in Japanese]. *Seishin Shinkeigaku Zasshi* 114, no. 6 (2012): 673–80.

Kreeft, Peter. *Making Sense out of Suffering*. Ann Arbor, MI: Servant Books, 1986.

Kuharski, Mary. *Prayers for Life: Forty Daily Devotions*. Notre Dame, IN: Ave Maria Press, 2014.

Langer, S. J. *Theorizing Transgender Identity for Clinical Practice: A New Model for Understanding Gender*. Philadelphia: Jessica Kingsley, 2019.

Lawrence, Anne A. "Sexual Orientation versus Age of Onset as Bases for Typologies (Subtypes) for Gender Identity Disorder in Adolescents and Adults." *Archives of Sexual Behavior* 39 (2010): 514–45.

Lewis, C. S. *A Grief Observed*. San Francisco: HarperCollins, 2001.

———. *Mere Christianity*. In *The Complete C. S. Lewis Signature Classics*. San Francisco: HarperSanFrancisco, 2002.

Littman, Lisa. "Correction: Parent Reports of Adolescents and Young Adults Perceived to Show Signs of a Rapid Onset of Gender Dysphoria." *PLOS ONE*, March 19, 2019. https://journals.plos.org/plosone/article?id=10.1371/journal.pone.0214157.

———. "Parent Reports of Adolescents and Young Adults Perceived to Show Signs of a Rapid Onset of Gender Dysphoria." *PLOS ONE*, August 16, 2018. https://journals.plos.org/plosone/article?id=10.1371/journal.pone.0202330.

———. "Rapid-Onset Gender Dysphoria in Adolescents and Young Adults: A Study of Parental Reports." *PLOS ONE*, August 16, 2018. http://journals.plos.org/plosone/article?id=10.1371/journal.pone.0202330.

Lyons, Kate. "Gender Identity Clinic Services under Strain as Referral Rates Soar." *Guardian*, July 10, 2016. https://www.theguardian.com/society/2016/jul/10/transgender-clinic-waiting-times-patient-numbers-soar-gender-identity-services.

Malone, William J. "No Child Is Born in the Wrong Body . . . and Other Thoughts on the Concept of Gender Identity." 4thWaveNow, August 19, 2019. https://4thwavenow.com/2019/08/19/no-child-is-born-in-the-wrong-body-and-other-thoughts-on-the-concept-of-gender-identity/.

Marsden, Paul. "Memetics and Social Contagion: Two Sides of the Same Coin?" In *A Memetics Compendium*, ed. Robert Finkelstein, 1145–60. Self-published, 2008. http://citeseerx.ist.psu.edu/viewdoc/download?doi=10.1.1.731.4497&rep=rep1&type=pdf#page=1145.

McCall, Thomas. *Forsaken: The Trinity and the Cross, and Why It Matters*. Downers Grove, IL: IVP Academic, 2012.

McGill, Arthur C. *Suffering: A Test of Theological Method*. Philadelphia: Geneva Press, 1968.

Meadow, Tey. *Trans Kids: Being Gendered in the Twenty-First Century*. Oakland: University of California Press, 2018.

Merton, Thomas. *No Man Is an Island*. New York: Harcourt, 1955.

Moser, Charles. "Blanchard's Autogynephilia Theory: A Critique." *Journal of Homosexuality* 50, no. 6 (2010): 790–809.

Mother Mary Francis. *Come, Lord Jesus: Meditations on the Art of Waiting*. San Francisco: Ignatius, 2010.

Mouw, Richard. *Consulting the Faithful: What Christian Intellectuals Can Learn from Popular Religion*. Grand Rapids: Eerdmans, 1994.

———. *Restless Faith: Holding Evangelical Beliefs in a World of Contested Labels*. Grand Rapids: Brazos, 2019.

Murib, Zein. "Transgender: Examining an Emerging Political Identity Using Three Political Processes." *Politics, Groups, and Identities* 3, no. 3 (2015): 381–97.

Navasky, Miri, and Karen O'Connor, dirs. *Frontline*. Season 33 (2015), episode 1, "Growing Up Trans." https://www.pbs.org/wgbh/frontline/film/growing -up-trans/.

Nouwen, Henri. *The Life of the Beloved: Spiritual Living in a Secular World*. New York: Crossroad, 2002.

———. *The Return of the Prodigal Son: A Story of Homecoming*. New York: Doubleday Dell, 1994.

Olmsted, Thomas J. "Complete My Joy." Catholicculture.org, December 30, 2018. https://www.catholicculture.org/culture/library/view.cfm?recnum =12046.

Paris, Jenell. *The Good News about Conflict: Transforming Religious Struggle over Sexuality*. Eugene, OR: Wipf & Stock, 2016.

Philippe, Jacques. *Interior Freedom*. New York: Scepter, 2002.

———. *The Way of Trust and Love*. New York: Scepter, 2012.

Priest, Maura. "Transgender Children and the Right to Transition: Medical Ethics When Parents Mean Well but Cause Harm." *American Journal of Bioethics* 19, no. 2 (2019): 45–59.

Rafferty, Jason. "Ensuring Comprehensive Care and Support for Transgender and Gender-Diverse Children and Adolescents." *Pediatrics* 142, no. 4 (October 2018). http://pediatrics.aappublications.org/content/142/4/e20182162.

Rosenthal, Stephen M. "Transgender Youth: Current Trends." *Annals of Pediatric Endocrinology and Metabolism* 21, no. 4 (2016): 185–92.

Ruttimann, Jacqueline. "Blocking Puberty in Transgender Youth." *Endocrine News*, January 2013. https://endocrinenews.endocrine.org/blocking-puberty -in-transgender-youth/.

Ruzicka, Diana L. *Redemptive Suffering in the Life of the Church: Offering Up Your Daily Suffering to Cooperate with Christ in Redeeming the World*. Self-published, 2015.

Sheen, Fulton. *The Power of Love*. New York: Image Books, 1968.

Solovitch, Sara. "When Kids Come in Saying They Are Transgender (or No Gender), These Doctors Try to Help." *Washington Post*, January 21, 2018. https://www.washingtonpost.com/national/health-science/when-kids-come-in-saying-they-are-transgender-or-no-gender-these-doctors-try-to-help/2018/01/19/f635e5fa-dac0-11e7-a841-2066faf731ef_story.html.

South, Susan, Amber M. Jarnecke, and Colin E. Vize. "Sex Differences in the Big Five Model Personality Traits: A Behavior Genetics Exploration." *Journal of Research in Personality* 74 (2018): 158–65.

Sri, Edward. *Pope Francis and the Joy of the Gospel: Rediscovering the Heart of a Disciple*. Huntington, IN: Our Sunday Visitor, 2014.

Stackhouse, John, Jr. *Can God Be Trusted?* 2nd ed. Downers Grove, IL: InterVarsity, 2009.

Stein, Edith. *Essays on Woman*. Translated by Freda Mary Oben. 2nd ed. Washington, DC: ICS Publications, 1966.

Stryker, Susan. *Transgender History: The Roots of Today's Revolution*. 2nd ed. New York: Seal Press, 2017.

Talbot, Mark. *When the Stars Disappear: Help and Hope from the Stories of Suffering in the Scripture*. Suffering and the Christian Life 1. Carol Stream, IL: Crossway, 2020.

Tanner, Lindsey. "More U.S. Teens Identify as Transgender, Survey Finds." *USA Today*, February 5, 2018. https://www.usatoday.com/story/news/nation/2018/02/05/more-u-s-teens-identify-transgender-survey-finds/306357002/.

Thompson, Curt. *The Soul of Shame*. Downers Grove, IL: InterVarsity, 2015.

Tushnet, Eve. "The Botany Club: Gay Kids in Catholic Schools." *American Conservative*, May 30, 2012. https://www.theamericanconservative.com/2012/05/30/the-botany-club-gay-kids-in-catholic-schools/.

———. "Pope Francis Wants the Church to Apologize to Gay People. Here's What That Could Look Like." Vox, July 1, 2016. https://www.vox.com/2016/7/1/12070954/pope-francis-lgbt-apology.

Wadman, Meredith. "New Paper Ignites Storm over Whether Teens Experience 'Rapid Onset' of Transgender Identity." *Science*, August 30, 2018. http://www.sciencemag.org/news/2018/08/new-paper-ignites-storm-over-whether-teens-experience-rapid-onset-transgender-identity.

Weisberg, Yanna J., Colin DeYoung, and Jacob Hirsh. "Gender Differences in Personality across the Ten Aspects of the Big Five." *Frontiers in Psychology* 2, no. 178 (2011): 1–11. https://www.ncbi.nlm.nih.gov/pmc/articles/PMC314 9680/pdf/fpsyg-02-00178.pdf.

White, Randy. *Encounter God in the City: Onramps to Personal and Community Transformation*. Downers Grove, IL: InterVarsity, 2009.

Whittle, Stephen. "A Brief History of Transgender Issues." *Guardian*, June 2, 2010. https://www.theguardian.com/lifeandstyle/2010/jun/02/brief-history -transgender-issues.

World Health Organization. *International Classification of Diseases*. 11th ed. Geneva: World Health Organization, 2018. https://icd.who.int/browse11/l -m/en.

Yarhouse, Mark A. *Understanding Gender Dysphoria: Navigating Transgender Issues in a Changing Culture*. Downers Grove, IL: InterVarsity, 2015.

Yarhouse, Mark A., and Dara Houp. "Transgender Christians: Gender Identity, Family Relationships, and Religious Faith." In *Transgender Youth: Perceptions, Media Influences, and Social Challenges*, ed. Sheyma Vaughn, 51–65. New York: Nova Science Publishers, 2016.

Yarhouse, Mark A., and Julia Sadusky. "A Christian Survey of Sex Reassignment Surgery and Hormone Therapy." Center for Faith, Sexuality, and Gender. 2018. https://www.centerforfaith.com/resources.

———. "The Complexities of Gender Identity: Toward a More Nuanced Approach to the Transgender Experience." In *Understanding Transgender Identities: Four Views*, ed. James K. Beilby and Paul R. Eddy, 101–30. Grand Rapids: Baker Academic, 2019.

———. "Gender Dysphoria and the Question of Distinctively Christian Resources." *In All Things*, January 30, 2018. https://inallthings.org/introduction -to-gender-dysphoria/.

INDEX